ALSO BY VICTORIA GLENDINNING

Vita: The Life of Vita Sackville-West
(1983)

Edith Sitwell: A Unicorn Among Lions
(1981)

Elizabeth Bowen
(1978)

A Suppressed Cry
(1969)

REBECCA
WEST

REBECCA WEST

A Life

VICTORIA GLENDINNING

ALFRED A. KNOPF · NEW YORK 1987

Grateful acknowledgment is made to the following libraries for permission to reprint material from their collections: Harry Ransom Humanities Research Center, The University of Texas at Austin; Beinecke Rare Book and Manuscript Library, Yale University; Dorothy Thompson Collection, George Arents Research Library for Special Collections, Syracuse University; Lilly Library, Indiana University; and the Henry W. and Albert A. Berg Collection, The New York Public Library, Astor, Lenox and Tilden Foundations.

Excerpts from unpublished letters of H. G. Wells reprinted by permission of AP Watt on behalf of the Literary Executors of the Estate of H. G. Wells.

Grateful acknowledgment is made to the following for permission to reprint previously published material: *Harcourt Brace Jovanovich, Inc.*: Excerpts from *The Letters of Virginia Woolf*, Volumes 2, 3, 5, and 6, edited by Nigel Nicolson. Excerpts from *The Diary of Virginia Woolf*, Volume IV, edited by Anne Oliver Bell. Reprinted by permission of the publisher.

Little Brown and Company: Excerpts from *H. G. Wells in Love*, edited by G. P. Wells. Copyright © 1984 by the Executors of the Estate of H. G. Wells. Reprinted by permission of Little Brown and Company.

AP Watt Ltd.: Excerpts from *H. G. Wells and Rebecca West*, edited by Gordon N. Ray. Reprinted by permission of AP Watt on behalf of the Literary Executors of the Estate of H. G. Wells.

———   Library of Congress Cataloging-in-Publication Data

Glendinning, Victoria.
Rebecca West, a life.

Bibliography; p.
Includes index.
1. West, Rebecca, Dame, 1892–1983—Biography.
2. Authors, English—20th century—Biography. I. Title.
PR6045.E8Z65   1987   828'.91209 [B]   87-45252
ISBN 0-394-53935-4
Manufactured in the United States of America
FIRST AMERICAN EDITION

For Stanley Olson

All good biography, as all good fiction, comes
down to the study of original sin, of our
inherent disposition to choose death when we
ought to choose life. (RW, *Time and Tide,* 1941)

I wonder if we are all wrong about each other,
if we are just composing unwritten novels about
the people we meet? (RW to Marie-Noële Kelly, 1970)

Everyone realizes that one can believe little
of what people say about each other. But it is
not so widely realized that even less can one
trust what people say about themselves.
(RW, *Sunday Telegraph,* 1975)

CONTENTS

Illustrations follow page 172.

ILLUSTRATIONS

Winnie, Cissie, and Lettie at Streatham Place (courtesy Alison Macleod)
Charles and Isabella Fairfield, c. 1890 (courtesy Alison Macleod)
Winnie, Cissie, Lettie, and Jessie Bidgood (courtesy Alison Macleod)
No. 2 Hope Park Square, Edinburgh (author)
No. 24 Buccleuch Place, Edinburgh (author)
Winnie Fairfield (courtesy Alison Macleod)
Cissie at George Watson's Ladies' College (University of Tulsa)
George Bernard Shaw at a Fabian summer school (University of Tulsa)
Dr. Letitia Fairfield in uniform (courtesy Alison Macleod)
Fairliehope, Hampstead Garden Suburb (courtesy Alison Macleod)
Rebecca in her late teens (courtesy Alison Macleod)
H. G. Wells in 1920 (BBC Hulton Picture Library)
Rebecca and Anthony at Quinbury (University of Tulsa)
Quinbury and the path across the fields to Braughing (University of Tulsa)
H. G. Wells outside Quinbury (University of Tulsa)
Southcliffe, Marine Parade, Leigh-on-Sea (studio 2000)
Anthony and Rebecca in 1916 (courtesy Alison Macleod)
Rebecca West (author)
Lord Beaverbrook in 1921 (photograph by E. O. Hoppe, Mansell Collection)
Sylvia Lynd (courtesy Maire Gaster)
G. B. Stern (photograph by E. O. Hoppe, Mansell Collection)
Fannie Hurst (BBC Hulton Picture Library)
Rebecca West (University of Tulsa)
Rebecca West, by Wyndham Lewis, 1932 (© Estate of the late Mrs. G. A. Wyndham
    Lewis. By permission, National Portrait Gallery, London)
John Gunther (courtesy Jane Gunther)
Anthony and Rebecca with their dog (University of Tulsa)
Pamela Frankau in France (University of Tulsa)
Rebecca with June Head in France (courtesy Mrs. June Fenby)
Anthony and Rebecca in France (courtesy Mrs. June Fenby)
Henry Andrews as a child (University of Tulsa)
Mrs. Andrews in her youth (University of Tulsa)
Rebecca and Henry on their wedding day (courtesy Alison Macleod)
Rebecca soon after her marriage (University of Tulsa)
Ibstone House (courtesy Lady Ashton)
Rebecca in her prime (University of Tulsa)

The drawing-room at Ibstone (University of Tulsa)
Henry and Rebecca at Ibstone, 1957 (courtesy Anne McBurney)
Rebecca after Henry's death (University of Tulsa)
Rebecca West, 1982 (reproduced by kind permission of *Vogue* © The Condé Nast Publi-
     cations. Photographer: Snowdon)

ACKNOWLEDGEMENTS

My first thanks are to Dame Rebecca West's executors for their support, in particular to Professor G. E. Hutchinson, and to Alan Maclean, Dame Rebecca's publisher at Macmillan for many years, who over lunch on 22 August 1984 persuaded me that I might be able to do what seemed then too difficult. Particular thanks are due to members of Dame Rebecca's family: Dr. and Mrs. Marion Macleod, and Alison Macleod (Mrs. Jack Selford), who gave me hours of her time, and in whose hospitable house I worked through family letters and papers. Anthony West talked and wrote to me at length, and gave me access to much material, as did Lily West and Katharine Church: I respect and value their candour, and am extremely grateful to them.

Special thanks too to Kim Lowenthal, who consulted the Emma Goldman papers in Amsterdam for me, and to Laura Mayhall, who reported on some correspondences in the Humanities Research Center of the University of Texas at Austin and on the records of Culpeper County, Virginia. I am grateful to the Master of Saybrook College, Yale, where I stayed when consulting the Rebecca West material in the Beinecke Library; to Messrs. Gamlens, Solicitors, of Lincoln's Inn, in whose offices I worked while Dame Rebecca's London archive was in safe keeping there; to Diana Stainforth, then secretary to Dame Rebecca's estate, who was my companion among the filing-cabinets at Gamlens's and guided me through them; and to Bruce Hunter, agent, friend, and critic.

A great many people have talked and written to me about the life and work of Rebecca West. Many have been generous in sharing their memories, and in allowing me to use their own or their families' letters from her. For original material, information, insight, and practical help I should particularly like to thank the following: Angelo J. Accornero, J. B. Allcock, Yemaiel and Ben Aris, Nicholas Bagnall, Carol Barash, Elaine Bate, Lord Bauer, Nora Beloff, Nancy Bignell, Emily Hahn Boxer, Nicolas van den Branden, Freda Bromhead, Hubert Butler, Christina Byam

Shaw, Carmen Callil, Mina Curtiss, Marcia Davenport, Gwenda David, Lady Donaldson, Vincent Dowd, Janet Dunbar, Pat Evans, June (Head) Fenby, Margaret Forster, Olga Franklin, Madge Garland (Lady Ashton), Maire (Lynd) Gaster, Simon Glendinning, Jonathan Grace, Jane Gunther, Lady Harrod, Sir Rupert Hart-Davis, Joan Haslip, Lady Selina Hastings, Tara Heinemann, Margaret and John Hodges, Michael Holroyd, Diana Hopkinson, Frankie Howerd, Elizabeth Lady Iddlesleigh, Annabel Imrie-Swainston, Brian Inglis, Evelyn Irons, Yvonne Kapp, Lady Kelly, Linda Kelly, Robert and Muriel Langford, Gerd Larsen, Marghanita Laski, Justin Lowinsky, Sheila Macdonald, Susan Lowndes Marques, Anne (Charles) McBurney, Mary Melville, the late Tessa Monro, the late Greta (Wood) Mortimer, Lady Mosley, Rabbi Julia Neuberger, Richard O'Donoghue (of RADA), Stanley Olson, Ursula Owen, Marjorie Parr, Sir Leslie Porter, Dr. Gordon N. Ray, Elise ("Timmy") Richardson, Dr. Richard Roberts, Martin and Merle Rubin, Hilary Rubinstein, Anne Sebba, Hilary Spurling, Clare (Lowinsky) Stanley-Clarke, Leslie Stokes, Alan Taylor, A. J. P. Taylor, Margot Lawrence Thompson, Mary and Julian Trevelyan, Raleigh Trevelyan, Kathleen Tynan, Marjorie Watts, Teodora Weber, the late Professor G. P. Wells, Vanessa Whinney, Chester Williams—and, last but always first, Terence de Vere White.

INTRODUCTION

The story of Rebecca West, who lived from 1892 to 1983, is the story of twentieth-century women. She was both an agent for change and a victim of change. In a very early article, "Things Men Never Know," she described how girls were reproached for having weaker bodies, weaker brains, weaker wills, and weaker emotions than boys; but if a girl decided to put this right, and to become strong and clever and brave, then she was told she had lost her "real value" and that no one would love her.

This was the trap in which she herself felt caught. Both her analysts were Freudians; but C. G. Jung's paper "Women in Europe" (1927), about the gains and losses made by emancipated women, might have been written for and about Rebecca West. It is not only Jung's appositeness in the "case" of Rebecca West that is striking, in all his writing about women, but his underlying prejudices and preconceptions, which may be taken as typical in that he did not recognize them. Rebecca West, who was doing her main work during the same decades and who belonged to the same European tradition, suffered from some of the same prejudices and preconceptions, having been conditioned to do so. She was thus fighting against herself a lot of the time.

Rebecca West's most passionate concerns were art, morality, history, and politics. Jung wrote that any love of an abstract "thing," as opposed to a person, was not part of a woman's true nature but of a man's: "If one lives out the opposite sex in oneself one is living in one's own background. . . . A man should live as a man and a woman as a woman." This is painfully limiting to a woman. Equally painful is the knowledge that Rebecca West too longed for "men to be men and women to be women," was made anxious by her own comprehensiveness and nostalgic for some ideal simplicity.

She worked in so many genres that she cannot be categorized. Some of her writing was "masculine" in that it was about world affairs. A woman who takes up a masculine profession, wrote Jung, "develops a kind of rigid intellectuality based on so-called principles, and backs them up with a whole host of arguments which always just miss the mark in the most irritating way, and always inject a little something into the argument that is not there." Such a woman, according to him, is injuring "the meaning of her femininity," which leads to neurosis and to sexual difficulties.

Readers of this story may feel that it is impossible not to glimpse Rebecca West in this harsh profile. Equally, it is impossible not to recognize Jung's patronizing tone, which is like H. G. Wells's when he was writing about militant feminists: behind the criticism, there is in both cases a suppressed guffaw which would drive any serious woman to hysteria, as would Jung's implicit definition of femininity: "Masculinity means knowing what one wants and doing what is necessary to achieve it." Rebecca West was not cut out to be a *femme inspiratrice,* a muse to man's genius, which Jung, Wells, and most "great men" of her youth thought was the best way for a woman to use her gifts.

Jung's theory of the *animus* is nevertheless useful as one way of understanding Rebecca West's difficulties in her personal life. She wrote that any account of an ordinary person "must be as the map of a jungle, in which there range many beasts, some benign, some abhorrent." Her son, Anthony, with an animosity equalling her own, too often saw only the negative side of the mother-figure in Rebecca—devouring, controlling, malign. They fulfilled each other's awful expectations in a way that would be ludicrous if it were not so sad.

If Rebecca West had been a mediaeval woman, and rich, she would have been a great abbess. If she had been a seventeenth-century woman, and poor, she would have been burnt as a witch. There are several ways of explaining her, and none. There is little that a woman could have achieved, enjoyed, and suffered during the decades when women's lives were being transformed that she did not achieve, enjoy, and suffer. There is a great deal to be learned from her experience. But she is not just an emblem of modern woman. As Wells wrote of his first meeting with her, when she was a mere girl, "I had never met anything like her before, and I doubt if there ever was anything like her before."

She was ninety when she died, and her last twenty years were as eventful as any other period of her life; I knew her for the last ten years, and saw her often with pleasure. She left a signed request that two biographies of her should be written: a short one by myself, and a "full" biography by Stanley Olson. I have concentrated on the early and middle years, since to give equal weight to every phase would have made too long a book. There is room not only for a detailed biography in the future, but for studies of aspects of her life and work which this first biography has not been able to cover fully.

Dame Rebecca had hundreds of friends and acquaintances—writers, theatre people, academics, tycoons, politicians, men and women in private and professional life, rich and poor, of every race, all over the world. To name all these, or even many of these, would have made her biography read like an international telephone directory. The few must stand for all, with apologies to those unmentioned whose friendship she valued. Those who knew her in her later years may regret the omission of their favourite "Rebecca stories," and a complete account of the griefs, triumphs, exploits, and interests of her old age. I feel that the extraordinary story of her life as a whole will be sufficient compensation.

It has turned out to be a sadder story than I expected, on account of the way she felt about the things that happened to her. She felt like Job, persecuted by God (and by man, woman, and child), and any friend who played the part of Job's comforter got short shrift from her. But her positive was as strong as her negative: "Yet I like dresses, and the wide light *salons* where one buys them. I like hats, I like rooms with walls the colour of autumn leaves. . . . I like strawberries; the people whom I like I love."

Music, the first of all the arts, is one possible metaphor for Rebecca West's life and work, as it was for her best-known novel, *The Fountain Overflows*. She had the gift, in her writing, of making frightening situations a little ridiculous, and ridiculous situations more than a little frightening. This is one way to look at the drama of her life. She wrote in *Black Lamb and Grey Falcon*: "I remembered that when Mozart wrote *The Magic Flute* in exploitation of our love for the crypto-cavern and the solemn symbol, he and his librettist had finally to turn their backs on the unresolved plot and go home whistling with their hands in their pockets." Rebecca West lived her life operatically, and tinkered endlessly with the story-line, the score, and the libretto. The plot remains unresolved.

REBECCA

WEST

PROLOGUE

Summer 1975. There is a small lunch party in a comfortable flat in Kingston House, a large block facing Kensington Gardens in London. Geraniums are rampant on the balcony outside the sunny drawing-room, which has a unique porcelain fireplace painted with flowers in turquoise and white. A painting by Lowry hangs over the fireplace, and on other walls are two paintings by Dufy, two Vuillard pastels, and a Bonnard street-scene. There is a small sofa with swan arms; the hostess herself always settles in one of a pair of Regency gilt chairs with claw feet and the armrests carved into lions' heads.

Three women sit at the shining mahogany table in the dining-room, which forms part of the large entrance-hall. The hostess is in her eighties; her sister is ninety; the third person is in her thirties. The eldest woman, who looks and moves like a healthy seventy-year-old, is doing most of the talking. She has been a distinguished public-health doctor, and also qualified as a barrister; her stories centre on long-ago battles with ministers and administrators. She speaks softly but is hard to interrupt.

The hostess's manner is quite different. Her voice is emphatic and theatrically modulated, her comments wickedly acute. She is behaving badly, sighing loudly, casting her eyes up to heaven, looking at a non-existent watch on her wrist, while her sister's voice winds on. She throws in irreverent interpolations, which are not acknowledged. Both the old women are equally deaf, or affecting to be. Neither responds directly to anything the other says, but directs her fire at the younger guest—crossfire, at cross-purposes. The younger guest feels she is playing two games of tennis at once, and has a sense of disloyalty to her hostess, to whom she is devoted, when she dutifully returns the service of the elder sister.

The elder sister does not defer or refer—why should she, perhaps?—to the personal fame or professional achievement of the younger one, who is falling ever deeper into the well-rehearsed role of recalcitrant

little sister. The elder sister's conversation shifts to left-wing politics before World War I, when she held office in the Fabian Society and argued
with George Bernard Shaw. (The younger sister had known Shaw too; he
had written that she could "handle a pen as brilliantly as I ever could,
and much more savagely.")

The two come together at last on the subject of snobbery, baying in
counterpoint about the vulgarity of Evelyn Waugh, who had the nerve to
call other people common. They treat the younger guest, in the next,
apparently unconnected breath, to a rundown of their own aristocratic
connections. They cannot agree even on this, but argue over titles and
relationships, calling each other "dear" with emphatic frequency.

The elder sister leaves early, to visit a friend in hospital. Immediately the door closes, the hostess says to the remaining guest: "Now you
see. She's always been like this. I've had to listen to her all my life. Her
hair's that same colour, you know, under the *wig*, reddish-yellow." (The
hostess also has a wig, worn for special occasions, of bouffant white-grey
curls.)

Hostess and guest drift into the kitchen. She talks about psychoanalysis, and of the anti-woman bias of even women analysts. In the
kitchen bookshelves are the works of H. G. Wells. She reads them sometimes while the kettle boils, and is no longer sure if they are any good.
She regrets the fact that no one will let her forget her affair with Wells:
"Just how important is something that ends when you are thirty?"
She would rather talk, affectionately, about her late husband, Henry
Andrews.

She wants gossip now, as lurid as possible, and her rich voice swoops up
and down as she makes a small scandal sensational. She wants to know
what her guest will give her family for supper, and how she will prepare
it; she wants to know if her guest has tried the new variety packs of
breakfast cereals, the pleasure of which, she says, prevents her from
suicide. Her eyes are bad, which makes it hard for her to write, though
she never stops writing.

"I should like to have been a novelist. I should like to have been a
historian."

"But you are a novelist, you are a historian."

"Not in the way that I wanted."

The elder of the two sisters at the lunch party is Dr. Letitia Fairfield. The younger one, the hostess, is Dame Rebecca West. The other guest is myself.

PART ONE

Cissie

1

In the year 1900 the three Fairfield girls were fifteen, thirteen, and seven. Their names were Letitia, Winifred, and Cicely Isabel, known in the family as Lettie, Winnie, and Cissie. They lived with their parents at 9 Hermitage Road, Richmond-on-Thames, an unremarkable house in the ancient town on the south-western edge of London. All three children were intelligent and good-looking. They were attending Richmond Church of England High School; in a group photograph, Cissie is sitting in a white smock with the smallest pupils in the front row. Lettie, who loved and indulged this turbulent youngest sister, identified the small boy beside Cissie in a note on the back as "Edward, her adoring boy friend." Cissie did not enjoy school. She was outraged when required to fall on her knees with the headmistress and pray, as a consequence of her misdemeanours, and she herself caused outrage by her irreverent reaction to this performance. Cissie is the future Rebecca West.

The Fairfield family had plenty of books, music, and animated talk about ideas, the arts, politics, and current events. What they did not have was money, and the possibility of catastrophe lay just below the surface. The girls felt different from other children. People who were as poor as their parents were not usually so fiercely articulate and intellectual, while people with their interests and aspirations mostly had newer clothes and better houses. They were not well established in Richmond; their parents' married life had been nomadic. Papa, who was a journalist, had not been lucky.

The girls were precocious readers, steeped from an early age in literature and history: *The Three Musketeers* and *The Count of Monte Cristo* "taught one in the nursery what romance was." So did their own family history. Cissie was to describe herself in print as "an Englishwoman," but she was Scots-Irish, a Celt. Their father was Anglo-Irish, from a family that had served the British Army in Ireland since the seventeenth century. Their mother was Scottish, and the pair had met and married in

Australia, where the two elder girls had been born. The youngest by more than five years, Cissie may have represented a final bid on her parents' part to make their marriage work. After her birth, they ceased to share a bedroom, and in 1901, the year Queen Victoria died, the girls' father left home.

2

Charles Fairfield was a romantic figure to his daughters. With his tales of past glories he filled their heads with pride of family and the sense of a "real life" that should properly be theirs. They never relinquished this image of paradise lost. As he walked with them in Richmond Park, he told them about long-ago Fairfields and his own childhood in Ireland, interspersing his stories with instruction on gentlemanly topics such as the points of a horse.

The early history of the Fairfields is hazy. In 1948 Cissie met one Wynne Fairfield, who had been looking it all up: "Apparently we lived for something like three hundred years on the product of the thrift and intelligence of a Southwark butcher called John Fairfield who died in 1498, having bought land which was finally surrounded by London." Papa's father, Charles George Fairfield, had, like his grandfather, been a military man, and came from County Longford in Ireland. There was a family legend about Charles George's parentage; it was said that he was the natural son of a member of the royal house of Hanover, and that a personal allowance from the royal family accounted for his relative prosperity. Charles George was said, in his turn, to have been the natural father of the famous journalist George Augustus Sala, whose mother was an opera singer—thus providing Papa and his brothers with a distinguished if unacknowledged half-brother. Neither story is verifiable.

Charles George Fairfield married Frances Crosbie, from a well-established County Kerry family. She died, and in 1833 he married Arabella Rowan, the grandmother of the three girls walking with their father in Richmond Park. They heard how their father and his three brothers had ridden and swum and fished in the Kerry countryside. They heard about the sociable "Kerry cousinhood"—the network of Protestant gentry, Fairfields, Rowans, Crosbies, Blennerhassetts, Dennys, some of them powers in the land and some of them rough and wild. The girls' grandfather had bred greyhounds, and became High Sheriff of Kerry. A Denny and a Crosbie had fought a famous duel in the eighteenth century; a Denny ancestor had been cousin to Sir Walter Raleigh; a connection with the Sackvilles gave them descent from an aunt of Anne Boleyn.

Charles Fairfield bequeathed to his daughters an addiction to exotic genealogy. In her old age, Cissie would trace their exiguous connections with noble families all over the British Isles. Lettie, who became a Roman Catholic, was to work out their lines of descent from St. Margaret of Scotland, St. Louis of France, two Russian saints, and a Spanish one. These pedigrees gave them a sense of continuity; the Fairfields had become displaced persons. The Ireland of their father's youth was the promised land never to be regained, especially for Winnie and Cissie. Lettie got to know the real Ireland, and had friends there in political circles. Cissie only went to Ireland once in her life, and not until she was seventy-nine.

Charles Fairfield was actually born at 2 Day Street in Tralee—a small house, "pinched Georgian," as Cissie described it when, with Lettie, she finally searched for her father's roots. Charles and his brothers were brought up between Kerry and Dublin; in Kerry they also had a "shooting-lodge" at Mounteagle, north of Tralee in Stack's Mountains— which the girls all their lives rendered as "Stag Mountains," proof that their family history depended on word-of-mouth tradition. (When Cissie and Lettie tracked the shooting-lodge down in 1971 they found "a tiny cottage in a glade in a cleft of the moors, looking down on what had been a lawn surrounded by rhododendrons.") In 1853, when Charles was twelve, his father died, and all the property reverted to the family of Charles George's first wife. His second wife and her sons were homeless.

Arabella Rowan Fairfield was a devout woman, and after her husband's death she joined the Plymouth Brethren, a sect whose austerity further curtailed the family's possibilities. The story was that she declined to go on taking the royal annuity on discovering that it had its roots in immorality. Her chief source of income was rents from run-down prop-

erties along the quays in Dublin acquired by previous generations of Fairfields. These rents, badly administered and irregularly paid, were often
all that the girls' mother, in her turn, was able to rely on in the bad years
ahead. Cissie found the family's decline unbearably sad: her grandfather,
she said, probably never knew who he really was, her father and uncles
grew up in social isolation, "and there was my mother and my sisters and
I living the most terrible kind of isolated life—we knew nobody."

Arabella Rowan Fairfield brought her boys over the Irish Sea to London. Only the youngest, Edward, was sent to school; the others had the
benefit of an unusual tutor. This was Elysée Reclus, one of two brothers
who were exiled from France on account of their atheistic and revolutionary teaching. Arabella Fairfield apparently thought they were persecuted
Protestants. Her boys, as a result, had a rigorous grounding in geography, political history, and modern languages. Political science became
Charles's passion. Because of this, Cissie wrote, "and because my father
was handsome and eloquent, I cannot remember a time when I had not
a rough idea of what was meant by capitalism, socialism, individualism,
anarchism, liberalism and conservatism."

The eldest of the four Fairfield brothers, Digby, went into the Royal
Artillery, and died of cholera in India in 1863, still in his twenties. Arthur, a year older than Charles, became a civil servant in the Board of
Trade; Edward, the youngest, had a legal training and became a clerk in
the Colonial Office.

Charles, like Digby, joined the army. According to the Army Lists,
he became an ensign in the Prince Consort's Own Rifle Brigade at
twenty-two, in the year Digby died. According to the stories he told his
daughters, he was sent out as an observer to the American Civil War, and
served as a stretcher-bearer. He was a musketry instructor, and was
posted to Vienna, to St. Petersburg, to Canada. But he did not rise above
the rank of lieutenant, and is listed as having sold his commission in
1867. He returned to America as a civilian and an adventurer. He spent
time in Mexico; he ran a sawmill in Virginia.

It was only after his death that his family discovered that in Virginia
he had married a Miss Allison of Culpeper County, and had a son by her.
When Charles, restless again, went west, apparently to manage a mine,
they were divorced. That, at least, was Cissie's version of events, and she
told her family later that on one of her first visits to America she traced

their American half-brother, whose name was Stephen. There is no available documentation of this piece of lore, and if Charles Fairfield really was married in America it was not on his bride's home ground. There is no record of the marriage to be found in the Culpeper County archives, and no record there of the birth of Stephen Fairfield, or any other Fairfield.

In the early 1880s Charles sailed for Australia, accompanied by a boy, said to be the orphaned son of friends, whom he was escorting to relatives. No more is known of this child. What is certain is that Charles settled in East Melbourne as an artist on the Melbourne *Argus;* like his brother Digby, he had a talent for drawing and watercolour painting, rather in the style of Edward Lear. In Melbourne he met a Scottish woman, Isabella Campbell Mackenzie, and they were married there in St. Peter's Church on 17 December 1883. Both lied a little on the marriage certificate; Charles gave his status as "bachelor," and his age as thirty-nine. He was, we may assume, a divorcé, and he was forty-two. Isabella, who was twenty-nine, also took a year off her age.

Their youngest daughter, Cissie, was later to characterize their union as "the marriage of loneliness to loneliness."

3

Isabella Mackenzie came from Edinburgh. Her mother, born Jessie Watson Campbell, had, like her new husband's mother, been left a widow with a large family, of whom Isabella was the youngest. Isabella's maternal grandfather was a prosperous lace-merchant, and her grandmother the daughter of a tanner.

Isabella's father died when she was three. His name was Alexander Mackenzie, and he came from a less comfortably off background than his wife; these Mackenzies were "crofters turned underprivileged urban dwellers," but Alexander was talented. He played traditional Scottish music on the violin, collected and arranged reels and ballads, and became leader of the orchestra at the Theatre Royal in Edinburgh. He wrote music for the theatre's pantomimes, and was in demand to play at balls and assemblies. When he died, his friend the craftsman-poet James Ballantyne, whose verses Alexander Mackenzie had set to music, published a poem to his memory in *The Scotsman*. While he lived, the Mackenzie household—in Northumberland Street and then Nelson Street, in Edinburgh's New Town—was a lively one.

His Campbell father-in-law had a retail lace-shop in George Street, then as now one of the finest streets in Edinburgh. Campbell put his widowed daughter into the shop as manager. When Cissie came to write up this story, based on her recall of her mother's reminiscences, she emphasized the tragic predicament of her maternal grandmother, attributing the lace-shop to her courageous enterprise, and creating out of Jessie Campbell Mackenzie a brave, unsupported provider like her own mother, Isabella Fairfield, in the next generation. But without help from the comfortable, commercial Campbells, the fatherless family would never have been able to live, as for thirty years they did, at 41 Heriot Row, the most prestigious residential street in Edinburgh. Heriot Row represented the high point of the Mackenzies' life, and took its place in family history as another lost Jerusalem, if a less glamorous one than wild, aristocratic County Kerry.

Isabella grew up in Heriot Row; her eldest brother, Alexander Campbell Mackenzie, went farther. He studied music in Germany, married a girl who worked in his mother's lace-shop, developed his career abroad, and finally settled in London, where he was Principal of the Royal Academy of Music for thirty-six years. This illustrious uncle of Cissie's composed oratorios, operas, and a violin concerto—works seldom performed today—and Lewis Carroll invited him to compose the music for an operetta based on the *Alice* books (but never came up with the libretto). He worked with Gilbert and Sullivan, knew all the composers and performers of his day, and had his career crowned by a knighthood in 1922. He took absolutely no interest in the less successful members of his family.

Isabella inherited the musical talent, and was a fine pianist; Cissie was to remember particularly her mother's playing of Schumann. As a female, Isabella was not given the same opportunities as the boys. After some mild European travel, she took a post in London with Mr. and Mrs.

Heinemann, who had a house in Eaton Square and a country place in Sussex. Emil Heinemann was a rich Jew, born in Hanover but naturalized British, and the family was cultivated and cosmopolitan. Mrs. Heinemann was American, and they had eight children; Isabella was "musical governess" to the two girls, Emily and Clara.

Isabella was happy in London, but after an unfortunate entanglement (according to Cissie) she left the Heinemanns and returned to Edinburgh—unwell, unwed, and far advanced in her twenties. She went out to Australia both for her health's sake and to check up on one of her brothers, John, who had been sent out in the hope that the dry air and warmth could cure his tubercular tendencies. Like Willie, the stay-at-home brother (another one had gone to Canada, and died), Johnny was not a lot of good by Heriot Row standards. Both were on their way to becoming chronic drunks. Isabella found Johnny integrated happily enough in the coarse gold-rush life, working with a troupe of variety artists and allied to Lizzie Wheeler, a cheery member of the company. Isabella travelled with them for a time, playing the piano; but it was hardly surprising that she accepted the proposal of Charles Fairfield, the dark, clever, intense Anglo-Irishman she met at Fitzroy.

4

The new couple settled at 26 Acland Street—a small pre-fabricated wooden house, with a little garden—at St. Kilda, Melbourne. The earliest extant family letter is from Jessie Campbell Mackenzie in Heriot Row, thanking the son-in-law she had never seen for sending her news about the baby, Lettie, born in 1885. "I will live in hope I will see the wee pet." Two years later a second daughter, Winnie, was born.

Charles Fairfield was no longer drawing for the Melbourne *Argus*, but had become a staff journalist, contributing under the pen-name "Ivan" long articles on current affairs, economics, and public controver-

sies. It was work that suited his interests and energies. His articles were
full of anecdotes and illustrations, not only from history and literature
but also from his own varied career. A typical Charles Fairfield sentence,
in an article about the relationship between bad legislation and excessive
profit-taking, began: "I remember a dear old Barcelona Jew, whom I used
to know in Havana . . ."

Nothing lasted with Charles. He lost favour with the newspaper
management. According to Lettie, this was because he supported Roman
Catholic schools; he was violently anti-Catholic, but believed in freedom
of choice. According to Cissie, it was because he leaked the news of a
forthcoming bank crash. Neither daughter had the means of knowing for
sure, and their explanations reflect their characteristic preoccupations.

Soon after Winnie's birth, they returned, penniless again, to Britain, and went to Scotland to be near Isabella's family. Charles found work
on the Glasgow *Herald,* and continued to send contributions back to the
Argus in Melbourne. He speculated with what money he had on mining
enterprises overseas. Cissie wondered why, in later life, jagged mountain
ranges made her uneasy—until she realized they reminded her of graphs
of the rise and fall of copper prices, anxiously scrutinized by her father.

Glasgow was a shock after the sunny beach-life of Australia, and
Isabella was delicate, suffering from eye-trouble. When she became pregnant again, the Fairfields moved south, to make a new start in London.
Mrs. Heinemann, Isabella's former employer, paid the rent of the furnished house they took in Westbourne Park, near Paddington Station.
The previous occupant of 28 Burlington Road had been a druggist's sales-
man, and most houses on the street were let out in rooms. The third and
last baby was born there on 21 December 1892; her father registered her
ten days later as "Cicely Isabel" (though the spelling of her first name
was often rendered later as "Cicily"). Isabella's ex-pupil Emily Heinemann, now Mrs. Bolland, stood godmother.

5

The first house that Cissie remembered, and with ecstasy, was 21 Streatham Place, off Brixton Hill in South London, where the family moved before she was two. This is the house described in her novel *The Fountain Overflows*, except that number 21 had no coach-house. It had, unusually, stables beneath the house, in an under-croft; but in any case the Fairfields could not afford to keep a carriage or horses. It was an early-nineteenth-century semi-detached villa, and the area was still semi-rural, with farms, market gardens, and fields of buttercups within walking distance. Roses climbed up their pillared porch, and there were chestnut trees at the bottom of the unkempt back garden. There was even—essential, for this family—an ancestral connection: Charles's great-grandfather Richard Fairfield, an eighteenth-century East India merchant, had described himself as "of Streatham Hill."

Here the Fairfields collected some decent but shabby furniture and family portraits, as described in *The Fountain Overflows*—the chairs of peeling red leather and the portrait of an ancestor by Lawrence, which hung over Cissie's bed. This soon had to be sold. It was the best home they ever had, and seemed to the children, in retrospect, like heaven. If the two elder girls were aware of tensions between their parents, Cissie was less so. Papa wrote in his study, and went out on strange errands at all hours; Mama worked her fingers to the bone for the family, and played the piano.

Cissie thought her mother had the professional air of a concert pianist, though she never was one. She knew that both her parents, who were not young, looked even older than they were. Isabella Fairfield was nervous, bony and dark, not pretty, badly dressed, "a shabby eagle." (In retrospect, Cissie thought she might have been anorexic.) Sometimes she looked and behaved so unconventionally as to seem eccentric. Cissie never underestimated this "ugly, witty, fascinating and intelligent woman." But Papa, "a shabby Prospero" and the only male in the house, was the more glamorous parent.

Mrs. Fairfield had relations in London, notably her successful musician brother, though he did not bother with them. At the seedier end of the social scale was her cousin Tom Mackenzie, a commercial traveller who lived with his wife and daughter, Dorothy, in Earlsfield, another South London suburb. Tom Mackenzie was an excellent amateur flautist but an "odious" and vulgar man; the Fairfields were frankly ashamed of him. There were more cousins, the Joseph Mackenzies, in Chiswick; he was a civil engineer married, according to Cissie, to a woman of gypsy origin.

Charles Fairfield's brothers were also in London. The girls liked Uncle Edward and Uncle Arthur, who talked to them about horse-racing and the glory of the British Empire. But Cissie in particular disliked and feared Arthur's wife, Aunt Sophie (née Blew-Jones), a handsome, dominant woman who was kind to Isabella Fairfield but spread an atmosphere of disapproval, especially of Charles's shortcomings as a provider. She may have had a poor opinion of all Fairfields; her husband's career at the Board of Trade ended in dismissal.

Cissie's picture of her father became with time a mixture of nostalgia and wish-fulfillment. She said, in her seventies, that her first memory of him was of his "great strength" when he pulled her out of the sea as a small child.* His "physical maleness" impressed her, as it impressed all females; she noticed, at five, how the girl at the farm where they went for milk flirted with him. Charles Fairfield was chronically unfaithful to his wife. He belonged not to the family but to the outside world; but he brought the world of newspapers and current events home with him, talking to the children as equals and insisting that they be literate and articulate.

Charles's politics were romantically conservative and individualist. He called himself a Liberal Unionist. His heroes were the eighteenth-century political philosopher Edmund Burke and, among his contemporaries, the sociologist Herbert Spencer, with whom he corresponded. He belonged to an anti-socialist society called the Liberty and Property De-

---

*She elaborated this and other memories of her father in *The Birds Fall Down* (1966), attributing them to her heroine, Laura, and Laura's father.

fence League, led by the Earl of Wemyss and Lord Bramwell (Charles wrote the article on Lord Bramwell in the *Dictionary of National Biography*). Though he was in favour of education for women, on the principle that a woman's duties were performed better by a well-informed person than an ignorant one, he was against women's suffrage, as his articles in the *Argus* attest: he called the women suffragists of the time "unsympathetic and repellent," "strange, shipwrecked lost souls."

His conservatism was in marked contrast to his own manner of life, which was non-conformist to the point of raffishness. Cissie later wrote that what Edmund Burke and her father had in common was that both "went on and on about order and stability while they reeled through space like a couple of drunken comets." ("Drunken" is to be taken figuratively; she said that Charles had a horror of alcohol.) A man without capital or property, he defended the rights of proprietors. A gambler, he wrote portentously in the *Argus* in the year Cissie was born that "about the great stock-markets of the world hovers the twittering marsh-light which gamblers know . . . and its flaring brightness distracts the eyes of men and women from the many puddles and black pools full of dead and wounded, in the path."

Ten years after his death, Cissie had a letter from an old Richmond friend of his, Tom Pillans, lamenting the grief it would have been to Charles, his "dearest and most intimate friend," to see his youngest daughter "a socialist and a suffragist." Pillans told her how "entrancing" Charles's company had been, and how exhilarating their discussions. "Your father was by far the cleverest, best-informed and most interesting man I ever knew." Cissie inherited his fine eyes and many of his contradictory characteristics.

When she was five, her daydream was to become a general in the British Army, after which, she imagined, Queen Victoria would gratefully make over to her the vast Tudor palace of Hampton Court. One of her memories of her father is more revealing of her character than of his. He came upon her in the Streatham Place garden digging up conkers which she had previously buried. When he asked her why, she replied, "I am God, and they are people, and I made them die, and now I am resurrecting them." He watched her for a while, smoking his pipe, and then asked why she had buried them in the first place, if she meant to dig them up again. Why not just leave them alive? She replied, "Well, that would have been all right for them, but it wouldn't have been any fun for me."

The point of the story for Cissie was that he went on watching her because he loved her, and, realizing this, "I dropped my trowel and ran over to him and put my arms round his neck and was swung up into his warmth." When he left home, she was, like many children in the same situation, afraid it was because she had been bad, or because he had not loved her enough. She blamed her elder sisters, probably unfairly, for implying that this was the case; she tended to attribute unhappiness to some outside enemy, as a defense against her low self-esteem: "I have naturally a strong sense of guilt. I have the type of mind that in less favourable conditions than mine would conceive the idea that it had been guilty of the sin against the Holy Ghost." Constantly seeking proof of her father's love, she found it in the memory of how he had turned to her in a grief of his own.

In 1897, the year Cissie became five, Lettie and Winnie were both seriously ill with meningitis. Charles's arrangement with the Melbourne *Argus* came to an end, and though he still contributed to the Glasgow *Herald* and occasionally to the *St. James's Gazette,* his income was further reduced. The hypocrisy and injustice of the Dreyfus case in France was one of Charles's great topics in the 1890s, and in this bad year of 1897 the Fairfields had a Dreyfus case of their own. Charles's younger brother, Edward, had become an assistant under-secretary at the Colonial Office, with special responsibility for South Africa. In the inquiry following the indefensible Jameson Raid launched in December 1895, Colonial Secretary Joseph Chamberlain's prior knowledge of the plan was suppressed, and Edward Fairfield was made the scapegoat, blamed for failing to understand or pass on messages from Africa.

Edward was deaf, which lent weight to the charge, and under strain in the period leading up to the inquiry; he collapsed and died in April 1897, leaving the field to his detractors. His case was not helped later by the ill-informed interventions of his other brother, Arthur, with the se- lect committee of inquiry.

After Edward's death, Cissie remembered, her father came to her room and lay down beside her, talking to her about his brother and their childhood in Ireland, and weeping. Her recollections suggested to her older self that he had "a close if demented relationship with me." When she was psychoanalysed, in her thirties, she uncovered what seemed to be an even earlier memory of her father standing naked beside the bars of her crib. She believed this, and its disturbing sequel, to be fantasy rather than true memory. She was not generally adept at telling the two phenomena apart.

Her sisters were more alive than she to the other causes of her father's troubles, and to their mother's unhappiness. When Winnie read *The Fountain Overflows,* which is a fictional version of the Streatham years, she commented that Cissie had minimized the unbearable sadness, since "no one could read the truth." But for Cissie they really were happy years, and 21 Streatham Place and its surroundings an enchanted site. She never ceased to believe in the superiority of South London—its light, its air, the special greenness of the trees.

They had left Streatham Place for reasons of economy by early 1898, and moved to the cheaper and less pleasant house in Richmond. There Charles's prospects deteriorated further—though Cissie's last book, *1900,* opens with an account of them all walking up Richmond Hill in May of the year Gladstone died, very much a family, her parents discussing the old statesman's passing earnestly and amicably. On the facing page in the book is a photograph of little Cissie, sitting among bracken and long grass, surrounded by older sisters and cousins. Her eyes are closed, her mouth is open, and Winnie is feeding her with blackberries. It is a picture of a trusting, petted child.

6

"The detachment of my father from the consequences of his actions was almost a cause, like his anti-socialism. The whole strength of his being was turned in a direction which led him away from his wife and children." When Charles Fairfield left them in 1901, he went out to Sierra Leone in West Africa to launch a pharmaceuticals factory. To judge from the impact on his family, his departure was more

definitive than a temporary job abroad would suggest. Mrs. Fairfield
used to copy her daughters' verses out in a book. In the year that Charles
went away, eight-year-old Cissie wrote two sadly knowing poems, "He"
and "She," in which each voice reproaches the other for betraying their
love. She probably could not have told whether "She" was her mother or
herself.

Charles had moved out before he set sail, writing to sixteen-year-
old Lettie from an address in Kensington: "This is a *venture,* indeed, on
which I go. . . . Thank goodness I am very well and active. It is not
much use discussing the future now." He would be back soon if things
went well, if not, "it will be a longer time before I see you."

Mrs. Fairfield took her girls back to Edinburgh, where the living
was cheap. While the move took place, Cissie was despatched for a term
to Helsington Towers, a Bournemouth boarding-school where Mrs. Fairfield's cousin Jessie Watson Campbell taught French. Cissie liked Aunt
Jessie but not the school. Her mother got together some money by working for the American evangelists Torrey and Alexander on their British
tour, and the Heinemanns, hearing of her plight, gave her a small regular
allowance, "and what we'd have done without it I don't know."

Cissie was taken to meet the Heinemanns in Eaton Square before
the move to Edinburgh, and remembered Emil Heinemann* as a "tall,
impressive, ugly man with very beautiful manners" and a strong German
accent. She remembered too their "glorious, stodgy, comfortable house"
with butler and footmen, red damask wallpaper in the dining-room, damask panels in the drawing-room. Their kindness to her mother seemed to
her in retrospect "amazing," since Isabella had only worked for the family
for two or three years.

Charles Fairfield was back from Sierra Leone, "that luckless place,"
sooner than anyone anticipated. After only four months he was writing
to Lettie again, from Liverpool. "As you advise I *will* write to mamma in
a day or two, but I want first to 'settle down' a bit and be able to tell her
some good news or other. I shall not ask her for anything except shirts
and collars." His friend Tom Pillans had been up to see him, and he was

* It is likely that Emil Heinemann and his ménage contributed to the creation of Mr.
Morpurgo, the kind and generous Jew who helps the Aubrey family in *The Fountain
Overflows* and its sequels.

finishing a painting of Sierra Leone commissioned by Sir Alfred Jones.*
He told Lettie that he was hoping to get work in connection with the new
Manchester-to-Liverpool rail link, since he knew the solicitor to the railway company. He asked about the girls' new schools, but did not suggest
that he would rejoin them soon.

Charles Fairfield stayed in Liverpool for the next five years, in failing health and fortune. His last note to Lettie, in October 1906, is addressed to her at her grandmother's house in Edinburgh, which suggests
that his wife did not choose to let him know exactly where they were
living. It is a pathetic pencil scrawl from 71 Upper Stanhope Street in
the Toxteth area of Liverpool, a poor street of artisans' dwellings and
lodging-houses. "Good bye Lettie, Winnie, Cissie. I am dying I loved you.
Papa." On the back was a note from the doctor: "Come immediately. Bad
news."

Isabella Fairfield went alone to Liverpool to bury the husband she
had not seen for over five years. He was taken from his lodgings to Toxteth Cemetery in a horse-drawn hearse; this, with the polished oak cof-
fin, robe, bearers, gratuities, and a brougham for the single mourner,
cost £9.3.0. The grave remained bare until 1927, when Lettie arranged
for it to be dignified with a stone kerb and a carved inscription: "Charles
Fairfield, died October 1906, aged 63 years. Rest in peace."

7

"I had a glorious father, I had no father at all." Cissie
wrote in her old age that she remembered her mother coming home from
the funeral with scraps of paper on which he had written words of love,
and telling the girls how she had met a young clerk in the lodging-house

---

*Jones was senior partner in the Elder Dempster shipping line, chairman of the Bank of
West Africa, and founder of the Liverpool School of Tropical Medicine. He was probably
behind Charles's pharmaceuticals project.

who had spoken of Mr. Fairfield with the deepest respect. Isabella brought very little else home: his watch, his studs, cuff links, and dressing-case had all gone. "If he had been found dead in a hedgerow he could not have been more picked bare of possessions."

Cissie was nearly fourteen when her father died; clever, and mature for her age, she won the Best Essay prize, junior section, at her Edinburgh school that year. She was capable of remembering what happened with accuracy. She wrote later of the bitterness her mother felt at her father's abdication from any attempt to support his family—a resentment conveyed to the girls and shared by Lettie, who had played the painful role of go-between. Winnie suffered by sympathizing with both her parents. Going through their father's papers after his death, she found "many frantic letters from young girls," a fact that she only revealed to Cissie after she had read *The Fountain Overflows*. Loyally, Winnie stressed that it was the girls who seemed to be doing all the running. For Cissie, her father's seeming rejection of his family was so painful that she later devoted much emotional energy to denying that it had happened; and, indeed, from the meagre evidence it seems possible that Isabella had played her part in the separation by giving him some kind of ultimatum.

Cissie was to compose countless written versions of her parents' marriage and its unhappy end, in drafts of her memoirs, in memos, notebooks, and diaries, in letters to friends, and in fierce communications to writers seeking biographical information about her. Most often the version that she wanted the public and her own descendants to accept was the one that she needed for her own comfort. Her father, she said, stayed in Liverpool at her mother's suggestion, since she was busy nursing her own mother. He lived in a "comfortable family hotel." He was not responsible for his insolvency. Most important, "nobody abandoned anybody." She repeatedly stated that he died from a heart attack "soon" or "very shortly" after his return from West Africa. For the most painful fact of all was that her parents had lived apart for five years and presumably would have continued to do so.

The failure of this flawed and gifted man makes a pitiful story, and any daughter might wish to defend such a father from the glib judgement of strangers. Cissie, though she took her mother's side as the girl, could not, as a grown woman, reject him. She created a myth out of the wonderful father she had and did not have.

The impossibility of knowing exactly what had happened between her parents made her ambivalent about the opposite sex. She longed for men to be strong and supportive, while believing that they were generally inadequate and destructive. She was to guard her independence ferociously, while expressing resentment towards the men who encouraged her to do so. Because her father had left the family penniless and *déclassé,* money, clothes, and food became her emotional currency, carrying an inflated symbolic value.

She was frequently to say that human beings did not have enough information about the conditions of their existence, and that as a writer she tried to discover it for herself. The versions, or stories, that she told herself out of her need to handle this first crisis are reflected in all her writing. An artist, she wrote, is goaded into creation "by his need to resolve some important conflict, to find out where the truth lies among divergent opinions on a vital issue." His work is often "a palimpsest on which are superimposed several incompatible views about his subject."

She made such a palimpsest not only in her work but out of the story of her life. The need to make a pattern out of random happenings led her to interpret her experience as if it were a dream, and to restructure her past as if it were, as she said, "a bad book" which had to be improved. Although she drafted and redrafted the raw material of her life until she was on her deathbed, she knew it was a hopeless task. Destiny, she wrote, cared nothing for the orderly presentation of material; "it likes to hold its cornucopia upside down and wave it while its contents drop anywhere they like over time and space. Brave are our own human attempts to correct this sluttish habit." But it is "only by making such efforts that we survive."

She wrote that the *Confessions* of St. Augustine were too subjectively true to be objectively true. There were things in Augustine's life "which he could not bear to think of at all, or very much, or without falsification, so the *Confessions* are not without gaps, understatements and misstatements." She could have been describing her own autobiographical process. Like many artists, she most revealed herself when describing someone else. She wrote, for example, of Ford Madox Ford that although he was a fantasist he was not a liar: "Liars see facts as they are and transform them into fantasies, but in Ford's case facts changed to fantasies in the very instant of their impact on his senses." Her own fantasies were something that her enemies held against her and her allies enjoyed or took in their stride.

Yet she was to be, among much else, one of the best and most successful investigative journalists of her generation, with an energy for research and a hunger for dry facts beyond the normal range. These conflicting strands are united by her heightened sense of the drama of life. In *The Fountain Overflows* the mother teaches her daughters that life is "as extraordinary as music says it is," and the actions and feelings of ordinary people are all as significant as those of "people in Shakespeare."

The story of Cicely Fairfield, who became Rebecca West, is not only a narrative but a web of perceptions, constantly modified. Part of the purpose of telling it is to disentangle what really mattered to her from what did not. There are some events which become experience, she wrote, and "many more which do not." There is also often a gap between what she felt, or decided, had happened and how it seemed to somebody else. Human beings felt insecure, she wrote, unless they could find out what was happening around them. "That is why historians publicly pretend that they can give an exact account of events in the past, though they privately know that all the past will let us know about events above a certain degree of importance is a bunch of alternative hypotheses."

8

Edinburgh is a beautiful and proud capital. Its setting, its architecture, its history, and its intellectual tradition give it a stature equal to that of any city in northern Europe.

But it is, within the context of the United Kingdom as a whole, a provincial city and a relatively small one. There has been, among its better-off inhabitants, a streak of petty snobbery and a puritan rejection of the social-rule breaker that could be experienced as constricting. In the early 1900s social class was an inescapable fact of life.

In the graceful streets, squares, and crescents of the New Town, laid out in the late eighteenth century, lived the upper and the successful professional classes. Scottish landowners had their town houses here, and advocates, judges, physicians, surgeons, professors, and rich trades-men lived orderly lives behind doors which displayed larger expanses of highly polished brasswork than the doors of any city on earth.

South of the New Town, beyond Prince's Street and dominating it, stands the Castle on its high crag, and clinging to the rocky farther side of the crag is the Old Town. Before the New Town was built, rich and poor lived here hugger-mugger, literally on top of one another—in the high, ancient, smoke-blackened tenements whose stone stairs were but extensions of the street, and in the closes and courts linked by alleys and stairways cut into the rock. By the turn of the century, the Old Town, insanitary and ruinous, had been abandoned to the growing population of urban poor and the rowdy hopelessness of drink, crime, and prostitution.

South of the Old Town, on level ground again, is more fine eigh-teenth-century planned development, of an indigenous and simple kind: George Square, where Sir Walter Scott lived and where Cissie was to go to school, and Buccleuch Place, where the Fairfields were to find a home. In her novel *The Judge* Cissie was to describe Buccleuch Place as "a street of tall houses separated by so insanely wide a cobbled roadway that it had none of the human, close-pressed quality of a street, but was desolate with the natural desolation of a ravine." In the years before World War I, many of the tall Buccleuch Place houses were run-down, in multiple occupation, chiefly by Jewish refugees. This area had already lost out to the prestige of the New Town on the other side of the Castle Mound; the Victorian residential streets that were added to the South Side became lower-middle-class territory, genteel but not smart. In Edinburgh, social inequalities were if possible even more apparent than elsewhere in Brit-ain at the same period. It was a stratified city where a family was irrevo-cably "placed" not only by which street it lived in, but which side, and which end, of that street.

In later life Cissie was to write and speak about the poverty of her childhood in a way that suggested she had been seriously deprived. When it transpired that she was chiefly complaining about having less good clothes, or less good parties, than some other children, critics were quick to accuse her of snobbery and bad faith. In comparison with millions of others, she had a reasonable childhood. But those who were rooted in one class or culture had less of a problem: it is easy to feel proud, and even grateful, about a solid working-class background. It was those who were on a cusp, without acknowledged status in any section of the community, who felt social differences most painfully. Cissie was of a generation by whom these groupings could not be forgotten or disregarded. "In any class I feel at home, and I am never accepted, because of the traces I bear of my other origins. This does not, instance by instance, cause me any pain, but my experience of rejection has been an agony."

Mrs. Fairfield, brought up in Edinburgh, knew its tribal customs. To the girls it was all new. Their grandmother, having retired from her lace-shop, was no longer in the New Town but at 5 Duncan Street, a terraced house built around 1825, on the then undistinguished South Side. Old Mrs. Mackenzie was bedridden, cared for by the girls' cross old great-aunt Eezie (another Isabella); also living there was unmarried, ageing, alcoholic Uncle Willie. The four Fairfields moved in with them until they found a temporary house of their own nearby for £16 a year: 2 Hope Park Square.

This is Ellen's house in *The Judge*, and the square is, as the novel describes it, "the queerest place, hardly forty paces across, on three sides of which small squat houses sat closely with a quarrelling air." The fourth side looks over railings onto the open space called the Meadows, and the dark little square—more of a courtyard—can only be approached under an archway from a lane. Today Hope Park Square (which, like 24 Buccleuch Place, is now part of Edinburgh University) seems pictur-esque; in 1902 it was nearly a slum, and the lanes around it were dark and dirty.

To Cissie, the Edinburgh set-up seemed "deplorable." Her grand-mother's house in Duncan Street, occupied by "a dough-faced prisoner in a four-poster, her hunchbacked jailer, and my whisky-sodden uncle," held no attractions. The Scottish relations seemed a depressing lot. In com-parison with absent Papa and the Fairfield uncles, they were not "edu-cated" people with contacts in the wider world—though their unmitigated Scottishness, Cissie liked to believe, had been enlivened in the eighteenth century by African blood from a Berber bride brought back by a soldier ancestor, "but alas, my nearer ancestors were ashamed of this and destroyed all traces." Cissie, who was startlingly dark-skinned when young, thought she herself looked a bit like Pearl Bailey; but this family myth is unverifiable, like so many others.

Only in distant retrospect was Cissie able to acknowledge the courage and kindheartedness of the Mackenzie women at least, and their traditional Scots qualities and household skills. "All these people spoke broad Scots among themselves, and used a different, more formal Scots tongue, Scots more by accent than vocabulary, when they dealt with strangers, and in both cases with eloquence and good manners, and even a certain grandeur." But in spite of learning to appreciate her Campbell and Mackenzie ancestry, "I could happily have discarded many of my relatives on this Scottish side." Uncle Willie seemed particularly horrible to a little girl, "not distinguishable from the stumbling brutes I saw pushed out of public houses if I happened to be out late at night"; he brought the family frighteningly close to "the slumdwellers who would foregather about the rotting doors of dead men's mansions" in the Old Town—as Cissie was to describe them in *The Judge*.

The girls adapted to the new situation. Lettie and Cissie both had above-average looks, talent, and energy, and responded to circumstances with a determination to excel. Winnie, the middle sister, shared their gifts but lacked their drive. Troubles drove her in on herself; never robust, she tended to withdraw from social encounters and never used her talents to the full. She won, however, a scholarship to Cheltenham Ladies' College, a prestigious English boarding-school; although Cissie made fun of her "fancy" Cheltenham ways, Winnie remained her favourite sister. She admired Winnie's imaginative gifts, and was grateful for her ready affection. Winnie repressed a lot of her disappointments. During her last illness she said to Cissie: "Oh yes, I am Anne Brontë" (Anne having the reputation of being the mildest and least talented of the Brontë sisters). Cissie then felt as if Winnie's banked-up resentments were suddenly revealed: "it was as if I had opened a furnace door and stood in the blast of burning air."

Only Cissie had to take the full force of the Edinburgh experience. She and Lettie both went to day school—but Lettie only for a year, before starting to train as a doctor at the Edinburgh Medical College for Women on a Carnegie scholarship. Lettie took her position as head, as she saw it, of the family very seriously. Blonde, pretty, and ambitious, she qualified in 1907 with a first prize in clinical surgery and several medals.

Cissie became a pupil at George Watson's Ladies' College in George
Square, with a scholarship that took care of all fees, when she was
eleven. George Watson's, a nineteenth-century Merchant Company foun-
dation, was only a minute's walk from the flat at 24 Buccleuch Place,
where the family moved around this time. It had an excellent music department—larger than any other department in the school—and employed male teachers as well as female. Cissie liked best Mr. Budge, fat
and balding, the inspired English teacher; she also liked her handsome
Latin teacher, Miss Macdonald. The school offered mathematics, science, art, French, and German, but not Greek.

For the time, it was as good an education as could be found for a
girl. Cissie became a fair Latinist but had little talent for modern languages. She never spoke French very well, even after a lifetime as a Fran-
cophile and long periods spent in France. An interviewer for *Le Figaro
Littéraire* was to write charmingly that *"Notre langue, dans sa bouche, ras-
semble les gazouillis et les décalages d'un idiome de l'Ile de Pâques."* ("Our
language, on her lips, acquires the twitters and dislocations of an Easter
Island tongue.") She took typing as an extra, having begun on her mother's machine at home; Mrs. Fairfield was making ends meet by typing
music theses for Edinburgh University students.

In her "Recitations" book Cissie copied out poetry she learned by
heart: passages from Browning, Shakespeare, Newbolt, Whitman, Yeats,
Tennyson. She and Winnie were fluent versifiers in the Romantic mode;
at thirteen, Cissie expressed the excited restlessness of early adolescence
in terms of nymphs and satyrs, whose company she longed to join: "I hate
this thin blood—slow and pale!"

She had piano lessons at George Watson's with Dr. Ross, and prac-
tised on her mother's piano in the Buccleuch Place flat. Mrs. Fairfield
took the two younger girls to first-class concerts; they heard Saint-Saëns
and Debussy perform. But though she did well at everything, Cissie had
only one close friend at school, Flora Duncan. For the first few years in
Edinburgh the world outside the family circle seemed too threatening.
Visiting her godmother, Mrs. Bolland, in the English Midlands, she felt
an outsider and very much the "old governess's child." This was around
the time her father died, when the family's concealed stress and distress
were most intense.

After his death Cissie's energies and emotions were released, and she embarked on a high-spirited and adventurous girlhood. Feminism,for the Fairfield girls, was a self-evident fact of life. They all three became radicals: socialists and suffragists. It was Winnie who wrote (but never published) a passionate "Letter to Hilaire Belloc by a Suffragist." Six years older than Cissie, she now left home to train as a teacher at the Maria Grey College. It was Cissie, aged only fourteen, who burst into print.

She wrote a letter to *The Scotsman,* signed with her own name and published on 16 October 1907. Headed "Women's Electoral Claims," it defended the split of the National Women's Social and Political Union (NWSPU) from the Liberal Party, which had disappointed their hopes, and stressed "the profound national effects of the subjection of women on the nation." She pointed out that the position of women in industry— with special reference to the Cradley Heath chain-makers and the white-lead workers—"affected the Empire itself." She drew attention to the "sex degradation implied in manhood suffrage."

It is not impossible that she had a little help from her new friends with this solemn and impressive letter. It was written shortly after a women's suffrage demonstration in Edinburgh which attracted four thousand marchers, to whom young Cissie had attached herself. Winnie was away in Alençon, teaching English and perfecting her French, and wrote to her little sister: "I like to hear of my Baby playing with the swell dogs; no doubt the suffragettes like to attach to themselves babies with a promising physique." To their mother, Winnie wrote that "Cissie seems to have become a 'féministe enragée'; much as I approve of the cause, I shouldn't like a relative of mine to become a martyr to it."

Cissie's "promising physique" and exuberance were exercised in tomboyish ways too. She described to Lettie, now a clinical assistant at Birmingham City Asylum, how she had walked with Flora Duncan from Balerno in the Pentland Hills back to Buccleuch Place; another day they walked from Balerno to Colinton, and climbed the waterfall barefoot. These adventures in the hills were to be her best memories of Scotland, and she relived them in imagination through Ellen Melville in *The Judge,* the only novel in which she used Edinburgh as a setting; and the heroine, like herself, is a fiery teenage suffragette, eager for excitement, and finding what she needed in the women's movement: the "sense of love and power that comes from comradeship."

The WSPU leaders were Cissie's romantic heroines. At fifteen, she put her hair up, and looked older than her years. She joined the Votes for Women Club in Edinburgh—"a sort of secret militant society," as she told Lettie. She sold the WSPU journal, *Votes for Women,* on Prince's Street, and wore a "Votes for Women" badge to school. She went south to Harrogate in Yorkshire on a propaganda exercise with Lettie, and was taken up by one of the leaders, the Leeds schoolteacher Mary Gawthorpe, whom Cissie admired greatly and called "Lovey Mary." Cissie became a mascot, and a promising recruit, to the northern suffrage workers; after one meeting Mary Gawthorpe ("very pretty and funny") called Cissie up on to the platform "and we had a talk."

Cissie went to Harrogate again, on her own, and reported to Lettie on a "splendid meeting": "Both Christabel [Pankhurst] and Lovey Mary at their very best." Christabel was "very decent indeed, and not at all sarcastic." Cissie was also active in Newcastle, where there was a bye-election, and stood outside the polling booth shouting "Keep the Liberals out!" for eight hours. Lovey Mary was there too: "How the crowds adored her! But Mrs Pankhurst had a wonderful hold on them."

In December 1909 there were violent scenes in Edinburgh on the occasion of a visit from Sir Edward Grey.* At his meeting in Leith, "Miss Hudson addressed the crowd and led them against the doors." Miss Hudson was struck in the face repeatedly by the police but kept coming back. Then, Cissie told Lettie (who was now doing a stint at a Manchester asylum), the police led a baton charge: "It was a disgusting sight." Blood flowed, and Miss Hudson was taken away, still holding the purple, white, and green flag of the WSPU above her head. Cissie carried the dramatic story back to headquarters. She never came into conflict with the law herself, though once, outside the House of Commons in London, she had to wriggle out of her coat, leaving it in the hands of two policemen, and escape by crawling away through the crowd.

From a conservative adult's point of view, this vital seventeen-year-old was running out of control. School and home life were suffering. Mrs. Fairfield was ill (with exophthalmic goitre) and when she had to go into the Infirmary, Cissie, with her elder sisters away, was on her own. She

---

*Foreign Secretary. A particular enemy of the suffragettes, since it was after a disturbance at his meeting in Manchester in October 1905 that demonstrators had first been sent to prison.

was getting on badly with her mother anyway. Mrs. Fairfield was even more anxious than Winnie on seeing her youngest daughter becoming a *feministe enragée;* it is impossible to overstress the distaste and horror with which the militants were regarded by the majority of both men and women. Nor did Cissie get on with her headmistress, Miss Ainslie, who made few allowances for her home situation or her political commitment. There was some sort of trouble at school, and a spell of illness—a tubercular infection of the left lung. Cissie left school under a cloud, with no mention of further education. Sensible Lettie suggested that she look for office work.

9

Music was central to the Fairfields' life, but for Cissie it came second to the theatre. She had been thrilled, at ten, by Sarah Bernhardt in *La Dame aux Camélias,* and in her teen-age years she saw Mrs. Patrick Campbell, Ellen Terry, and the singer Yvette Guilbert. She found time, in addition to her suffragette activities, not only to see plays but also to act in them. Both plays and protest marches were in a sense public appearances, and perhaps complemented one another; theatre stories in her letters to Lettie come hard on the heels of her accounts of demonstrations. She saw nearly every production that came to Edinburgh, including the risqué *What Every Woman Knows* by J. M. Barrie.

She belonged to an amateur dramatic company run by Graeme Goring, for whom she had little respect. He was "a perfect and entire Ass, with an absorbing reverence for the romantic drama," though she acknowledged that he had something to teach her about "the voice." She despised the little-girl parts she was inevitably asked to play, and described to Lettie the "awful ordeal" of having to "enter the room dancing, my hands behind my back, singing."

When, at fifteen, she went backstage at the King's Theatre in Edinburgh while the Christmas pantomime was in production, she thought

that both she and Flora Duncan were "better looking than the actresses,"
as she told Lettie. Cissie had fine dark hair, a wide forehead, a wide
mouth, large bright dark eyes, and a well-developed if stocky figure that
was to cause her problems later—"my sturdy pack-horse build," as she
was to call it. Her own opinion was that although she was not a beauty
she was "capable in certain conditions of reminding people of beauty,"
although "I have ugly feet and ankles, I have always known it."

She had both the appearance and the temperament to make a career
on the stage, though there were counter-indications. One of these was,
paradoxically, her tendency to react histrionically to crises in ordinary
life. She was claustrophobic; she tended to express emotional strain by
physical collapse; her high-strung nervousness also showed in a skin-
irritation on her wrists and hands, and a slight involuntary facial
grimace, both of which affected her under stress. Her "twitch," Winnie
candidly said, was enough in itself to prevent her from being a success on
the stage. Cissie's sisters, though they marvelled at her exploits, refused
to be impressed by her.

In April 1910, aged seventeen, she went to London to audition for
the Academy of Dramatic Art in Gower Street, which had been founded
only six years before. (Later it became the Royal Academy of Dramatic
Art, known as RADA.) "I fainted in the Tube going up, at Baker
Street. . . . Three very nice women came and looked after me, and one
asked, 'Are you going to meet anyone who'll look after you—a sister?'
'No', I muttered piteously, 'A theatrical manager', and closed my eyes. I
then heard a whisper. 'Poor child—an actress!'"

After this fine performance, she was seen and heard at the Academy
by the administrator, Kenneth Barnes, and three others. "Oh, the 'manner'! They all sat and looked 'brilliant'. They were kind, though." She
was accepted, to begin at the end of the month. She collapsed again afterwards on the doorstep of a friend of Lettie's in York Road, Lambeth, and,
the friend being out, was succoured by her room-mate, Chris Hartley.

Chris Hartley, older than Cissie, shortly married and became Chris
Bishop; she was to be a close friend. It was with Chris that Cissie went
to the first London performance of Chekhov's *The Cherry Orchard,* when
the audience, after howling with derision during the first act, ended up
applauding wildly. The Bishops belonged to the Fabian Society, and it was

on that initial meeting in York Road that Cissie first heard scandal about the famous author and former Fabian H. G. Wells.

Chris told Cissie, and Cissie reported to Lettie, that in his novel *Ann Veronica* "Wells has given every particular of the proceedings c.f. Amber Reeves, after she became insane from over-study." What Wells, a twice-married man in his forties, had actually depicted in his novel was his passionately sexual affair with young Amber, the daughter of his friends and fellow-Fabians Maud and Pember Reeves. This had been published six months before; the current scandal was in fact the recent birth of Amber's daughter by Wells. Obviously, Cissie had not yet read *Ann Veronica*; and her new friend had censored the gossip for the young girl's ears.

10

Cissie's Edinburgh life was over. Like both her sisters, she left the scene of her eventful girlhood without a tear. She rarely talked about Edinburgh, and rarely wrote about "the Scottish blight that ruined my early life." It was connected with fatherlessness, with being poor and socially uneasy. Her mother's bitterness against her husband had infected those years, and fuelled Cissie's ecstatic feminism. In her Edinburgh-set novel, *The Judge*, the young heroine remembers "no good of her father," who is depicted as an emptily boastful Irishman, "a specialist in disappointment."

The Fairfield household moved back to London. Winnie had qualified as a teacher, and took a post in a boys' preparatory school. Lettie was employed by the London County Council as medical officer for schools. They found a small semi-detached house in Chatham Close in the Hampstead Garden Suburb, on the extreme northern edge of the capital. It was a brand-new development of cheap, cottage-style housing; there was a long way to walk to shops or public transport to the city centre, but it was quiet. They called the house Fairliehope, after a farmhouse with a view over the Forth they had liked in the Pentland Hills.

The new house was not far from where Aunt Sophie and Uncle Arthur Fairfield lived in Golders Green. Before her mother moved south, Cissie had to stay with Aunt Sophie, and hated it. Both Cissie and Winnie believed that Aunt Sophie was a morphine addict. This forceful woman approved of Lettie, who was hardworking, responsible, and successful, and disapproved of headstrong Cissie, who in turn resented her bitterly.

Cissie tended to externalize her problems, attributing failure or unhappiness to a malign fate. One of the last friends in her long life was the comedian Frankie Howerd. In the car after a lunch with him in the 1970s, she asked him whether he felt that the fates were against him— clearly expecting the answer "Yes." When he replied that he felt that anything that had gone wrong was generally a result of his own mistakes, she was silent. It was not just fate that Cissie blamed for her own troubles but, very often, a particular person, the intimate enemy. Aunt Sophie had been generous during the difficult years, but for Cissie, whose fragile self-esteem she had damaged, she became the prototype of a series of monsters in human form. "The darkness and fear of my childhood was due to one person; who became several."

Cissie attended the Academy of Dramatic Art for three terms (the full course was four), from April 1910 to the end of March 1911, at 12 guineas a term. By her own account, she did not do well there. She had come with a recommendation from the actress Rosina Filippi, who had heard her recite in Edinburgh. Miss Filippi had taught at the Academy, but left before Cissie arrived; Cissie ascribed her own lack of success to the fact that Filippi and the administrator, Kenneth Barnes, had parted on bad terms. She was also self-conscious about her "twitch," and felt at a disadvantage because she could not afford good clothes. The greatest friend she made there, Greta Wood, recalled three-quarters of a century later how half Cissie's false moustache fell off while she was playing Antonio in *The Merchant of Venice,* humiliating her in front of Mr. Barnes, who was not kind.

But Cissie, always articulate and outspoken, learned at the Academy how to control and project her voice. Though she still had the light voice of a young girl, it became resonant and expressive, any Edinburgh intonation—"that delightful pinched Edinburgh accent"—eradicated. She left the Academy "beaten," as she felt, but determined, at eighteen years of age, to find work in the theatre for herself. She got the part of Regina in a production of Ibsen's *Ghosts,* and a small part in *Phyl,* a play by Cicely Hamilton which was performed in Eastbourne and in the theatre on Brighton's West Pier during the summer season.

She became a writer "without choosing to do so—at home we all wrote and thought nothing of it." She was still at the Academy when her first journalism was published: a review of Gorky's play *The Lower Depths,* for the London *Evening Standard.* The regular theatre critic was unable to go, and gave her the two free tickets (she took Lettie with her) on condition that she send in a notice. After this successful coup she called on the London bureau chief of the Melbourne *Argus*—the same man who had employed her father—and asked him for work. He told her to "find something more suitable to do than writing," and proceeded to give a job to the child of another former colleague, who happened to be a boy. But Cissie found a better platform.

The first issue of *The Freewoman,* a feminist weekly, appeared on 23 November 1911. The editor and leader-writer was a young woman from Lancashire, Dora Marsden, whom Cissie thought "one of the most beautiful women I have ever seen." She was a close friend of Mary Gaw-thorpe, Cissie's patron and heroine, who at this stage was co-editor though she soon fell out with Dora Marsden over the latter's critical at-titude to the WSPU. In the second issue of *The Freewoman,* on 30 No-vember, there was a review of a book about the position of women in Indian life; the reviewer was Cicily (*sic*) Fairfield, and she began her piece with a bang: "There are two kinds of imperialists—imperialists and bloody imperialists." (Shaw's *Pygmalion,* in which the phrase "Not bloody likely" elicited gasps of scandalized laughter from the audience, was not performed until 1913.) She liked to go for the jugular in her first sen-tence, as in a review of Strindberg's published plays: "Writers on the subject of August Strindberg have hitherto omitted to mention that he could not write."

It was the following spring when Cissie began using a pseudonym, chiefly in order to pacify her anxious mother. Much could be made of her choice of the name "Rebecca West," a character in Ibsen's play *Ros-mersholm* who is the mistress of a married man and compels him to join

her in a melodramatic double suicide by drowning. Cissie Fairfield was
no one's mistress, and she came to regret the Ibsen connection, insisting
that she chose the name in a hurry when the paper was going to press,
and that she liked neither the play nor the character. It was Ibsen, she
wrote in middle life, who first taught her that it was ideas that make the
world go round, but soon "I began to realize that Ibsen cried out for ideas
for the same reason that men call out for water, because he had not
got any."

But no one would choose to sail under a flag that she actively repudiated, and, indeed, Ibsen's Rebecca West speaks some lines which (as
her friend the columnist Bernard Levin said at her memorial service in
1983) might have been written to sum up her flesh-and-blood namesake:
"Live, work, act. Don't sit here and brood and grope among insoluble
enigmas." Many of those unfamiliar with Ibsen's work, and who only
knew this marvellous girl as Rebecca West, assumed from the name that
she was Jewish. She was in fact, both by temperament and circumstances, an honorary Jew. The Hampstead Garden Suburb and the adjacent suburb of Hendon were favoured by members of the Jewish
community who were less impoverished than those in the East End of
London but less prosperous than those who lived in Hampstead or in
Golders Green. Many of Rebecca's closest friends, from girlhood on, were
Jewish.

Hers was an instantly successful pseudonym. She was transformed
into Rebecca West not only in professional but in personal life as well, at
least with new friends. To her family, she remained Cissie.

11

Rebecca met new people at *The Freewoman*'s fort-
nightly discussion circle, where she was a lively presence—it was too
much like being in church, she thought—always seeking to open feminist questions out to include literature and philosophy. In May 1912 she

read an ambitious paper to the circle on "Interpretations of Life," about duality between man and woman and between God and man.

God existed, then and later, for Rebecca. Her quarrel with Him as a girl was that He did not take the responsibility for crimes committed in His name. A "new God" would grow out of man's humanity to man—that is, out of socialism: "If we see that life is ordered so that humanity may flower unstinted by poverty and unhappiness . . . a God will come to us born of the human will." Her socialist feminism found fault with the established church, which panicked "if women show any signs of having close relations with Christ."

Lettie had joined the Fabian Women's Group as soon as the Fairfields moved to London, and as a woman doctor was particularly welcomed. Her younger sisters joined the Fabians in her wake, and Rebecca, still in her teens, met luminaries such as George Bernard Shaw, a frequent speaker. She admired his "greyhound" appearance, his athletic bearing, his voice, and his eloquence. "The effect he created was more stupendous since in those days every well-to-do man wore stuffy clothes, ate too much, took too little exercise, and consequently looked like a bolster." But she did not, in her maturer years, admire his work: "I passionately resent the fact that God gave him a beautiful style and that he used it to preach tedious and reactionary ideas." Nor did she continue to admire him as a male specimen: on account of his sexless marriage, he became "a eunuch perpetually inflamed by flirtation."

In September 1912 Rebecca West wrote two articles which had important consequences. One was a notice of *The New Humpty-Dumpty* by Ford Madox Hueffer, until recently editor of *The English Review*, in which her piece appeared. Hueffer had published the book under a pseudonym; Rebecca's humorous notice made the book's true authorship clear to anyone who could read between the lines, and Hueffer asked her to tea.

Or, rather, Violet Hunt did. She and Hueffer were living in London as man and wife at her house, South Lodge, 80 Campden Hill Road. Violet Hunt was a novelist with private means, well past her first youth, who had had many lovers (including H. G. Wells). She and Hueffer entertained young literary people—"*les Jeunes,*" as they called their protégés—and Rebecca became part of the group. Violet Hunt recorded her first impression of an ingenue Rebecca, in a pink frock and a "country-girlish" straw hat that hid her "splendid liquid eyes." She sat with her feet planted firmly together, her satchel-like handbag in her lap; she was "the ineffable schoolgirl," with a voice like milk and honey. She was "quite superiorly, ostentatiously young"—yet, said Violet Hunt, she already had Fleet Street at her feet. Her articles and reviews were making "not so much a splash, as a hole in the world." Rebecca West, in short, was news.

In *The English Review,* from which he had recently been dislodged, Hueffer had published new work by Thomas Hardy, Henry James, H. G. Wells, D. H. Lawrence, and Ezra Pound; Rebecca in retrospect thought it "the most impressive periodical ever to appear in our language." She found Hueffer wanting as a man—"stout, gangling, albino-ish"—and told G. B. Stern, the ebullient young Jewish woman novelist whom she met at South Lodge and who became her best friend, that being embraced by him was like being the toast under a poached egg. Yet she admired him not only as an editor but also as a writer, hailing what was to be his best-known novel, *The Good Soldier,* when it appeared in 1915 as "a much, much better book than any of us deserve." (By this time, on account of the war with Germany, he had changed his name to Ford Madox Ford.)

Violet Hunt was a poor man's Lady Ottoline Morrell both in her appearance and her way of life. In her drawing-room, decorated with William Morris wallpaper and chintzes, she gave the tea parties where, in the ensuing months, Rebecca was to meet, among others, the writers Compton Mackenzie, Somerset Maugham, and May Sinclair.

It was Wyndham Lewis, another South Lodge regular (he painted a red abstract panel to hang over Hueffer's study mantelpiece), who was the first to publish Rebecca West's fiction—a lurid story of sexual antagonism entitled "Indissoluble Matrimony," begun when she was still an aspiring actress and turned down by both *The English Review* and *The Blue Review.* Lewis printed it in the first issue of *Blast* in 1914. Much later, in 1932, he did a drawing of her, which she kept until she died."*

Brigit Patmore, one of the young women guests of whom Hueffer was particularly fond, described Rebecca at the South Lodge parties making "incredibly hair-raising and wicked" observations in her soft, musical voice. A lot of the conversation was radical and feminist: Violet Hunt was a suffragist and wrote for *The Freewoman*—which came to an abrupt end

* Now in the National Portrait Gallery, London.

from lack of funds only a month after Rebecca had joined the South Lodge circle. W. H. Smith, the major news-agent chain, had declined to stock it, and Dora Marsden, while remaining editor, was moving out of London. Dora was moving away from current issues towards the idealistic philosophy which was to occupy her for the rest of her life—a distressing development which Rebecca combatted in print under the transparent alternative pseudonym "Rachel East."

Rebecca wrote to Harold Rubinstein, a young solicitor with literary leanings with whom she went out and about and who attended the *Freewoman* discussion circle, that the collapse of the paper was a great shock to her; she was "almost mad with depression." She was desperate to get *The Freewoman* re-established, and hopefully collected donations at the discussion circle, wearing "a new hat with 5 pink ostrich feathers." More realistic backing was found in the United States and from a rich unmarried Englishwoman, Harriet Weaver, who became treasurer. *The New Freewoman* was inaugurated in June 1913, as a "humanist," and later an "individualist" review. Rebecca was appointed assistant editor, at £52 a year.

Though she wrote a passionate piece for *The New Freewoman* on the death of the suffragette Emily Davison, Rebecca was already distancing herself from an exclusive concern with the cause. After going through back numbers of *The Freewoman*, she complained—not for the first time—to Dora Marsden that the paper had no real literary content. "I don't see why a movement towards freedom of expression in literature should not be associated with your gospel. Tell me, did you ever try to get any short stories or literary essays? . . . And did you try to get any poetry?"

But "*where* are the women who can write?" She had been amused and impressed by the young Ezra Pound at South Lodge, remembering him later as "resolutely acting the dandy after the prescription of Baudelaire, but Baudelaire born again as an innocent child." She got him taken on at *The New Freewoman* as literary editor. Pound, who took no payment for his own work published in the paper and paid his contributors out of his own pocket, used *The New Freewoman* as a vehicle for promoting French criticism and *imagiste* poetry; Rebecca wrote a piece on the aims of the *imagistes*, in his behalf, in the second issue. After the paper died yet again, to be reborn as *The Egoist*, with Harriet Weaver as business

manager, Pound used it to publish James Joyce, to whom Miss Weaver
was to devote much of her life and substance.

Rebecca herself resigned from *The New Freewoman* after only four
months. She had been horrified by the proofs of the first issue: "My lord,
the printing! The carelessness, the dirt, the shakiness! . . . And can't we
stop attacking the WSPU? The poor dears are weak at metaphysics but
they are doing their best to revolt." The "parish pump" aspect of feminist
politics should be avoided, she told Dora Marsden, disrespectfully—"particularly as your facts . . . are not strictly accurate."

Disagreement between Dora Marsden, Pound, and herself about
the aims of the paper was her ostensible reason for leaving. She had other
outlets already for her own work; she was writing regularly for the *Clarion,* a socialist newspaper whose wider interests suited her. Her best and
most astringent early writing was published in the *Clarion.** She chas-
tised the politicians, both Labour and Liberal, for their pusillanimity over
votes for women. Though she deplored Christabel Pankhurst's anti-sex
bias, she announced in the *Clarion* that "Oh! Men are miserably poor
stuff." She reported on social conditions and labour problems; she defended the trade unions, but warned against the evolution of a caste system in political life and of the destructiveness of "hunting in packs."

Her strength was that she was both well informed and funny—
brutally, effortlessly funny at the expense of received wisdom, at the expense of the great and good of the establishment. Abrasive humour does
a better demolition job than earnestness. The writer she most wanted to
be like was Mark Twain; she had read his attack on Christian Science,
"and I thought, if I wanted to attack anything, I would like to attack it
neatly and precisely like that. . . . I knew what satire was." She knew,
because she was a romantic idealist. A satirist must have a vision of the
glorious alternative to the situation he excoriates.

She was also an *enfant terrible* having a wonderful time, overturning
the values and attitudes in which she had been brought up, furiously
aware than an England "black with industrialism, foul with poverty, iri-
descent with the scum of luxury" had been "held up to my infant eyes as
the noblest work of God and the aristocracy." She wrote with the fear-

*See *The Young Rebecca: Writings of Rebecca West 1911–1917,* selected and introduced by
Jane Marcus, Virago/Viking 1982.

lessness of the very young who have nothing to lose—but also with the authority and intensity that characterized her last writing as much as her first. Rebecca West found her "voice" as a critical writer the moment she found a platform.

She had also begun contributing regular book reviews to the *Daily News*. The literary editor there was an attractive Irishman, Robert Lynd; Rebecca made friends with his wife, Sylvia (daughter of A. R. Dryhurst, one of the original Fabians), after meeting her at the house of another Irishman, the playwright and critic Saint John Ervine, in Golders Green. She could do without *The New Freewoman* now. She departed precipitously, without taking salary due to her. "As Miss Marsden has let me go, I think the least I can do is to go without looting the till!"

The real reason why she could not continue as assistant editor was that her private life had become inordinately complicated.

PART TWO

Panther

1

H.G. Wells was one of the most famous authors not only in England but in the whole world. He was a subscriber and an occasional contributor to *The Freewoman*—it was, he said, "even at its worst a wholesome weekly irritant"—and a regular visitor to South Lodge. But Rebecca West did not meet him there.

In September 1911, when she had written the review that brought her into the circle of Hueffer and Hunt, she had also reviewed Wells's latest novel, *Marriage,* in *The Freewoman.* Harold Rubinstein jokingly prophesied that Wells, like Hueffer, would want to meet her. He was right.

She was invited to lunch at Little Easton Rectory on Lady Warwick's estate, Easton Park, in Essex, where Wells was living with his second wife, Amy, known as Jane, and their two sons. Rebecca, writing from her own home in the Hampstead Garden Suburb, reported to Harold: "I found him one of the most interesting men I have ever met. He talked straight on from 1.15 till 6.30 with immense vitality and a kind of hunger for ideas." His wife, she thought, was "charming but a little effaced."

Some weeks later she had something else to tell Harold. Wells had sent her a "most thrilling" issue of the Chicago *Evening Post* "which had a leader on my review of *Marriage* comparing me to Emerson! and is splashed all over with quotations from me. Fame!"

And in the new year of 1913, shortly after her twentieth birthday: "Our drawing-room was hallowed yesterday by the presence of Wells, who dropped in suddenly and stayed 2½ hours! Wasn't it glorious?" The famous author had found his way to the Hampstead Garden Suburb, just to see her.

Wells, in his mid-forties, valued and even loved his second wife, Jane, but his sexual needs were not satisfied in his marriage. His wife tolerated his infidelities, was kept informed of the state of play, and made herself indispensable in other ways. Wells's principal liaison at the time he met Rebecca was with the novelist Elizabeth von Arnim, "Elizabeth of the German Garden." The pair had made love under a tree, lying on a page of the *Times* in which the moralizing novelist Mrs. Humphry Ward had denounced the moral tone of a rising young writer named Rebecca West. They were on the young writer's side, though they did not then know her. Rebecca's attack on Mrs. Ward, which had provoked the older woman's outrage, had been in the first *Freewoman* piece to which she had appended her new name.

In the aftermath of his intense and painful previous affair with Amber Reeves, Wells had embarked on a series of "discussion" novels in which he investigated the relations between men and women in a changing society, advocating a free comradeship between the sexes (in which the man somehow always ended up as the freer comrade, both sexually and intellectually). He was using his own experiences as raw material, in a way that those in the know found shocking. Beatrice Webb, with her husband, Sidney, one of the earliest members of the Fabian Society, had broken with him after the Amber affair and his subsequent novel *Ann Veronica*; the Webbs themselves had then been caricatured by him in another novel, *The New Machiavelli*. Rebecca's long review of his latest book, *Marriage*, was under these circumstances provocative. She called him "the Old Maid among novelists," and wrote that "even the sex obsession that lay clotted on *Ann Veronica* and *The New Machiavelli* like cold white sauce was merely the Old Maid's mania."

Writing up the history of his complex love-life in his old age, Wells made many factual errors about his mistresses' backgrounds, including Rebecca's. But his accounts of the women themselves have at least a subjective truth. At that first lunch at Easton, he was struck by her "curious mixture of maturity and infantilism." She had "a fine dark brow and dark, expressive, troubled eyes, she had a big soft mouth and a small chin"; she talked well, had read a lot, and remembered what she had read. "I had never met anything quite like her before, and I doubt if there ever was anything like her before." When she came to see him again, at his London house in Hampstead, "face to face with my bookshelves . . . and apropos of nothing, we paused and we suddenly kissed each other."

It was hardly an unusual occurrence for Wells to kiss an attractive, admiring, clever young girl with whom he found himself alone. For Rebecca, inexperienced and excited, it was very different. She knew Wells's reputation by now; small, plump, and middle-aged, he nevertheless seemed to offer what she wanted, and his vitality mirrored her own. A letter Wells wrote to her makes it clear what she asked of him: "I suppose I shall have to do what you want me to. But anyhow I mean to help you all I can in your great adventure." He would take the risk of "it" being known about and misunderstood, though he was trusting her to be discreet.

Then, because of pressure from Elizabeth von Arnim, he changed his mind about making Rebecca a free woman sexually, and went abroad with Elizabeth. Mrs. Fairfield and Lettie were appalled by Rebecca's despair; to take her mind off Wells, her mother took her away to Spain for a month. Explaining her absence, Rebecca told Dora Marsden that her problems were "both tragic and ludicrous"; her life was "in a tangle just now. Entirely my own fault."

Not quite understanding the situation, Miss Marsden later asked her to get Wells to write something for the paper. "Really and truly I cannot ask him for an article. . . . It is over two months since I heard from him and I have no desire to dig up the corpse."

The letters and postcards Rebecca sent to her sisters show that she was badly depressed at the outset of the European journey ("I hate Paris"). But they travelled to Madrid by train in company with "beautiful boof* toreros"; she was excited by the Prado, and by a bullfight and "disreputable" cafés in Seville; she enjoyed a high mass in Burgos cathedral, and the cool coastline at San Sebastian: "I don't want to come home."

But she was not cured. She wrote to Wells on her return: "During the next few days I shall either put a bullet through my head or commit something more shattering to myself than death." Her long letter was a mixture of defensive self-irony ("I refuse to be cheated out of my deathbed scene") and defenceless appeal. "I don't understand why you wanted me three months ago and don't want me now." She said that he had ruined her, and that she had twice tried to kill herself. "Your spinsterliness makes you feel that a woman desperately and hopelessly in love with a

---

* Boof: the Fairfield girls' word for an admirer or any attractive male, from "boof'l young man."

man is an indecent spectacle." She would give her whole life to feel his arms round her again. "I wish you had loved me. I wish you liked me."

She may never have sent the letter. She frequently relieved her violent feelings in unmailed letters; she decided, for example, not to publish a riposte to a man who had criticized her theatre reviewing in *The New Freewoman*—on the grounds that "I am old-fashioned enough to think that a superior cow ought to refrain from attacking an inferior bull."

Later that summer she published in *The New Freewoman* a story called "At Valladolid," about a girl who had made two suicide attempts: one by taking an overdose of Veronal in her North London home, the other by shooting herself in the house of her lover. It is unlikely that Rebecca attempted suicide, though she rehearsed it. In old age she said that "At Valladolid" was "an externalization of internal events in my life," a response to a series of rejections—from the drama school, from disapproving Lettie, from Wells. "I can assure you that I did not shoot myself, I did not go to see a doctor in Valladolid, I did not take veronal. I thought of doing all these things. . . ."

She also published some lively travel articles, in which she acknowledged she had left England "with the sort of fatigue that becomes a frenzy," and that she found relief in the drama of Spain: "It was exactly what I had always expected life to be like. I had always been a little disappointed with things."

Wells responded to her travel pieces as he had not to her personal pleas. "You are writing gorgeously again. Please resume being friends." He trusted that she saw now how excitement and "complete living" were to be found elsewhere than in him, and that he had been right to refuse to "let you waste your flare-up—one only burns well once—on my cinders."

He liked too the independent line she was taking in the *Clarion* about the suffragist leadership, criticizing their narrow fanaticism (though she still supported their cause). Wells called himself a feminist, but repeatedly made fun of the militants for their political ignorance, weak arguments, and—worst sin of all, where he was concerned—their physical unattractiveness. Wells found it impossible to think of women except in their relation to men, and considered "independent women" ridiculous and pathetic. The freedom he wanted for them was sexual freedom, which meant in practice sexual availability. This aspect of his egotism was to cause trouble between him and Rebecca. As she wrote— using a characteristically theatrical image—"the woman who is acting the principal part in her own ambitious play is unlikely to weep because she is not playing the principal part in some man's no more ambitious play."

She wrote those words in her review for *The New Freewoman* of Wells's next novel (he was writing one and sometimes two a year), *The Passionate Friends*. Though there was much in it, she wrote, to annoy feminists, this novel was "infinitely nobler" than *Marriage,* and "Mr. Wells is more exciting than anybody else in the world." Mr. Wells responded by telling her that her review was "first-rate criticism." He was discontented with Elizabeth von Armin, and he now wanted Rebecca.

Soon after Rebecca returned from a dreary visit to Aunt Jessie in Bournemouth—"crumbly cliffs, a hinterland of suburban red brick slums, interspersed with patches of waste ground where bathing machines hold protest meetings"—they began seeing each other again. "I must say I like Wells. He hasn't made love to me and it's fun watching his quick mind splash about in the infinite." Within a few weeks, in the autumn of 1913, they were lovers. Rebecca told Dora Marsden that "a physical basis" had been discovered for her nervous disorders, and that she was "being treated for it and would be much better in future."

Rebecca thought in retrospect that she had been drawn to Wells, paradoxically, not so much for her excitement as for security and approval: the paternal virtues. Her mother and Lettie were both wary of the deceptions of men, and hostile to sexuality. Rebecca, on the other hand, always felt that "the mind of man is on the whole less tortuous when he is love-making than at any other time"; it is when he "speaks of governments and armies that he utters strange and dangerous nonsense to please the bats at the back of his soul." She wanted to leave home anyway, and build her own life away from family pressures.

New Woman though she was, she had thought of escape in terms of marrying, which was the only socially acceptable reason for a girl to leave home in 1913. But her young men "were mostly Jewish, and would never have thought of marrying a Christian, or they were Left Wing and didn't mean to marry. Professional men were out; because in those days

they did not marry girls without money or useful connections." She believed that the Fairfield daughters' inability to fit anywhere in the British
class system made them virtually unmarriageable.

She pinned her hopes for independence plus security on Wells.
When they became lovers, she moved out of Fairliehope into lodgings.

The breach hurt all parties. Though Rebecca was a rebel and found
the social values of the Hampstead Garden Suburb as constricting as
those of Edinburgh, she had Edinburgh genes of her own. As with the
young heroine of her novel *The Judge*, "it was one of the least of her
demands that she should be well thought of eternally and by everybody."
She spent that Christmas, and her twenty-first birthday, with Violet
Hunt at her cottage at Selsey, in Sussex, "an ever so depressing and sallow guest."

From there she had to go into a nursing-home in London, with a
recurrence of the lung inflammation that she had had at school. She
wrote to Sylvia Lynd that the doctors disagreed about her "incipient
pthisis" but agreed that her "inside" was "all wrong." What was "all
wrong" was that she was pregnant.

2

The baby had been conceived only the second time they
were together, in Wells's new flat at St. James's Court, Westminster.
According to Wells, there was a danger of interruption, and he failed to
take his usual precaution.

However much they were to diverge in their accounts of their life
together, Rebecca and Wells were at one on the point that the pregnancy
was inadvertent and unwanted by Rebecca. "Nothing of the sort was our
intention. . . . It should not have happened, and since I was the experienced person, the blame was wholly mine," wrote Wells. Once, later,
Rebecca suggested that the child had been forced on her by Wells "in an
angry moment"; sometimes she said that he had wanted to make her preg-

nant in order to bind her to him—which was unlikely, considering the
obloquy that he had suffered as a result of Amber Reeves's pregnancy only
a few years before. In 1976, goaded into candour by a television interviewer, Rebecca declared brusquely and simply: "The child was not
intended."

She and Wells, in the early months, were happy lovers. He called
her Panther, she called him Jaguar, and they quickly evolved a private
mythology in which Panther and Jaguar played in a secret erotic world.
"There is NO Panfer but Panfer," wrote Wells in one of the notes which
he embellished with comic illustrations, or "picshuas," "and she is the
Prophet of the most High Jaguar which is Bliss and Perfect Being." She
was "the sweetest of company, the best of friends, the most wonderful of
lovers."

Wells's whimsical love-letters show that he had no intention of let-
ting her down. With the help of his solicitor and friend, E. S. P. Haynes,
he made and remade plans about where and how she would live after the
baby was born. She was to be Mrs. West, and he would visit her as Mr.
West. "Panther I love you as I have never loved anyone. I love you like a
first love. I give myself to you. I am glad beyond any gladness that we are
to have a child."

But, as he wrote much later, they were "linked by this living tie"
before they had had time to get to know each other properly, and as things
turned out, "we never achieved any adjustment of any sort." It was harder
for Rebecca, without marriage or the support of her family, to be "glad
beyond any gladness" about the baby. She cannot have been naïve about
the possibility of pregnancy. Two of her angriest articles for the *Clarion*—
in early 1913, months before she became Wells's mistress—were about
the injustice done to unmarried mothers by respectable society and the
law of the land. She had no romantic illusions about the difficulties that
faced both mother and child. An unmarried mother, she wrote, "is the
most outcast thing on earth," and an illegitimate child "has a bad time
before it." The child "sees its mother shunned by the godly, associates
itself with her disgrace and grows to think of itself as a pariah." At the
time of her initial rejection by Wells, she had been much preoccupied by
the plight of a penniless, pregnant, unmarried friend in the *Freewoman*
circle; and at the time of her reconciliation with him, she described to
Dora Marsden the "quaintness" of a member of the discussion circle who

was "always jumping up demanding that we be kind to illegitimate children, as if we all made a habit of seeking out illegitimate infants and
insulting them."

The fact remains that the unmarried mother and her child were
occasions of shame and embarrassment in the public mind, and only a
saintly man could be expected to take such a girl on as a wife—in the
middle classes, at least. Rebecca in old age grieved for the disappointment
she had been to her mother. "How I wish I could have made her happy
by marrying early and never meeting H.G."

Wells, while campaigning against sexual hypocrisy in the novels he
was writing, urged total secrecy on her, and she confided in almost no
one outside her family. He went away to Russia, and on his return found
lodgings for her in Hunstanton, a small seaside town in remote north
Norfolk, where she spent the rest of her pregnancy—six long months.
He spent as much time with her as he could spare from his work and his
family; his wife, Jane, was in his confidence over everything that was
happening. Rebecca's isolation was voluntarily deepened by a further
break away from her earliest political allegiances. She had already dis-
tanced herself from the single-mindedness of the suffragists, though she
remained friendly with Dora Marsden and wrote to her from Hunstanton
wishing "Good luck to *The Egoist*"—to which she became an occasional
contributor. She now left the *Clarion,* after voicing her growing distrust
of the "pack system"—by which she meant all single-issue politics, and
all blind loyalty to class, creed or party. "There is nothing behind the race
but individuals." Her father would have agreed; it was also a reflection of
her own situation.

She wanted now to succeed as an author on her own merits. "I
loathe and hate journalism." She began to write her first book, a critical
study of Henry James. The story Wyndham Lewis had taken for *Blast*
appeared while she was working in purdah at Hunstanton, and the letter
she wrote to Violet Hunt, thanking her for her congratulations on the
story, shows that she was still keeping the real reason for her seclusion
even from this kind but gossiping friend.

The house in which she was marooned was called Brig-y-don, on
Victoria Avenue, a straight street of newish red-brick, bow-windowed,
semi-detached villas of a severe kind, set back from and at right angles to
the esplanade and the wide, windy beach below. Her landlords were a

postman and his wife, who needed the money. On 4 August 1914, the day on which Britain declared war on Germany, her baby was born in the house, with the help of the local doctor, an Irish midwife, and chloroform. He was named Anthony Panther. Wells, hurrying to Hunstanton from London, conveyed to his wife that it had been a difficult birth; she told him to give her dear love to Rebecca "if you can." Sixty years later Anthony Panther, visiting Hunstanton, sent his mother a picture postcard: "What a surprising place to have been born in. It doesn't appear to be aware of its important place in history. Bless you."

3

Lettie came to look after Rebecca, as did Mrs. Townshend, a friend of Wells's who had sometimes sheltered the lovers at her house in London, and Wilma Meikle, a suffragist friend of Rebecca's. Mrs. Fairfield too paid a visit, but mother and daughter were not reconciled. During her last illness, in 1976, Lettie dictated a statement about the family's attitude towards Anthony, designed to refute the allegations of rejection that he repeatedly made when, as an adult, he, like his parents, became a writer.

"It was my mother's desire," said Lettie, "and the desire of my sister Winnie and myself, that Cissie should bring Anthony home to live with us, in spite of all the social difficulties, much greater, of course, at that time. We longed to give her little boy the best chance in the world. But Cissie chose, quite naturally, to have her own establishment and keep her little boy with her. She chose also to continue her relationship with H. G. Wells, which, as my mother rightly foresaw, would lead her into innumerable difficulties."

If the price of her family's support was giving up Wells and returning home as a penitent, Rebecca was not prepared to pay it. She did not go back to Fairliehope again until Anthony was three. Lettie's suppressed disapproval hurt her more than her mother's, which was to be expected.

There is nothing in Rebecca's numerous girlhood letters to her eldest sister to suggest anything but affection on both sides. The three girls, in spite of the spread in ages, formed a close unit, reinforcing their solidarity with private slang and nicknames: Lettie was Cow, or Frisk; Winnie was Podge; their mother was Lily; and Rebecca signed nearly all her letters to her sisters, all their lives, with the name "Anne." This was short for Anne Telopé, in memory of a childish pseudo-erudite mistake she made in pronouncing "antelope" at the age of eight.

But later Lettie joined Aunt Sophie in Rebecca's mind as someone who had ruined her life. Lettie is extravagantly portrayed as the complacent, conformist, talentless Cordelia in *The Fountain Overflows*, whose "white look" of rejection reduces her youngest sister to despair. In her memoirs, Rebecca wrote that Lettie, in childhood, "never ceased to convey to me that I was a revolting intruder in her home." Rebecca thus backdated her paranoid feelings; she came to believe that Lettie had destroyed her confidence in her looks, capacities, social behaviour, and professional prospects. Diatribes against Lettie, in Rebecca's later life, filled many pages of notebooks, typescripts, and letters to friends. Rebecca downgraded Lettie's impressive professional achievements, disliked hearing her praised, and granted her no virtues—except, secretly, the most terrifying virtue of all, that of being in the right. She resurrected a memory of seeing Lettie dancing at school, "so lovely, so cool, so innocent. . . . If she denounced me she must be right." Simply by being herself, Lettie inflamed Rebecca's raw self-doubt, and was never forgiven for it.

The feeling that Lettie "must be right" in a conventional moral sense went deep. When, in 1946, Winnie's daughter, Alison, as a young journalist, became an unsupported mother, Rebecca took on Lettie's role and criticized Alison for behaving "as if there was not only no public opinion, but no law and no penalties"; she suggested that Alison was bringing unendurable pain and shame on the family—which was what she felt she herself had done.

Rebecca's original plan had been to have her baby fostered while she established herself as a writer, but when it came to the point she could not part with him. With hindsight, she regretted this decision, and begged Winnie to dissuade her Alison from doing the same thing. "I made a great mistake by not sending Anthony away for the first year to some nearby place—round the corner would be best—and not getting on with my work. As it was I had to work hard later on, so that I could not give Anthony all the time he needed when he was a little older." One enviable change between 1946 and 1914 was the difference between Winnie's attitude and Mrs. Fairfield's. Rebecca admired "beyond anything" Winnie's supportive loyalty to her daughter: "It's just what poor Mother, with all her virtues, did not practise towards us."

But her more open bitterness against Lettie made a rumbling accompaniment to her thoughts and intimate conversations all her life. On another level, she was aware of her unfairness. Anne Charles, Rebecca's secretary from 1946 to 1953, once saw on her desk a paper on which she had written: "I know I have largely invented my sister Lettie."

Lettie stuck by Rebecca and made a good relationship with little Anthony, but she let Rebecca know that she found the whole business infinitely regrettable. She liked Wells as an acquaintance—he was "funnier than Chaplin," as Winnie said—but not as a lover for her young sister. Wells's own interpretation was that the "intense man-hatred of the mother" had imposed itself on the two elder daughters (though Rebecca did not complain about Winnie). Lettie, Wells believed, had a suppressed jealousy "not for me but for physical love. She adored her sister and also now she hated her."

4

Rebecca was never sentimental about maternity. "Life makes itself," she wrote in old age; "I cannot see that childbirth is creative at all, one is just an instrument, and it's none the worse for that." In a long, confused letter to Violet Hunt written a few days after Anthony was born, she said that the doctor had told her she might easily miscarry, because of her lung condition and poor general health. The implication was that he was prepared to bring about the miscarriage. "However I insisted on having my child," and her health had mended as the pregnancy progressed. She justified to Violet Hunt her campaign of secrecy. Had she been candid about her pregnancy, "Pale Fabians would say that I was The Free Woman and that I had wanted to be the Mother of the Superman." She rejoiced in "the possession of a son whose appearance defies description. I can only say that were he a Pekinese he would be worth his weight in gold." She was going to keep him with her, in a home of her own, "from which domesticity I will occasionally emerge and lead a maiden existence in Fleet Street."

Mrs. Townshend took it upon herself to impress on Wells, who favoured the fostering plan, that it would be "a thousand pities" to separate Rebecca from her baby. "She's not a bachelor-woman but all that there is of the most feminine," and not "the kind that keeps sex in a watertight compartment." Mrs. Townshend warned Wells that "a lover at discreet intervals isn't enough for her . . . though I admit she would like a 5th of you better than the whole of anyone else."

A lot of the trouble that developed between Rebecca and Wells stemmed from the fact that he did keep sex "in a watertight compartment," and wanted her to do the same. He did not want domestic life with Rebecca; he already had a family to which he was sufficiently devoted, and a comfortable, well-run home. Jane Wells, during the summer Anthony was born, enlarged and improved the house and garden at Easton Rectory, which was renamed Easton Glebe. Wells's discomfort and irritation while the alterations were in progress meant that he spent more time with Rebecca; but once completed, the family home became attractive to him, and an ideal setting for the exuberant weekend parties he enjoyed. He needed Rebecca as an amusing young companion and as a lover. His wife, in his words, "regarded my sexual imaginativeness as a sort of constitutional disease; she stood by me patiently, unobtrusively waiting for the fever to subside." What this endlessly repeated act of stoicism cost her, no one can know. Wells asked a lot of Jane, and she gave it.

He asked a lot of his mistresses too, those transitory projections of what he called "the Lover-Shadow," now embodied in Rebecca: "She was to be a lovely wise and generous person wholly devoted to me." Wells's mistress was, in fact, to be the very opposite of a "Freewoman." She was to be what Dora Marsden, in the first fighting issue of her paper, had called a "Bondswoman"—a secondary creature, "a kind of human poul-

tice" for the male. Wells wanted Rebecca to get on with her writing in a
discreet setting—preferably in the bosom of her family, though this was
not possible—and build her separate social life—preferably all-female,
since he was possessive—and be available to him whenever he was free.

A furnished house was found in east Hertfordshire, not far across
country from Easton. Quinbury was a solid, creeper-covered, late-
nineteenth-century farmhouse attached to a working farm, in a valley,
just outside the village of Braughing. It lay on its own in the midst of
fields; Rebecca could see the spire of Braughing's fifteenth-century
church through trees half a mile away. There was a rough track from the
farmhouse leading to the hamlet of Hay Street and the country road that
passed through Braughing on its way to join the main London road. The
pretty little River Quin flowed past the farm down to the village, where
it was crossed by picturesque fords and footbridges.

At Quinbury, Rebecca was only thirty-odd miles from London, but
she might as well have been five hundred miles away. Rural and remote,
her hideaway was the perfect setting for a rustic idyll. She was to call the
adorable boy in *The Fountain Overflows* Richard Quinbury (always abbre-
viated to Richard Quin), as if in memory of days of hope and happiness
with Wells and her baby. They were happy exploring the countryside
nearby, and happy on excursions farther afield—to the Monkey Island
Inn on the Thames, loved by Wells since his boyhood, which became
their special place.

But when winter came Quinbury was muddy, bleak, and lonely.
Wells was not always free to see her, and only trusted friends like Ford
Madox Ford and Violet Hunt were encouraged to visit. Violet Hunt offered a temporary home at South Lodge, but Wells did not want Rebecca
and the baby in London. Rebecca wrote jokingly to Harold Rubinstein
that she was trying to get sent to the front as a war correspondent, but
in fact, as she told Chris Bishop, "I rarely leave this hovel"; her printed
letter-head was largely to impress editors, notably Walter Lippmann of
The New Republic, who had signed her up as a regular contributor. Rebecca could not after all give up journalism, then or ever; she needed
both the money and the exposure.

Motherhood had not changed her style. Her piece for the first issue
of the prestigious new American periodical in November 1914 was headed
"The Duty of Harsh Criticism," not a duty that she had ever shirked.

Her irreverent treatment of established authors had been a hallmark of her reviews from the beginning, and seemed all the more provocative, and funnier, because of her extreme youth. Now she rallied against the "weak affability" of most English criticism, arguing that in time of war the life of the mind should be particularly "athletic"; she picked out "two great writers of today who greatly needed correction"—Shaw, and H. G. Wells.

In Wells's view, it was the arrangement of their private life that "greatly needed correction." Especially he did not enjoy dull evenings sharing Rebecca with Anthony's nanny and Wilma Meikle, who was a companion to Rebecca after she moved, when Anthony was a year old, to another furnished house—Alderton, in Royston Park Road, Hatch End. The only advantage of this large suburban villa was that Rebecca could get into central London easily, to find copy for her *New Republic* articles—such as "A Fable for Christmas" at the end of 1915, describing her experiences in Liberty's of Regent Street when a bomb fell nearby.

That article also reflected her sensual delight in the expensive clothes she longed for and could not afford, while coolly noting the squandering, luxurious instincts, incongruous in wartime, which diffused women's concentration and prevented them "from becoming geniuses"— a view of women often expressed by Wells in his fiction. She had a new woman friend, with whom she went to art galleries and on "hat-buying sprees," and who came to the small dinners Rebecca and Wells gave in London restaurants. Sara Tugander was, until in 1915 she married James B. Melville (later legal counsel for the Beaverbrook Press, and Solicitor General), the confidential secretary of Bonar Law, leader of the Conservative Party. By virtue of her political contacts, Sara was a woman of some influence and a source of gossip. She and Rebecca took riding lessons together, encouraged by the horseman-adventurer R. B. Cunningham-Grahame, who gave Rebecca a whip; in his house Rebecca met Joseph Conrad.

She wanted that kind of life far more than she wanted the nursery world that awaited her at home. Sylvia Lynd came to Hatch End to visit "darling Rebecca" and had her first glimpse of Anthony, "a baby in a red cap sitting up in his pram." His innocent existence was a trap for both his parents. "*I hate domesticity,*" Rebecca wrote to Sylvia after her visit. "I can't imagine any circumstances in which it would be amusing to order 2 ounces of Lady Betty wool for socks for Anthony." She loved the child, but "I want to live an unfettered and adventurous life like a Bashibazouk, and spend all my money on buying clothes in Bond Street." In Anthony, she said, she was "laying up treasure for the hereafter (i.e., dinners at the Carlton* in 1936) but what I want now is ROMANCE. Something with a white face and a slight natural wave in the dark hair and a large grey touring-car is what I really need." H. G. Wells did not fit this description; but she loved him too, more than she admitted to Sylvia Lynd.

At the Lynds' house in Hampstead, Rebecca made a new friend, the historian Philip Guedalla. In her social life as in her professional life, she was not wholly dependent on her lover. She picked up her political interests, attending the Fabian Summer Schools in the Lake District; Shaw, now over sixty, teased the actress Mrs. Patrick Campbell by telling her how he had struck up a "precipitous flirtation" there with Rebecca, who could "handle a pen as brilliantly as I ever could, and much more savagely. We fell into each other's arms intellectually and artistically." Rebecca gave a lecture on feminism, and rowed on the lake with other elderly Fabians.

She had been taken on by Wells's literary agent, J. B. Pinker, and in 1916 her *Henry James* was published. It sold only six hundred copies, but caused comment: the literary establishment found it offensive that a twenty-three-year-old should feel free to criticize the Master, particularly since he had been dead only a few months. Her short book still stands as a fair introduction to the man and his work. She faults James for his lack of intellectual passion, asking why "books about ideas" are generally so bad since "the genius of M. Anatole France and Mr Wells have proved that they need not be so"; it must be, she said, that most people "reserve passion for their personal relationships and therefore never 'feel' an idea with the sensitive fingertips of affection." She was funny about James's idea of women, and about the Jamesian sentence, "a delicate creature swathed in relative clauses as an invalid in shawls." Her criticism was more levelheaded than that of her mentor Ford Madox Ford, whose hagiographical *Henry James* had appeared four years before; her astringency was contained within a context that acknowledged the "white light" of James's genius.

---

* The Carlton Grill, a restaurant—not the Carlton Club, a Conservative stronghold.

H. G. Wells had an ambivalent friendship with Henry James—
their aims and techniques as novelists could hardly have been more opposed—and while Rebecca was writing her book he had been making
cruel fun of the Jamesian manner in *Boon* (also published in 1916). He
defended Rebecca's book, writing to the novelist Hugh Walpole that "my
blood still boils at the thought of those pretentious academic greasers
conspiring to put down a friendless girl (who can write any of them out
of sight) in the name of loyalty to literature."

Rebecca West, successful and attractive, might not seem a "friendless girl" but, as Wells understood, it was how she saw herself. As an
unmarried mother she was someone who many "nice people" would not
want to know. Socialists and Fabians tended to be puritan; it was not
among them that Rebecca was to find unquestioning acceptance, but
among more worldly people such as St. Loe Strachey of the *Spectator* and
his wife, Amy, and the society hostess Lady Colefax. One of her chief
champions was the thriller-writer Marie Belloc-Lowndes, the confidante
of fashionable London (Wells described her as "the most attractive tea-
cosy I have ever met"), who praised Rebecca's diffidence, touched by
seeing her blush "when I once told her that I regarded her short study of
Henry James as one of the best critical works in the language."

It was with Mrs. Belloc-Lowndes that Rebecca met the man to
whom Wells had defended her, Hugh Walpole. "Because he is a triffic
[*sic*] celebrity he sat still while Miss Stern and I handed round tea and
cakes to the old ladies." She had offended the "triffic celebrity" shortly
before, by an acid review. He had written her a petulant letter, to which
she replied that she did not conceal her feelings when she thought people
were writing nonsense, nor when she thought they were writing "sensi-
bly and beautifully"; "if people choose to remember the far less frequent
occasions of my dislike rather than the quite numerous occasions of my
appreciation it is hardly my fault!" Professionally, she was forceful. Privately, she was the friendless girl.

When as an elderly woman she read the account of her youthful
modesty in Mrs. Belloc-Lowndes's published letters and diaries, she
wrote in her own diary that she had loved Mrs. Belloc-Lowndes. "I think
she must have loved me a little. How dignified she was. I am not gentle
and I have had my dignity cut away from me, *sawn off*, by all the people I

have ever had anything to do with. . . . It was my loneliness. I had no one to back me."

Rebecca West was never complacent or conceited. As an old and famous woman she rarely referred to her own work, except when interviewers obliged her to do so, and then only to confess her difficulties. Those who found her imperious could not possibly know that she saw herself as an underdog. She fought her own corner, and she championed the cause of fellow-underdogs. "Were it possible for us to wait for ourselves to come into the room, not many of us would find our hearts breaking into flower as we heard the door-handle turn. But we fight for our rights, we will not let anybody take our breath away from us, and we resist all attempts to prevent us from using our wills."

5

In the year of her *Henry James,* Wells spent the late summer touring the French and Italian war fronts for a book. From abroad, he spelled out to Rebecca how their lives might be improved. "I wish we could fix up some sort of life that would detach us lovers a little more from the nursery." The way things were, "it's really a very severe test of my love for you." Above all, "Clear Wilma out. This is an ultimatum."

They made a new arrangement. Wells took rooms in a boarding-house at 51 Claverton Street, in the Pimlico district of London, where he and Rebecca could be together alone. In the spring of 1917 she and Anthony moved to a modest modern house on Marine Parade at Leigh-on-Sea on the Essex coast. The house was called Southcliffe; it was semi-detached, and covered in decorative woodwork. Marine Parade, on a cliff above the wide estuary of the Thames, commanded a magnificent view. G. B. Stern—Gladys, usually called "Peter," though Rebecca called her "Tynx"—took Wilma Meikle's place, and spent much of her time with

Rebecca, who was happier at Southcliffe, "a jolly little house" and the first home that she had liked.

Anthony could play down on the beach, where winkle-sellers had their huts. The railway at Leigh runs behind the beach, at the foot of the cliff on which Marine Parade is built; from her house Rebecca only had to walk down the steep grassy slope and cross a metal bridge to reach the station and the train to London. At Leigh, Anthony, seeing the red sun go down, said to his mother, "Do it again!," as if her power commanded the sunsets.

He was three that year, and only now did Rebecca feel able to take him home to see her mother in the Hampstead Garden Suburb. Mrs. Fairfield's pleasure in the child mended the breach. "Mother simply adored him, and gave him every privilege a favourite little boy can have." Mrs. Fairfield's extant letters confirm this version of her feelings for "the little precious." Only when she was terminally ill did she decline to see him, not wanting the child to remember her as disfigured. (It is typical of the opposing versions of his childhood that Anthony claimed only to remember seeing his grandmother on her deathbed.) Rebecca began to go to church again, for the first time in five years. "Anthony whiled away the time with his collection of winkles. I had no such consolations," she wrote in her diary; but she kept on going to church.

Her life was restless; she rarely spent as much as a week in one place. In Leigh she worked, and spent time with Anthony; in London, from their base in Claverton Street, she and Wells dined out, went to theatres, film and music halls. They saw his friends, mostly literary and political—Arnold Bennett (who never liked Rebecca, nor she him), E. S. P. Haynes (who suddenly kissed her passionately, "amazing incident")—and hers, mostly literary and theatrical—Violet Hunt (now "raving mad"), William Archer, the translator of Ibsen and "a dear creature," the actress and writer Fryn Tennyson Jesse, the impresario Nigel Playfair, Sara Melville, the Lynds, her sisters.

Rebecca's favourite restaurant was Le Petit Riche, "such a nasty place now," according to Sylvia Lynd after she and her husband first dined there with Rebecca on an occasion when the other guests were E. S. P. Haynes and his wife. "It was a strange party, joined later by Wells and Bennett," Sylvia reported to her mother. "Bennett is a rather vulgar and provincial-voiced person and smoked the last piece of his cigar stuck on the end of a pen-knife. He had been dining with Wells at the Reform Club and had swallowed a good deal of champagne, so perhaps that accounted for his vulgarity."

Wells, Sylvia Lynd thought, had much better manners, "full of deliberate impudences of course in his talk but not gauche and intentionally boorish like Bennett. Also he does not cut his conversation according to his company. A good mark for H.G." But in spite of her liking and admiration for Rebecca, Sylvia was "rather horrified" that Wells had come at all. "My sense of propriety believes in neat compartments and it was a flooding of the bulkheads. . . . Besides I like Janie [Wells], and all the non-jealousy business is humbug—only done as the price of the Pasha's company—converting all their sounds of woe to Hey nonny nonny."

Rebecca, in private, could not always suppress her sounds of woe. Her divided life, as Mrs. Townshend had foreseen, was not suiting her. Stress manifested itself in nervous illnesses and skin-trouble; she sought relaxation with face-massages, and found solace in impulse-buying—extravagant "silk evening knickers" and other luxuries, from the best shops.

Wells optimistically expected her London life with him, her home life with Anthony, and her writing life to be carried out harmoniously. He had already, in *The Research Magnificent* (1915), depicted the Rebecca he had first loved as Amanda, "the freest, finest, bravest spirit" the hero had ever met. Panther and Jaguar were playfully transformed into Leopard and Cheetah. But Wells used the novel to send Rebecca warning messages. There are serious temperamental conflicts between the life-enhancing Amanda and her lover: she is over-dramatic, undisciplined, always ill, and insufficiently supportive of his high intellectual purposes and need for order.

In 1916 Wells published *Mr Britling Sees It Through,* a war novel from the home front. His heroine—"it seemed unreasonable that anyone shouldn't be in love with her"—is actually named Cissie, and has a sister named Letty. He used the Fairfields' private slang ("boof'l young man") and placed a baby in Cissie's arms: "She looked like a silvery Madonna." But the baby belongs to Letty, who, in the novel, is married.

The fictional Letty's husband in *Mr Britling* is lost, or maybe amnesiac; Rebecca West's first novel, *The Return of the Soldier,* turns entirely on the partial amnesia of a shell-shocked officer, and the healing significance of parenthood. Her humble heroine was modelled, she said, on

Mrs. Vernon, their sympathetic landlady at Claverton Street; and the Monkey Island setting of the soldier's early love affair gave Rebecca the opportunity of describing, with lyric precision, the place where she and Wells were happiest. She referred in the novel to "Bert Wells" (H.G. was Herbert George), nephew to the innkeeper at Surley Hall—Wells's real-life uncle. The psychoanalytic doctor who finds a device for breaking through the soldier's amnesia is, in appearance, a playful portrait of Wells—"a little man with winking blue eyes, a flushed and crumpled forehead, a little grey moustache that gave him the profile of an amiable cat, and a lively taste in spotted ties." Wells and West conversed through their published work, always, as well as in person. *The Return of the Soldier* is a story about salvation through unselfish love.

In 1917, a year before it was published in London, where it went into a second printing within a month, *The Return of the Soldier* was bought by the Century Company of New York, who paid $1,000 for the magazine serial rights and 15 percent royalties on the book. Rebecca told her agent that "it is rather a Conradesque story and I suppose I ought not to say it is good but it is." She owed the introduction to Century, as she owed many of her professional contacts, to a family friend from the Hampstead Garden Suburb, S. K. Ratcliffe: "You have been an angel to me. . . . Thank you, thank you for the Century." (Ratcliffe was a self-taught radical intellectual who lectured and contributed to progressive journals on both sides of the Atlantic, and a fellow-Fabian.) Rebecca then sold the dramatic and film rights of her novel, which seemed promising; but they were bought and rebought by different companies so often over the years that when the film of *The Return of the Soldier* was finally made, in 1981, with Alan Bates, Julie Christie, and Glenda Jackson, Rebecca gained no financial advantage from it.

6

By the spring of 1917, German Gotha aircraft were threatening the home population. The bombers, making for London, followed the Thames inland from the east coast. Leigh-on-Sea was in their flight-path. Rebecca, from her bedroom balcony on Marine Parade, watched the searchlights picking out the enemy bombers as they flew along the estuary. "*Pretty* aeroplanes!" said Anthony. "*Lovely* guns!" Wells went again to Russia, where he met a young woman who excited him. On his return, he and Rebecca quarrelled. Air raids exacerbated their stretched nerves; both of them were physically run down, and Anthony had mumps, followed by a tonsillectomy. In between visits, Wells wrote what Rebecca in her diary called "awful letters."

It was hard to respond generously when her shy sister, Winnie, now thirty-one, announced her engagement to Norman Macleod, the son of an Edinburgh bookseller; they met at the Fabian Society, and he was, during the war, private secretary to a succession of Civil Lords of the Admiralty. It was a suitable match and, for Winnie, second-best. She was in love with an older man who had married her best friend, a man in the same unreliable mould as her lost father. But Norman Macleod loved her devotedly.

They married in the spring of 1918, and settled down near Mrs. Fairfield, on the Hendon borders of the Hampstead Garden Suburb. It was not the sort of marriage Rebecca wanted for herself—"I do hate virtuous poverty"—and she described the wedding ironically to S. K. Ratcliffe as "one of the dressiest affairs the Garden Suburb has ever seen." Winnie looked lovely, Lettie wore her uniform as medical officer in the armed forces, and Rebecca was "so effectively disguised as a lady that Mother shook hands with her with exquisite politeness and audibly en-quired of a neighbour who she was." All the family backed the bride up "in their sinister way," and Winnie now "does housework all day long, it seems to be nearly all the same housework. She seems very happy."

She was echoing Wells, who had already, in *The Wife of Sir Isaac Harman* (1914), poured scorn on "these hutches that make places such as Hendon nightmares of monotony" and "ridiculous sham cottages in some Garden Suburb, where each young wife does her own housework and pretends to like it." But however much she agreed with him, the Macleods' contented domesticity threw into relief her own ambiguous situation.

Shortly after Winnie's engagement, in the week when Century bought Rebecca's novel, there was a bad air raid over Leigh. Both Wells and Gladys Stern were with Rebecca. Then there was a daylight raid on a Sunday morning, when they were all out in the adjacent resort of Southend-on-Sea: an incendiary bomb fell only seventy yards away. "I suddenly found that though I had never been consciously afraid I was simply gibbering," Rebecca confessed to Sylvia Lynd.

The series of raids revealed deep differences between Wells and Rebecca. He was just as terrified as she was, but his instinct, as he wrote to her, was to "alter or avoid disagreeable things if that can be done and to sit tight and jeer if it can't." Rebecca had set up "loud and exasperating cries of 'Oh *God* oh *God!*' For which I detested you." Though he loved "your artistic vigour, your wit, your fat old voice, a real greatness and beauty that shines through you . . . and the perfect delightfulness of our embraces," he hated the way "Every disagreeable impression is welcome to your mind, it grows there." He was making a statement of "an absolute and incurable incompatibility. It is your nature to darken your world and blacken every memory. So long as I love you you will darken mine." The Panther and the Jaguar were "beasts of different species." Rebecca replied with an equally bitter letter which has not survived: it is believed that Wells burned most of her letters to him during the Second World War on learning they were both on the Nazi Black List.

Even before the bombings, Rebecca had been thinking of sending Anthony to board at a Montessori school in London run by a friend, Anne Hillyard. The Montessori method, she thought, recognized that "all intelligent children suffer continual agonies from the frustration of their will to power"; and Anthony's nanny seemed "inadequate for his active mind and body." The Southend bomb made up her mind for her; within ten days she had taken the child to the school in Courtfield Gardens, "and of course he is looking peculiarly adorable and babyish, and my heart is idiotically sore over it." She told Anthony's first wife, Kitty, long afterwards that Wells's threats to break with her were an added reason for her decision: "I had no money, no friends, and was in wretched health. I had to send Anthony to school in order to get on with my work." And, maybe, to salvage her relationship with Wells, who wrote to her around this time with sublime selfishness: "Panfer I love being with you always. I also love being with my work with everything handy. I *hate* being encumbered with a little boy and a nurse, and being helpful. I hate waiting about."

Rebecca stayed at Claverton Street and saw Anthony every day for

the first week, putting him to bed herself in his new surroundings. (Subsequently he came home for weekends; but after the bombs reached London, and the school was moved out to Wokingham, he came home less
often.) "Anthony has absolutely abandoned me. From the first wild glad
shriek, 'There are little girlies here!' he has preferred his school to his
home. He takes me out in the afternoon with an air of kindness and
condescension."

He was not yet four. In later life he was bitter about having been
sent away from home so early. He felt even more bitter about the damag-
ing mysteriousness of his parentage. Rebecca, known as Miss West, was
not acknowledged to be his mother; he was brought up to call her Panther, or Auntie Panther. "Nobody was more conscious than I that this
was not a very good arrangement," Rebecca wrote in the 1970s, "but it
was the best I could do." Wells thought it was the relentless disapproval
of Rebecca's family that forced these "idiotic lies and pretences" on her;
guiltily, she connived with them. The vague title "Auntie" was the accepted formula, in ordinary families, for legitimizing the presence of illegitimate offspring. Rebecca was an emancipated woman theoretically;
but she was still a Fairfield.

Wells said he deplored the evasion, even though he was not prepared
to acknowledge Anthony himself: the child was taught to call him Well-
sie. But Wells saw that it was because of the transparent pretence that
Rebecca was not the boy's mother that her servants exploited her. She
had endless problems with her ever-changing domestic help, who felt free
to be insulting, or even threatening, when it suited them. Rebecca, sensitive and proud, did not handle these situations well. There was a particularly humiliating episode with a housekeeper who came on the
recommendation of a friend of Jane Wells.

These domestic crises bored and irritated Wells, as did Rebecca's
chronic and emotionally expressive illnesses: ear-trouble, eye-trouble,
bronchial trouble, digestive trouble, and every infection going. He had
been through it all before, when he and Jane had lived together before
his divorce—continual ill-health in rented lodgings, not enough money,
and landladies ready to exploit the irregularity of the situation in unpleasant ways. His own unprivileged background had made him sensitive to
social snubs and, as Rebecca wrote, "full of justified proletarian resentments." But he had put all that behind him. His married home was calm,

with everything arranged for his convenience. Rebecca took the line that an irregular household such as hers was bound to be disorganized; Wells should put up with it, or stay away—or regularize the situation by divorcing Jane and marrying her (which was what she really wanted).

He was a demanding companion, even when Anthony was not there competing for Rebecca's attention. "H.G. is overworking and I am waiting for the collapse, which usually takes the form of the discovery of grave defects in my character, followed in a few days by an intimation that he will die at once if I do not immediately take him to somewhere that emphatically and inconveniently isn't here." She was busy herself, writing for numerous popular newspapers and the *New Statesman,* and reviewing plays for *Outlook.* Shaw had developed a "liking for my society," as she told S. K. Ratcliffe; at a Shaw lunch party she enjoyed the political talk but hated the way liberals, instead of grasping power themselves, told "mean little stories" about the people who did. They had been gossiping about Lord Beaverbrook, whom she had recently met; individual achievement such as his appealed to her more than party politics, let alone Russian communism: "Oh SKR! *ought* the D[aily] N[ews] to support the Bolsheviks after the publication of the Charter to send property-owners and the bourgeoisie into serfdom?"

Shaw was quoted as saying that *The Return of the Soldier* was one of the best stories in the language. Max Beerbohm was amused by this and, finding her articles strikingly Shavian in style, drew a caricature of Shaw and Rebecca West, "La Femme Shaw," as he "dimly and perhaps erroneously imagined her." Rebecca regretted that Shaw never gave her this drawing, after promising that he would.*

She had other admirers. Hugh Hart, who sought her out in Leigh to say goodbye before he went to the war, was a "rather spiritless" one, a cultivated businessman with a musical talent. Apsley Cherry Garrard, "a delicate flower of a young man" and a survivor of Scott's polar expedition, took her to see Scott's widow—who was "very disappointed in me, as she's heard I was a most scandalous person," as Rebecca reported to Sara Melville from the Sandringham Hotel in Hunstanton, where she and Wells were holidaying with Anthony in September 1918. "It's the deadliest

---

* In old age Shaw gave it to his secretary, Blanche Patch; Rebecca finally acquired it for £40.

place on earth, and it was where Anthony was born, so I got fed up with it last time. But he is awfully happy so it's all right."

Then there was Lieutenant Commander the Hon. Joseph Kenworthy, heir of Lord Strabolgi, a famous sportsman with political aspirations. Though "he professes a great interest in my 'wonderful mind', he seems even more interested in my body." She appreciated admiration from robust, non-literary males; as she wrote apropos of another spurned suitor: "I have never been able to make love with anyone but H.G. but there are lots of people that you feel have a right to ask you to. Men with square jaws who eat chops for breakfast and shoot and ride and have trained their sense perceptions chiefly on port; you feel that since society has allowed them the run of physical pleasure as an occupation they are quite justified in thinking that they might as well have this pleasure also."

7

At Christmas 1918, the war over, Rebecca took Anthony to see the pantomime on Brighton pier, and recognized on the stage her old friend from the Academy of Dramatic Art, Greta Wood (now Mortimer). Greta was surprised to be met after the show by Rebecca, with an unexplained four-year-old in a smart black fur coat. The two young women became from then on "a team," as Rebecca put it. She sometimes lent the struggling actress money, and passed on Anthony's outgrown clothes to her son. (Sylvia Lynd observed how beautifully dressed Anthony always was.) Greta helped Rebecca out in domestic crises, and looked after her when she was ill.

Convalescing from pneumonia in early 1919, Rebecca went away with Wells to Weymouth in Dorset. Wells wrote to Thomas Hardy asking whether he might bring Rebecca to see him; the old celebrity agreed, confessing that he had not read her novel and that she was "only a floating nebulous bright intellectuality to me." At his house, Max Gate, which seemed to Rebecca "an unspeakable dump," Hardy gave her a copy of his

Wessex Tales, on the flyleaf of which Wells later drew a "picshua" of the Hardys and themselves having tea, with balloons of dialogue. Rebecca sent Lettie a postcard reporting that Hardy had complained that the *Daily News* called his poems pessimistic, to which his long-suffering second wife had replied, "Well, dear, they aren't what you would call *hilarious.*"

Later that year Rebecca made a decisive move: she left Leigh and returned to London. No more anonymous outer suburbs, no more discreet provincial villas. With Anthony, and Ada Pears ("Peary") to look after him, she took a flat at 36 Queen's Gate Terrace in South Kensington, an address of mild and unimpeachable social acceptability. Her neighbours included army officers, physicians, a baronet, and a "private hotel" of the kind that sheltered the widows of colonial administrators. Wells, who paid part of the outgoings, visited her from his new London base at Whitehall Court for "long intimate halfdays and evenings."

But there was always a tension between them. Rebecca's family, and her own instincts, urged her to persuade Wells either to marry her or to break with her, alternatives that she attempted to set before him. But, as he kept saying, he wanted them to go on the way they were. The relationship was suffering from the emotional inertia that affects any longstanding, inconclusive love affair.

G. B. Stern had become Mrs. Geoffrey Holdsworth, and in the spring of 1920 Rebecca and Wells visited the couple at their cottage in Cornwall. There Rebecca slipped into an open cistern in the garden in the dark; a gash on her arm turned septic, and she was taken by horse-drawn ambulance to a nursing-home in Redruth. During her weeks there she passed into a disturbed mental state, probably exacerbated by fever, anxiety, and medication.

She described it as a disturbance of perception. Unable to sleep, she found herself incapable of "eliminating irrelevant impressions and coordinating those that remained." She perceived everything with exaggerated intensity, but disconnectedly. When she did sleep, she had nightmares about death and putrefaction. She dreamed—prophetically, as she believed—of seeing men come to remove another patient's corpse the night before this scene actually took place, and was convinced that she had against her will been caught up in the supernatural world.

She wrote a tense account of these phenomena immediately afterwards—not for publication, though in it she begged "those who deliberately seek such experiences to take warning from my case." She may have described her terrors to Wells, who, when analysing her qualities, wrote with some degree of truth that "Rebecca had a splendid *disturbed* brain." Its splendour owed something to its disturbance. There is always a price to pay.

Rebecca continued to believe that she had this undesired access to the paranormal. During the Second World War, she seemed to sense when there were going to be air raids on London with such accuracy, she said, that people observing her movements thought she must be a German spy. In *The Fountain Overflows* the child Rose has the gift of second sight, a dangerous faculty outlawed by her wise mother. People who believe they have second sight—and many novelists, including Rebecca—fear that by foreseeing, or imagining, a tragedy, they actually bring it about. Rebecca's belief in her unwanted powers added to her burden of guilt and fear.

The poltergeist in *The Fountain Overflows,* she claimed, had actually manifested itself in the house of her despised cousin Tom Mackenzie, who himself attended spiritualist séances. Lettie shared Rebecca's preoccupation with the supernatural; but, armed with her medical training and Catholic faith, she approached the matter with less terror and more method, under the auspices of the Society for Psychical Research; she became a specialist in witchcraft and exorcism. Neither she nor Rebecca had any leanings towards Cousin Tom's kind of spiritualism, particularly after they attended a séance in 1925 where the medium received messages from relatives called "West" asking for "Rebecca." But both of them sent instances of their paranormal experiences to Arthur Koestler for his book *The Roots of Coincidence.* "The supernatural keeps pounding at my door," Rebecca wrote in 1962.

While Rebecca was recovering from her psychic collapse, Wells met Margaret Sanger, the American birth-control pioneer, and became involved with her. He began to write the novel *The Secret Places of the Heart* "against Rebecca" as he put it, ascribing to a woman character, Martin Leeds, all the qualities in Rebecca that he saw as ruining their love, as well as her loveableness and brilliance; the hero's prickly relationship with her is contrasted with his carefree affair with a new woman. A few months later he went back to Russia, where, in Petrograd, he met Gorky's secretary, the twenty-seven-year-old Moura von Benckendorff (later Budberg), the girl who had caught his eye on his previous visit. Decades later,

Moura was to be the most important woman in his life; on this occasion, in Wells's words, "one night she flitted noiselessly through the crowded apartments in Gorky's flat to my embraces."

He told Rebecca about this brief encounter on his return, and she was strengthened in her resolve to go away by herself for a while, to regain her health and work on her second novel, *The Judge*. Arrangements were made for Anthony to board at school again, and to spend holidays partly with his grandmother and Lettie, and partly with Winnie, who now had a baby girl of her own. As soon as Rebecca made a show of the independence which Wells had seemed to urge on her, he made every effort to reclaim her: he didn't deserve love, he wrote mawkishly; "I've not kept faith: I've almost tried to lose you. You are probably the only person who can really give me love and make me love back. And because you've been ill I've treated you so's I've got no right to you any more. . . . Have I ever got into your arms to cry? I would like to do that now."

Their plan was to meet up later in Italy, though Rebecca was wary: "Men being what they are there may be some other lady in possession by then." Nevertheless, "I really do like him much more than most other men—besides loving him, as I do." Before they parted, Wells added a codicil to his will acknowledging Anthony Panther West as his son and leaving him £2,000. (A year later Rebecca persuaded him to increase this to £5,000.) While Rebecca was away he wrote to Winnie several times about the child. Anthony, now six, could not yet read. "This is really shocking. He's naturally a very bright little animal and it is really damnable that he should be made into that most desolate and unhappy of living things, a *backward* boy." He blamed the Montessori method, and had no opinion of Peary; he canvassed Winnie's support for transferring Anthony soon to a preparatory school, with the idea of his following his older half-brothers to Oundle, their public school. He asked to have the bills from Anthony's present school sent on to him.

Rebecca, though she boasted that Anthony "converses entirely in epigrams," was aware of "the cub's" reading problem. She wrote on one of her postcards to Anthony from abroad (signed always "Panther"): "Darling I have had three letters from you all at once and I do believe you wrote one of them with your own paw. Get Aunt Winnie to give you a big hug. You're a dear good Anthony." She too worried, in a letter to her mother, about Anthony growing up "totally illiterate." But the precise strategy of his education was becoming yet another occasion for disagreement between his parents.

8

Rebecca went to Capri, to stay with Faith Compton Mackenzie at the Casa Solitaria. Faith's husband, the novelist Compton Mackenzie (always called "Monty"), who was clever, handsome, and in his late thirties, had been paying marked attention to Rebecca. Although she realized he wanted nothing more than a flirtation, she found him attractive, which added to Wells's unease.

Rebecca liked Faith too, and gratefully accepted the invitation to Capri. Faith then heard rumours of the flirtation, and drew back; but finally the two women travelled out together, with the Russian singer who was Faith's current escort. Rebecca wrote ecstatically to her mother that she was better already. Capri "is the most beautiful place on earth and I am sure this is the most beautiful place on it." It was the autumn of 1920, and Capri society was at its most exotic. She was taken to tea with the lesbian painter Romaine Brooks, met exiled Russian princesses and Dr. Axel Munthe, author of *The Story of San Michele*, "a very distinguished old chap, a very high type of charlatan."

It was Faith who took to her bed, with a gynaecological disorder. Rebecca found herself cast as nurse, a role she was ill-fitted to play. She told her mother, with self-knowledge, that if Faith became seriously ill "I should probably become artificially (neurotically) ill myself." She wrote to Monty, asking him to come out to be with his wife, and had no reply. Then, in an ugly scene, the invalid accused Rebecca of spreading stories of Monty's infidelities around the island. Rebecca packed her bags and moved out to the Hotel Paradiso, explaining her predicament to Dr. Munthe. Island gossips spread the story that Faith had thrown Rebecca out after finding her *in flagrante delicto* with Monty—who was hundreds of miles away in the Channel Islands.

Rebecca left Capri in early 1921 in low spirits to meet Wells. He too was in need of comfort. His wife had had a hysterectomy and he himself had been, he told Winnie, "really very ill." He had written to Rebecca that he trusted he would find in Italy "a *bright ready kind* panfer" and not "a sick distraught female." En route, he wrote to Arnold Bennett from Paris, "I think I shall get through to Amalfi all right and there a warmhearted secretary [*sic*] will look after me night and day." Man to man, he thanked Bennett for his understanding "over my temporary [*sic*] hymenic indiscretions."

With jarringly different expectations, Wells and Rebecca stayed together at the Hotel Cappucini in Amalfi for some weeks. "No, I do not look back at that time in Amalfi as undiluted happiness," wrote Rebecca sixty years later. Wells, irritable and jealous, presumed she had stayed in Capri because of some man. But after he returned to London, the separation, as always, rekindled his ardour. "I love you more than any human being. You are my dearest companion. I love and admire you. . . . I am prouder of being your 'dear Jaguar' than of anything else in the world."

They had moved from Amalfi to Florence, where Rebecca stayed on alone. Increasingly, she was making friends on her own account. She liked Violet Trefusis, unhappy after the break-up of her affair with Vita Sackville-West—a liaison in which Rebecca, meeting Violet in Florence with her formidable mother, Mrs. Keppel, found it impossible to believe. Violet, grateful for her companionship, later wrote that this new friend had "a voice like a crystal spring and eyes like twin jungles." Rebecca had a novelist's eye and journalist's ear for the idiosyncrasies of the rich English and American residents of Florence; Wells had bought her a miniature diary in Naples, in which she had jotted down small amounts of lire lent to or borrowed from Jaguar, and which she now used to make notes of scraps of conversation and gossip. Of one expatriate socialite, for example:

Chief lover Sir Seymour Fortescue, but that according to Mrs Keppel "only a rough and tumble on the sofa". Like a sleepy pear. Mauve rouge. Still adored by her husband Barmy, who married her because the co-respondents had tossed up and he lost.

Wells was begging her to return to London, and "I want to see you and Anthony very badly," she told her mother; but she stayed on in Florence, her troubles and indecisions temporarily shelved, for several weeks. She made friends with Reggie Turner—an ugly, kind, ageing man who had been a loyal friend to Oscar Wilde and was now curator of the Palazzo Horne and one of the circle of expatriate homosexuals. He became Rebecca's "dearest Uncle Reggie," with whom she subsequently corresponded regularly. He and the novelist Norman Douglas took her to meet D. H. Lawrence; they found him typing in a cheap back room in a hotel on the Arno. "He made friends as a child might do," and Rebecca went for a walk in the country with him and Norman Douglas the following day.

She was made ill at ease on that occasion by Lawrence's intensity, but never wavered in her belief in his significance as a writer. Six years before, she had castigated Henry James in print for writing dismissively about Lawrence in *The Times Literary Supplement,* retorting that Lawrence was "the only author of the young generation who has not only written but also created, and created with such power that he would be honorable in any generation."

She only ever met Lawrence this once. When his *Aaron's Rod* came out the following year, she reviewed it as "a plum-silly book" by a man of genius, and she defended his allegedly pornographic exhibition of nude paintings, even though she did not think they were much good ("Mr Lawrence seems to have very pink friends"). Some years later, asked for a contribution to *The Quarter,* she offered an article in praise of Lawrence. When her article did not materialize, Lawrence himself wrote from Bandol to urge her on, diffidently, "because of course if you felt like doing it you'd have done it; and why bother about a thing if you don't feel like it!" He asked her if there was anything he could do for her. "I'm sadder and wiser, and perhaps might." He was very ill already; he was dead within months.

Rebecca compensated for her failure to produce the promised article by writing a powerful obituary piece, "Elegy,"* in which she described their meeting and stated his claim to "our reverence and gratitude." Law-

---

* "Elegy" first appeared in the American *Bookman* and was reprinted in pamphlet form on both sides of the Atlantic.

rence did justice to the seriousness of life: "He laid sex and those base words for it on the salver of his art and held them up before the consciousness of the world . . . and prayed that both might be transmuted to the highest that man could use." His prayer might, as she believed, have been in vain, but his life was "a spiritual victory."

She had Lawrence's letter to her framed,* as also the embroidered picture of a panther which he had worked and sent her. She never renegued on her loyalty to him, and in 1960 was to appear as a witness for the defence in the *Lady Chatterley* prosecution—or, as she put it, "said a good word" for what by then seemed to her "poor, sincere, dated, dowdy *Lady Chatterley's Lover.*"

9

Wells sustained his interest in Anthony when Rebecca returned from Italy, and in the summer of 1921, with Peary, they took another seaside holiday in north Norfolk, visiting Hunstanton again, and basing themselves farther east along the coast at Applehill, near Kelling. Wells produced a series of stories and rhymes about Anthony and their excursions, complete with "picshuas." Anthony, then and always, adored him. They were almost like a real family. Rebecca, being driven again through the once-familiar East Anglian villages in her late seventies, mourned in her diary how they recalled H.G. "Oh, if only I could have married him, if Jane had died *then,* he was the best I had ever got." When Jane did die, in 1928, Rebecca and Wells had been apart for five years.

It is unlikely that Wells would ever, under any circumstances, have married Rebecca, and he rejected any suggestion that he should divorce Jane. Rebecca was in the classic predicament of the "other woman," and

---

* The only other letters she ever framed were one from George Moore, whom she considered "a moral genius," and one from Virginia Woolf thanking her for a perceptive review of *Orlando.*

came to feel that she was playing a minor role in the main drama, which was the marriage between Wells and Jane. She never saw Jane after her very first visit to Easton, but as Wells's wife Jane loomed larger and larger in her imagination. It would have been easier for Rebecca if Jane had played the part of the wronged wife in the traditional way; her tolerance was infinitely harder to handle, as was Wells's professed regard for her. Rebecca saw herself as the sexual woman perpetually punished and sacrificed to the "Great White Mother," the non-sexual woman.

She came to hate Jane with a hatred that did not diminish over the long years. When books about Wells began to appear, it became apparent to her how much he had depended on his wife in his professional as well as his domestic life. Away from Jane, he wrote to her almost every day, even during his deepest absorption in the affair with Rebecca. She had had no idea of this at the time, and it hurt to discover it in the pages of books. (There was a lot about Wells to which, in spite of their intimacy, she never had access: "I still cannot make out exactly what happened over Amber [Reeves]," she wrote in the 1970s.)

She could turn on Wells for his monumental male selfishness, as she sometimes did. But the full force of her anger became displaced and fell on Jane, in reality no less a victim than herself. Jane became bracketed with Aunt Sophie and Lettie—three emblematic "evil" women whose inflated images reinforced her own doubts about herself, seeming to devalue everything that she had to offer.

Rebecca's mother, after three months' serious illness, died that summer from Graves' disease, and Rebecca brought Lettie back to the Norfolk holiday cottage after the funeral. Lettie, freed from the domestic duties she had performed in addition to her medical work, at once embarked on further professional qualifications. She read for the bar, and moved to a flat in Gray's Inn, while continuing her work as a doctor. It was now too that she became a Roman Catholic. "Do be tender with her," Rebecca wrote to Winnie about this. "She was so dominated by Mother that she was bound to go to pieces after Mother's death."

Rebecca was to dedicate *The Judge* to the memory of her mother. "She was a marvellous person, who had the most tragic life, and her death was a terrible business—though it's hardly fair to say that, for her courage under suffering was extraordinary and she seemed to have an absolutely serene and certain knowledge that she was going to live after death." To Reggie Turner, she acknowledged that her mother had been "the most irritating and irritable old devil that ever lived" as well as "the most loving and witty and generous creature you can imagine."

10

In the autumn of 1921 Wells went to the United States to report on the Washington Peace Conference; he wrote devotedly to Rebecca, but was seeing Margaret Sanger and assuring her that his New York plans were governed by his intention to be alone with her as much as possible.

Rebecca, in London, was one of the forty writers who attended the inaugural dinner of PEN, the world-wide writers' association, at the Florence Restaurant in Soho. PEN was the brain-child of sixty-year-old "Sappho" Dawson Scott, a prolific novelist and ebullient personality who was very fond of Rebecca: she was elected onto the first executive committee.* Rebecca also made another appearance as an actress, in a charity production of Edward Bulwer-Lytton's *Not So Bad As We Seem.* There was a special performance in front of Queen Alexandra at the Devonshire House Ball, and Ivor Novello, A. A. Milne, Mrs. H. H. Asquith (wife of the former Prime Minister), and the painter William Orpen were among the cast. Rebecca did not think she was very good, and confessed to Lettie that the whole production had been "a terrible failure."

In early 1922 Wells went from the United States to Spain, where Rebecca, having sent her manuscript of *The Judge* to her agent, had agreed to meet him. "I am happy being back in my beloved Spain, but sad about H.G.—who is really having rather a bad nervous collapse after his *succès fou* in America, also a physical collapse, for he has the most terrible nose-bleeding." He had been lionized in the States—"I really am famous

---

* PEN's first president was John Galsworthy; from 1933, when Wells took over as president, Rebecca was a member of the Council.

here, people turn around in the streets"—and arrived in Spain elated and exhausted, and as usual expecting a mistress who would act as custodian of his greatness. Rebecca found him hectoring and arrogant, and was outraged when he sent her upstairs to fetch his coat. She wrote to Lettie from Algeciras that she was thinking of leaving him; he was "whining and nagging like a spoilt child" and expecting "to be waited on hand and foot to an absolutely insane extent."

Wells was in a state that gave people who did not revere him every justification for their hostility. Beatrice Webb, after reading *The Secret Places of the Heart* with its "quite obvious portrait of Rebecca West," noted that he was no longer agreeable company. "He is deteriorating intellectually; he orates to any company he is in, never tries to discuss as he used to do, and never listens seriously to anything that is said." She supposed that all this was due to his "enormous earnings."

In Granada, Rebecca turned on him and called him a "nagging schoolmaster," which touched him on the raw; they came home unharmoniously. Afterwards, he answered an accusatory letter from her with one of facetious self-justification. He would no longer ask her to fetch his coat, but declined to inaugurate a "Better Jaguar Movement" on the grounds that a projected "Better Panther Movement" had never materialized. "And when he does not feel up to being improved by Panther and her Friends he will just have to keep away."

Rebecca's friends were a sore point. Wells, in his fifties, was a major public figure; he dined with ministers, interviewed foreign heads of state, and published his views on every subject under the sun. Rebecca enjoyed dancing, and sitting around talking with whoever was around until late into the night. Wells did not. He was scornful of her "little friends," who, in turn, showed him scant respect. He felt that they encouraged her to lead a life away from him, as indeed they did. Rebecca had already been to see one of Wells's own legal advisers about arranging a separation with financial support for Anthony; she had already told Mrs. Belloc-Lowndes she intended to make a final break.

The question of the "little friends" came to a head in the summer of 1922, when Rebecca and Anthony were on holiday in Somerset, staying at the Ship Inn in Porlock. Also in Porlock were Gladys Stern and her husband, Geoffrey Holdsworth, Hugh Hart, Lettie, and Richard O'Sullivan. O'Sullivan was a quiet, dull barrister, a married man who devoted himself chastely to Lettie for years: "I hate him for not living in sin with my sister," said Rebecca. Wells, whose wife was away, became jealous of Rebecca even in the company of these unthreatening people, suspecting that the Porlock party had been arranged specially "to give you a time with Hart." If she had been over-kind to Hart, she ceased to be so. Gladys Stern reported to Lettie that he was "rather blighted by Panther's thoroughly naughty neglect of him ever since Porlock."

Wells had swept down to Porlock and taken Rebecca off for two days touring round the West Country in his car. In the early 1970s, when she was explaining the Porlock episode to Gordon N. Ray for his book *H. G. Wells and Rebecca West,* she gave a dramatic account of this excursion which Anthony, in his own book *H. G. Wells: Aspects of a Life,* diagnosed as "phoney." There is a sense in which he was right, as he was right about the "phoney" nature of her accounts to Ray of what happened between her and Wells in Amalfi, or in Spain. Her stories have the authenticity and the inauthenticity of myth. They have poetic truth when they do not have objective truth. Thinking back over the years to these bad times, she remembered odd details and feelings of fearful unhappiness. Without a fraction of a second's premeditation, her story-teller's brain provided a narrative, and circumstantial detail to clothe it. These late stories about her past are miniature novels, encoded texts.

Porlock is the best illustration of this process. Ray quoted her as telling him that she and Wells had stayed a night "at a curious inn right in the middle of a barren moor, near a place which I think was called Box. This was kept by a man who was going out of his mind and who lived there alone with his despairing daughter." H.G., the landlord, and a commercial traveller had played cards all day, "and the daughter and I sat in the kitchen and she wept and we did the household chores together."

The only evidence of what really happened is a contemporary letter from Rebecca to Mrs. Belloc-Lowndes in which she said Wells was "in a terrible state" and that she had had to "take him home by gentle stages putting him down to rest whenever we found a decent inn." The weird later story is full of echoes. Box is in Wiltshire, not on a barren moor but just outside Bath, but the name, and the idea of the barren moor, may have sprung to her mind to express her trapped feeling.

The matter of the innkeeper and his daughter is more resonant. In her idylls with Wells at the Monkey Island Inn, Rebecca had been fascinated by the landlord, Mr. Tinker, and his "beautiful and passionate daughter," who used to "wander about the hotel caressing her opulent figure . . . and at night they used to have fierce sharp monosyllabic quarrels." Rebecca heard the landlord speaking out of the dusk: "If it were not for the great love of God in my heart I would strangle the damn bitch."

This early anecdote may itself have a touch of fantasy in it. Rebecca made the heroine of *The Return of the Soldier* the landlord's daughter from an inn based on Monkey Island; and she and Wells, in the days when she was to him "the warmest, liveliest and most irreplaceable of companions," played out a fantasy in which "she kept an imaginary public house and she was the missus and I drove a gig. There were times when we almost materialized that gig." In *The Fountain Overflows* and its sequels, a Thamesside pub, the Dog and Duck, and its inhabitants play a large and ambiguously symbolic role. Inns and their keepers had a lasting metaphorical significance for Rebecca, whatever happened and did not happen when Wells took her away from Porlock.

The snarl of memories and perceptions from which Rebecca reconstructed the past enmeshed Anthony as well. In an autobiographical newspaper article he wrote as a grown man, he cited, as an instance of his unsatisfactory upbringing, a period in a boarding-school for the children of theatrical people at Minster in Kent. When Rebecca first read this in a Sunday newspaper, she was angry and distressed. Anthony, she insisted, had been at no such school. The evidence is that she was right; in the spring of 1923 he left his first school and went to St. Piran's, a preparatory school between Marlow and Maidenhead chosen by his father.

But Greta Mortimer's children were at school in Minster, and though it was not specifically a school for theatre people, both she and her husband were on the stage. At some point in 1922 Rebecca was writing to Mrs. Belloc-Lowndes from Rose Villa, Monckton Road, Minster: "I am down here with the boy and we find it icy." This visit, and his knowledge of the school, may have coalesced in Anthony's mind.

All this is worth remarking only because it was on just such issues—and they are legion—that Rebecca and Anthony were to spend

half a century scoring points off each other. Anthony inherited his mother's imaginative fluency. He was capable of extrapolating from memory
and hearsay so readily that, as he conceded, he often had to remind himself, "You weren't there, it didn't happen."

11

Rebecca's long second novel, *The Judge,* came out dur-
ing the Porlock summer. Wells's reaction to it crystallized the antipathy
between them about writing. His novels were written to plan, the plot
and characters designed to cover a framework of political or social ideas.
He had no aesthetic ideals, and mistrusted all talk of inspiration, or even
of art, as pretentious and futile. Rebecca's dedication to her own way of
working and her own critical values seemed to him a personal rejection.
"She splashed her colours about; she exalted James Joyce and D. H. Lawrence, as if in defiance of me—and in despite of Jane and everything
trim, cool and deliberate in the world."

Rebecca, in turn, found his attitudes philistine. She did not think
he should have wasted his talents on his *Outline of History*—as Wells
said, she hated that book almost as much as she hated Jane, who helped
him with it substantially. The lovers were harming each other as writers.
It seemed to Rebecca that Wells was always nagging her to work, but that
his one aim when they were together was to prevent her from working.
He felt the same about her. Each believed the other had a touch of genius
which was being frittered away on unworthy or mishandled projects, and
each saw the other's work as a tiresome rival for time and attention. "And
in a distraught preoccupied way we are abominably fond of one another. . . . But we are both too busy to look after ourselves or each other."

What infuriated Wells about *The Judge* was Rebecca's failure to
stick to her original plan. The central figure, he knew, had been going to
be a judge who collapsed in a brothel, recognizing in his seizure that the
woman he is with is the wife of a man he sentenced for murder. That is

not what *The Judge,* as written, is about, although on beginning it Rebecca arranged, through Sara Melville's barrister husband, to sit in on an Assize Court.* She began writing the story too far back in time; the whole first half is about the Edinburgh background of the murderer's young mistress. She then switched to the life-story of the murderer's mother, and explored the experience and consequences of bearing an illegitimate child, the novel becoming a version of the Jocasta myth set on the Essex coast, where she had lived with Anthony. To quote Wells: "At the end of an immense mass of unequal but often gorgeous writing, she had reached no further than the murder, and there she wound up the book, still keeping the title of *The Judge,* because that had been announced by her publisher for two years." The need to justify her now inapposite title accounts for the epigraph, invented by Rebecca, which sits grimly against the dedication to her mother's memory: "Every mother is a judge who sentences the children for the sins of the father."

Rebecca West said that she wrote her novels to find out what she felt, not to display what she knew. It did not bother her that this one did not follow the original scheme. Some critics reproached her for switching the focus of the story so brusquely from the girl Ellen Melville in Edinburgh to the unhappy mother of Ellen's lover in Essex—but for the author the novel's true topic had become the point where "the tide of the older woman's fate met the younger one's." She told a friend that she could bear any criticism of *The Judge* "so long as you don't say it is unrestrained and too exuberant." She could have compressed it, but chose not to: "I don't see why you can't have rich complex beauty. I hate the indiscriminating pursuit of concentration. I believe it has been the dessication [*sic*] of many a talent."

Somerset Maugham, whose personal comments to authors on their books were always shrewd, wrote from Bangkok to compliment her on *The Judge* in a mildly barbed way. He praised her witty, unexpected use of metaphor, but warned her that a metaphor, "being a comment by the author, pulls up the reader and so for a moment destroys his absorbing interest in the narrative. It reminds him that it is not life that he is living but a book that he is reading." It is true that Rebecca's authorial per-

---

*She finally used the Assize Court material in her posthumously published novel *Sunflower.*

sonality was, in her early novels, stronger than any character she could create.

Maugham ended his letter by saying, "I do not think there is anyone writing now who can hold a candle to you." For most readers, the painterly richness of Rebecca's language, which repelled Wells, was precisely what drew them to her writing. Virginia Woolf told Lady Ottoline Morrell that *The Judge* was a "stout, generous, lively voluminous novel"; she had not been able to finish it, for it "burst like an over-stuffed sausage," but it made her curious about Rebecca West. "Mary Hutchinson met her in a furniture shop and says she looked like a large wet dog, in a mackintosh, very shaggy." Mrs. Woolf thought Lady Ottoline ought to get to know Rebecca West.

So, in October 1922, Rebecca was invited to Garsington. Mark Gertler the painter was there, and his friend John Currie, both of whom she had met before. Philip Morrell met her at Oxford station and drove her home in a carriage with two horses that bolted down the moonlit High Street. "I can't think of a better introduction to Oxford."* But she did not enjoy the weekend. Philip Morrell was unhappy, Gertler brooded, and Rebecca felt she did not fit in. Lady Ottoline, "a disconcerting hostess," loomed "so enormous she could have eaten me for breakfast."

Meanwhile, her relationship with Wells went on collapsing slowly in recriminations, reproaches, rows, occasional moments of sweetness, and lacerating nostalgia on both sides for "all the fun, endearment, tenderness, friendliness and love of ten years." Anthony, at eight and nine, watched his mother pacing up and down in their flat, raging aloud against fate and H.G., rubbing the nervous irritation on her wrists until the skin was raw.

She had announced her intention of going to the United States on a lecture tour. Rumours that she might literally be banned in Boston on account of her irregular domestic arrangements made her once more present to Wells her ultimatum of marriage or separation. He replied on 21 March 1923 that it was unfair of her to turn on him "with this growing mania of yours about the injustices of my treatment of you in not murdering Jane." He regretted having ever met her. "For ten years I've shaped

---

*She elaborated this memory of a night drive through Oxford in her posthumously published novel *This Real Night*.

my life mainly to repair the carelessness of one moment. It has been no good and I am tired of it."

On the same day, Rebecca was writing to S. K. Ratcliffe about the "appalling life" she led with Wells, his "increasing nervous instability" and fits of "almost maniacal rage" alternating with "weeks of childish dependence." Wells was not in such a desperate mental state as this would suggest—he had offered himself (unsuccessfully) as a Labour parliamentary candidate, and in 1922–23 he published four books and countless articles—but it was how he presented himself to Rebecca, in protest and appeal.

But they still could not keep away from each other. A few weeks later they entertained Sinclair Lewis and his wife, Gracie, and all Wells's possessive jealousy returned—"the humiliation it was to see Sinclair Lewis slobber his way up your arm . . . My Panther." At the first international conference of PEN on 1 May, Rebecca and he sat together, both turning their heads defensively away from the recording camera. It was more like planning a divorce than the end of an affair, as was reflected in Wells's phrase "You may marry again," and in Rebecca's comment to S. K. Ratcliffe that, "as I have a steady monogamous nature and would have been the most wifely wife on earth," it was always hard not to give in to Wells and "take the job" again.

There were fatal differences between them about what each wanted from the other, and from life. There were fatal similarities as well. They had the same broad humour. Both were socially unplaced, both had had patchy educations. Wells complained about Rebecca's inconvenient illnesses, but "disabling physical collapses had been his stock response to stress" also; and in anger "he became infected with the paranoia that often affects the persecuted." His "tendency to overrespond to personal criticism which became part of his character in his late fifties" raised "the explosive outburst to the level of an art form." These characteristics, which Wells would have been the first to pin on Rebecca, were ascribed to him by their son, Anthony—a prejudiced witness in his father's favour, so his remarks need not be read as overstatements. Rebecca's chief complaints against Wells—"his indiscipline, his disorderliness, his refusal to face facts, his capacity for magnifying the smallest mischance into a major catastrophe"—always sound exactly like Wells's against Rebecca.

Why did they not break up earlier, and more easily? Wells was age-

ing, and may have doubted whether he would ever again find a young
woman so sexually and intellectually exciting as Rebecca. Neither
wanted to be the one who was left: each wanted to be the one who made
the break. For Rebecca, Wells was her first and only lover, mentor, pro-
tector, enchanter. Being in his company, she recorded half a century later,
was "on a level with seeing Nureyev dance or hearing Tito Gobbi sing."
Anthony, and his need for two parents, was their joint concern and at the
root of Rebecca's desire for marriage with Wells. Marriage is of use,
wrote Rebecca in 1925, "for rivetting the fact of paternity in the male
mind" (in an article with the feisty title "I Regard Marriage with Fear
and Horror").

Rebecca in the 1920s was, as an American paper declared, "the
personification of all the vitality, the courage and the independence of the
modern woman," but her girlhood had been Edwardian and her parents
had been Victorians. The word "mistress" aroused expectations which
her life with Wells had not answered. "It is impudent of men to keep
women as luxuries," she wrote nearly twenty years later, "unless they
have the power to guarantee them the framework of luxury. . . . But if
they fail to keep that ambitious promise, which there was indeed no obligation to make, they should surrender the system and let women go back
to freedom and get what they can." Wells had failed her on both counts,
and held on for his own convenience. "I ought to have liberated her,"
he acknowledged in old age. "I realize I got much the best out of our
relationship."

12

When Wells and Rebecca were semi-separated in the
spring of 1923, he (without her knowledge) became involved with a young
Austrian journalist, Hedwig Verena Gatternigg, who had first approached
him on professional matters. She declared herself to be passionately in
love with him. He, flattered, and smarting from Rebecca's apparent flir-

tation with Sinclair Lewis, succumbed on numerous occasions, but then
determined to put an end to the tiresome affair.

The distraught Gatternigg, naked under her mackintosh, turned up
at his flat at Whitehall Court as he was dressing to go out to dinner with
Edwin Montagu, Secretary of State for India, and was shown into the
study. According to his own, much later account, Wells called for the
hall porter to have her shown out, whereupon she cut herself across
the wrists and armpits with a razor. The hall porter and two policemen
had the bleeding but still-voluble girl removed to hospital. There was
every danger of the story's getting into the press; reporters were soon
pestering both him and Rebecca in the hope of a major scandal.

Wells had given Gatternigg a letter of introduction to Rebecca, presumably to deflect her attention from himself, and the girl had called on
her before the visit to Whitehall Court. Rebecca had found her mani-
festly neurotic, and was quite prepared to help H.G. out in this crisis. "I
remember sitting with her in Kensington Gardens," Wells wrote, "on the
morning after the scene in my flat. . . . So often we had attacked each
other with unjust interpretations and unreasonable recriminations that
it matters very much to my memories that we sat and talked and were
very sane and wise." Rebecca agreed to speak to those newspaper proprietors whom she knew personally, and ask them not to carry the story. (This
was only partly successful.) She and Wells closed ranks conspicuously,
lunching together at the Ivy after their talk and attending a first night
that evening. Wells felt that the incident had drawn them closer together.
In fact, it only hardened her resolve to detach herself from him.

The Gatternigg affair boomeranged half a century later, causing Rebecca fresh pain and humiliation. She told Wells's official biographers and
Gordon Ray, author of *H. G. Wells and Rebecca West,* that Wells had only
a brief and trivial involvement with the Austrian girl, and that it had
been Jane Wells who discovered her in the flat and telephoned for the
police. Those who knew better—notably Gip Wells, H.G.'s elder son—
contradicted this story when it appeared in print; Rebecca was assumed
to have falsified her account. Jane Wells was at home in the country on
20 June; the previous night, she had given a party at Easton to celebrate
Gip's graduation.

Rebecca believed her account was true because it was what Wells
had told her when they were being "sane and wise" in Kensington Gar-

dens. It was Gordon Ray's manuscript that revealed to her the true nature
and duration of Wells's relationship with Gatternigg; she was specially
upset to learn that he had spent a whole weekend with the girl. She wrote
out her unhappiness in her diary, and in her private notebook tried to
take in the other lie he had told her: "It was not Jane who discovered the
body [sic], though H.G. told me that she did, it was H.G." His lies were
a sad time-bomb, exploding in the 1970s, when she was old.

   After the Gatternigg affair, Rebecca went to Marienbad ("a mixture
between Hell and Bournemouth") with two women friends, to take the
cure. Wells turned up, by arrangement, on his way to see President Masaryk of Czechoslovakia, and, disturbed himself, disturbed her peace of
mind. "You were happy at Marienbad before I came and spoilt it." On her
return, Rebecca confessed to Sara Melville that she had agreed to go back
to him. If she did, she told Mrs. Melville, he would give her £20,000 for
Anthony: "I don't gamble on making that myself because I feel dead beat."
She could, she said (quite untruthfully), "have made H.G. get divorced
and marry me, he wanted so much to get me back, but I thought it wiser
not to."

   Letters about this latest development whizzed between Lettie and
G. B. Stern, who regretted that money should have been a deciding fac-
tor "when it was a question of her own personal health and happiness."
But since marriage was out of the question, money for Anthony was Rebecca's considered priority. Going back to Wells in order to secure it was
part of a strategy. "After all," she wrote to Sylvia Lynd, "the way I stuck
to Wells for Anthony's sake . . . gives me, I think, the right not to be
considered hysterical and impulsive in these matters."

   Having secured support for Anthony, Rebecca was staking all on her
escape to America. She, Wells, and Anthony had a last holiday in the
summer of 1923 in Swanage, from where she warned her agent that
"there will be no book this autumn"; but she had just received from him
£875.9.0 in royalties on her two novels. Anthony went back to school
at St. Piran's in September. In October, Rebecca left on the *Mauretania*
for the United States. As Wells conceded, "the effective break came
from her."

   His letters followed her. He was more hurt to lose her, he acknowledged later, than she was to be quit of him. "Bored. Wants his Black
Pussy. His *dear* Black Pussy. His soft kind Pussy—all others being shams

and mutations. Wants to know when she is coming back to him." There was something else that Wells did not know. Rebecca, who had never been unfaithful to him, was interested in another man—an interest that was to become an obsession.

PART THREE

Sunflower

1

"I love America and I loathe it. . . . I don't know how long I'm staying. I don't feel like going home, it's all so interesting," Rebecca wrote to the Sinclair Lewises from Pittsburgh in December 1923, towards the end of the first leg of her lecture tour, which had been arranged through the Lee Keedick Agency. She had already spoken at colleges and women's clubs in Springfield, Philadelphia, Chicago, Minneapolis, Iowa City, Rockford, Illinois, Milwaukee, Indianapolis, and St. Louis, and was exhausted.

She had been predictably dazzled by her first sight of the New York skyline—the skyscrapers "white and slim like lilies." Reporters had tried to provoke her into making indiscreet remarks about herself and Wells, and she had attracted much undesired attention. She returned to the Town House Hotel on Central Park West in New York for a Christmas break. Wells was writing to her longingly from England and, unwilling to face up to the separation, told Arnold Bennett that he would "stick it out" at Easton Glebe over Christmas and then go abroad alone "because R. is having the time of her life in America and I don't want to interrupt it."

Lord Beaverbrook traced Rebecca to the Town House and they spent Christmas together. Rebecca, who had been fascinated by him for five years and falling in love with him for months, presumed this was the beginning of a permanent relationship, and responded accordingly. She was wretchedly mistaken.

William Maxwell Aitken, Lord Beaverbrook, always known as Max, was the son of a Scotch Presbyterian minister who had immigrated to Canada, where the young Max made his first fortune. Starting as a bond-salesman, he was soon trading in equities on his own account, orchestrating profitable mergers, and heading his own finance company. He was already a millionaire when he came to London in 1910, at the age of thirty-one.

He made a sensational entry into the British political and social scene. He gained control of Rolls-Royce, made a close friend of Rudyard Kipling and a closer one of Bonar Law, who became leader of the Conservative and Unionist Party in 1911. Bonar Law, a quiet and unglamorous figure, was Max's hero: "I loved him more than any human being." Law took Max Aitken on as his confidant and adviser, and Aitken was, briefly, a member of Parliament. He was given a knighthood in 1911, allegedly to persuade him not to return to Canada, and also, no doubt, in return for contributions to party funds. But his ambition was not to hold political office; what he enjoyed most was political influence, and his heart remained in business. He bought a bank, and in 1916 gained control of the *Daily Express;* by 1923 he had, as well as a chain of cinemas, an interest in the *Daily Mail* and the London *Evening Standard,* and it was as a newspaper tycoon that he was to be remembered.

In 1916 Max Aitken was given a peerage, and became Lord Beaverbrook. He had a large country house in Surrey, and enjoyed champagne, cigars, and expensive motor-cars. He was tough, dynamic, amusing, and generous, and had a genius for publicity. He was also highly strung and nervous about his health, and suffered from asthma. A lover of women, he had no obvious physical graces, being small, with a heavy torso and short legs, a puckish urchin face, and a wide mouth that was a gift to caricaturists.

There was also Lady Beaverbrook. He had married Gladys Drury in Montreal when she was nineteen and he twenty-seven. She was by all accounts a fine person, and she had a difficult time. She did not share his London life, but stayed at their country house, where he came on weekends; their relationship was comparable to that between H. G. Wells and Jane. Beaverbrook was like Wells in other ways—in his smallness, his male energy, his driving egotism, and his anxieties about his health. He was also like the businessmen of the new technological world who dominated Wells's fiction, and Wells was to immortalize his version of Beaverbrook as Sir Bussy Woodcock in *The Autocracy of Mr Parham* (1929); elsewhere, Wells summed Beaverbrook up definitively: "If Max gets to Heaven he won't last long. He will be chucked out for trying to pull off a merger between Heaven and Hell, after having secured a controlling interest in key subsidiary companies in both places, of course."

Rebecca West met Beaverbrook in 1918, when he was Minister of

Information and Wells too was involved in wartime propaganda. It was a brief involvement; Wells went off to write his *Outline of History,* a book which so impressed Beaverbrook that he took Wells up as he had already taken up Arnold Bennett. Wells's latest visit to Russia had been to collect material for a series of articles for the Beaverbrook Press.

In 1920 Rebecca and Wells had dined with Beaverbrook the night before she left for Capri. He had a tiny Tudor house called the Vineyard in Fulham, in west London, where he gave exclusive parties—there was no room for big ones, though the garden was large, with a tennis court. In the letter to Sara Melville in which Rebecca had stressed that she still preferred H.G. to all other men, she gave her impressions of their host: "I found him one of the most fascinating talkers I've ever met, and full of the real vitality—the genius kind that exists mystically apart from all physical conditions, just as it does in H.G."

In the summer of 1923, when she was in the process of separating from Wells, she wrote again to Mrs. Melville: "I had dinner with Beaverbrook and his wife last Thursday—it was so funny. I must tell you about it."

One wishes that she had told Mrs. Melville about it in the letter. What happened between the Beaverbrooks and Rebecca before she left for America is a mystery. Rebecca in her old age concealed the name of the man she loved after Wells, but she talked, and wrote, about the affair with "X" as a terrible tragedy. In the 1970s she wrote that shortly before she left England X's wife had visited her and told her she and her husband were going to divorce, and that her husband intended to propose marriage to herself, Rebecca. This is not likely; Gladys Beaverbrook may have conveyed to Rebecca that she was not happy and was going to travel abroad, as she did. However, when Rebecca and Beaverbrook met in New York at Christmas 1923, "it was on the understanding that they were in love." But during the next fortnight it became apparent that "they were completely unsuited to be husband and wife." Rebecca meant that physical relations between them had been a failure. Beaverbrook usually kept up with his former mistresses, and sent them £50 at Christmas and on his birthday. The list changed, but Rebecca was never on it.

Nineteen twenty-three was a bad year for Beaverbrook. Bonar Law, who had become Prime Minister in 1922, was dying of cancer of the throat; Beaverbrook was constantly at his bedside, and when Law died, soon after Rebecca went to America, he lost not only his dearest friend but his special position at the centre of political life. According to his biographer, he destroyed a large part of his correspondence for 1923— including his letters from Rebecca. Nor did she keep any of his from this period.

Common sense suggests that all Beaverbrook wanted from Rebecca was her stimulating companionship and, perhaps, a comforting, casual affair. She was not the only woman to whom he was paying attention at this time. The pianist Harriet Cohen, a great friend of Rebecca's, was frequently invited to dine alone at the Vineyard that autumn, and was being sent "a hundred or more roses" once a week. And she was not the only one. Beaverbrook did not divorce his wife, but within the next two years he was to establish a liaison with a married woman, who in the late summer of 1923 was at home in the country looking after a new baby. She was Jean Norton, *née* Kinloch, the daughter of a Scottish baronet and wife of the heir to Lord Grantley. Inexperienced and young, she was still malleable; Beaverbrook liked to transform or "make" people. Rebecca was thirty-one that Christmas, and she was not malleable. She was strong-willed, single-hearted, ready to love, and longing to exchange the uncertainty of her life with Wells for the stability and éclat of a conspicuous marriage.

Her confidante in New York was the novelist Fannie Hurst, "a Jewess of the most opulent Oriental type." Rebecca found her ambience exciting and sympathetic. "I want to be a Jewess with thousands of uncles and aunts and cousins, on the East Side," she told Fannie. Ten years after her first visit to New York, she wrote gratefully to Fannie that "all my present happiness and the vein of satisfying work I have struck I owe to you because you were patient with me in the years of distraction." Fannie gave parties in a room rich with icons and hangings; during Prohibition, there were always twice as many bottles of drink as there were guests, and a samovar of strong tea. She dressed exotically—in a crimson silk shawl over frilled knickers with rows of white lace from waist to hem, and black silk stockings.

Rebecca sent a note to Fannie from her hotel: "I don't think you need worry about your dinner tomorrow night. M[ax] called up and said he thought we wouldn't go tomorrow because we ought both to reconcile ourselves to the fact that life together in London is impossible and that it was torturing for him to see me." She had "no hope," and wished he had never come, "the poor old donkey." Rebecca was to be far more damaged by this episode than her note would suggest. She remained obsessed by Beaverbrook for years. Back in London the following summer, she wrote Fannie Hurst a letter that must be quoted at length, since it is the only evidence of what had happened. Max called at her flat in Queen's Gate Terrace and took her off to lunch at the Vineyard:

> We were alone. That was a queer thing, for nearly always he had a crowd around him. We had lunch, and we walked round the garden for a time. He then talked quite lightly of our past infatuation as if it were a tremendous joke. He laughed about it. I suddenly realised that he was physically quite indifferent to me. Fannie, I'm not telling you the truth. I'm leaving out the point. He casually implied in a phrase that when he had made love to me in London first he was drunk, and that it had been very awkward for him when he found I took it seriously. New York he didn't explain at all. Then we went back to town in the car, and he dropped me on his way. Later that afternoon I heard he is making ardent love to Gwen Ffrangcon-Davies, the young actress who is playing Juliet very successfully.

This has a ring of cruel truth. The letter goes on to worry at the puzzle of why he had set his secretaries to find out where she was in New York—"or was that only because he wanted to see me as a friend, and never told me he was making enquiries in case he revived the hopes he had raised in me when he was drunk?" She had loved Max, she claimed, for years. "It's over but I'm over too. . . . I thought at Christmas I'd got something to give Max—that there was something worth while to be got out of it. But why was he so stricken when I told him that I couldn't have a child? I shall go mad wondering." By the end of the letter Rebecca was facing the fact that "the New York business was I suppose a panic-stricken response to what he realised was my clinging to the idea he loved me."

In her distress when Beaverbrook left New York—after sending her the statutory load of roses—Rebecca became ill, and the rest of her lecture tour had to be delayed. On her recovery she went west, mildly con-

soled by the attentions of other men. One New York admirer wrote to her
of his bitterness that "what was so little a game to me was so much a
game for you," and supposed that by now "you will have vamped half
California, and the other half of California will have tried (unsuccessfully) to rape you. . . . Do be careful how you handle Charlie Chaplin—
they say he has quite a way with you intellectual women!" On the back
of this effusion Rebecca planned a dinner menu, starting with oyster
cocktail. She was resilient, capable of concealing storms of misery beneath a vivacious public persona. When the controls did break, it was
dreadful for everyone, but most of all for Rebecca herself.

Rebecca had met Charlie Chaplin already, with Wells, when Chaplin visited England in 1921. She thought then he was "a darling . . . a
very serious little Cockney" with "a serious little soul." She had particularly liked his description of his marriage: "You know, I dropped into it
with a blonde." This was his first wife, Mildred Harris.

In Los Angeles, Chaplin did make advances to her—so pressingly,
Rebecca said, that she went away to Santa Barbara to escape him. When
she met him again three years later, he explained that he had wanted to
sleep with her "because he had suddenly become terrified of impotence
and wanted to see if it were so." When she ran away, she reported to
Lettie, he "experienced one of the regressive movements he has had at
intervals all his life, and became interested in very young children—I
mean little girls of 13 and 14." It was later in 1924, the year she rejected
him, that he had married the under-age Lita Grey; and "for six months
afterwards he was impotent with mature women, and remained so till he
took up with Marion Davies."

She had fun with Chaplin on their later meetings—after a party in
New York, they broke into a boathouse in Central Park and rowed on the
lake in the dark. But the revelation of his fears struck a chord. A young
executive in the movie industry had accompanied her up to her room at
the Majestic in New York and made a scene. He told her she fascinated
him but that "he knew I made him impotent." This had a shattering
effect on her, since she connected these two incidents with the debacle
with Beaverbrook. She decided that it was his impotence that had been
the trouble, rather than his disinclination to embark on so purposeful
and permanent a relationship as she had envisaged. This theory to some

extent salved her self-esteem, but left her with the more insidious terror that there was something repellent about her as a woman.

2

Rebecca's first visit to the United States, in 1923–24, taught her that it was not a country in which she and Anthony could build a new life, as she had tentatively wondered. There had been some upsettingly intrusive press interviews; there had been complaints from conservative women about her irregular private life and, from progressive feminists, criticism for having accepted financial support from her child's father.

She had met, and liked, the twenty-five-year-old Scott Fitzgerald, but this friendship was temporarily spoiled by a mix-up over a party. The Fitzgeralds arranged a dinner in honour of Rebecca on Long Island; they issued the invitation by telephone, saying that someone would bring her out. Due to some misunderstanding, no one came to pick Rebecca up, and since she had no idea where the party was, all she could do was wait in her hotel room all evening. Fitzgerald, insulted by what seemed to him her deliberate failure to turn up, set up an effigy of her at her place at the table in the form of a pillow with a grotesque painted face, topped with a feathered hat, and spent the evening abusing it. This jape was the talk of the town. Rebecca was mortified.

But there were real and permanent friends made, besides Fannie Hurst. Alexander Woollcott, the dramatic critic, journalist, playwright, and actor, took her to his heart; he had admired her work ever since 1916, when an article of hers in *The New Republic* had made him laugh out loud in a Broadway trolley-car. Rebecca tolerated Woollcott's renowned irritability, and took his criticism. "I have no hesitation in owning that during my twenty years friendship with Woollcott he twice used language to me which was brutal and scarifying. In each case I deserved it," she wrote after his death.

Beatrice and Bruce Gould, who edited the *Ladies' Home Journal,* took her under their wing, and she went out with Konrad Bercovici, the Romanian short-story writer, and Carl Van Vechten, the playboy novelist and jazz-lover whose *Nigger Heaven* was a bestseller of 1926. Jerome Frank became "one of the people I was most fond of in the world," as did Tim Coward of the Bobbs-Merrill Company. Mina Kirstein (soon to be Mrs. Harry Curtiss), the teaching, writing sister of Lincoln Kirstein, was another kind friend: "I really do remember our midnight talk and rummage in the icebox as one of the most warm and friendly things that happened to me in America," Rebecca wrote to Mina after her first visit.

Emanie Sachs,* novelist and biographer, and wife of the banker Walter Sachs, wrote on Rebecca's departure: "We fell in love with you, you know. And if you are so fascinating when you are living through a tragedy, you must be dangerous indeed now that it is over. But I wonder if you want peace really." Rebecca spent weekends with Emanie on all her subsequent visits to America and they remained lifelong friends. But Rebecca clearly confided the story of her "tragedy" with Beaverbrook to quite a few people; Mina Curtiss knew about it, and in 1978, when she made a veiled reference to the affair in her autobiography, *Other People's Letters,* and sent Rebecca the pages in proof for her approval, Rebecca insisted that she remove the offending anecdote.

She had met the most important new friend of all at the very beginning of her tour, in Chicago. John Gunther was to become world-famous as a political journalist and author, but in 1923 he was a university student. He was dazzled by Rebecca, and she responded to the tall, blue-eyed boy, "a young and massive Adonis with curly blond hair." In Chicago she stayed at the Drake Hotel, and found its view of the lake more impressive "than anything I've seen since Spain." She used to amuse her family with a story of how she had stayed a night, not alone, in a Chicago hotel and, because she had only a scanty evening dress, had remained in the hotel room all the next day until night fell again. It must have been

* After her divorce Emanie Sachs called herself Emanie Arling; later she married August (Toby) Philips and became Emanie Arling Philips.

a hotel other than her own, and it may not have happened on her first visit.

The most practical good that came out of her first American visit was an arrangement with the New York *Herald Tribune* to spend in New York one month in the spring and one month in the autumn, writing book reviews for the paper. This she did for many years, and Irita Van Doren, editor of the literary section, became a valued friend. During the next two years she made similarly useful arrangements with *Bookman* and with the Hearst organization, controllers of *International Cosmopolitan, Good Housekeeping,* and *Harper's Bazaar;* these journals were, over the years, to publish her feature articles and short stories. At a fancy-dress ball in New York in 1924 she met William Randolph Hearst himself, then aged sixty; looking like "a petrified giant," wooden-faced, he danced a "surprisingly agile" Charleston solo.

3

"I've had two very pathetic letters from Anthony," Rebecca wrote to Lettie in March 1924. They decided her to return to England as soon as possible, and not to stay over, as she had intended, to report on the Democratic Convention in June. Anthony had told his mother he wanted to become a Roman Catholic. She referred him to his aunt Lettie; she herself had no objection, "but I'm afraid it will raise an awful dust with H.G."

Anthony, nearly ten, was an insecure child and therefore a difficult one. He did not make friends easily, and was jealous of other children. The headmaster of St. Piran's wrote to Lettie, since Rebecca was on her way home, that "Anthony's latest escapade is to cut his sheets with a pair of scissors. . . . He is certainly an extraordinary youth who needs firm handling at the moment." Anthony meanwhile wrote to Lettie, "I am so glad I can become a catholic" (though he did not), and "Only twelve more days before a panther may be back!"

Conscientious Winnie felt she had to remind Rebecca, on her return, to send jam and honey to Anthony at school: "I haven't sent anything since you came back." It was to Winnie that Wells wrote that spring, to find out how his son was. He had not heard from Rebecca for six weeks, "except for a vague cable that seems to be intended sarcastic. I hear she's had a very good time." He was now spreading the news of the separation among his aquaintances. One of these, the writer Enid Bagnold, commented: "Why he wants to blare his break with Rebecca to people he hasn't seen for years I don't know. It seems a little noisy. I wrote back . . . that it was a good thing for Rebecca really to have done with being cumbered about with affections that weren't under her roof. The strain of them, I mean."

All summer Wells sent Rebecca wistful notes: seeing her in a London theatre "has left me sick and sorrowful with love for you." She was his "Dear Sweet Phantom Panther," with whom he would always be in love. It was mainly rhetoric: he found comfort elsewhere. As for Anthony, he told her, "You've got him on your hands. I'm not very likely to see very much of you from now on and I don't see how we can hope to cooperate in so subtle and complicated a matter of his upbringing. What is there to write about now? We've broken. Am I to tell him that?" But in the event Wells did keep in touch with Anthony, taking him out to lunch at Thamesside hotels, and joining Rebecca and Anthony in trips to the cinema and other entertainments. Rebecca was always anxious that the child should sometimes see his parents together.

Max Beaverbrook went on asking Rebecca to his parties even after the traumatic private lunch in June. To be with Wells and Beaverbrook at the same time was hard to take. On 31 July 1924 she sent a telegram to the Vineyard: "If you put me next Wells at dinner I will wring your neck. Many of your friends are deadly but at least I have not lived with them for ten years." Beaverbrook also invited her to his grand Election Dinner in October, during which the results of a Conservative victory came through. This party was "utterly dreary and stupid," she told Winnie. Her host had put her next to Lord Birkenhead, "and I am pleased to say he complained bitterly afterwards of the insolence of my manner."

Seeing Beaverbrook always upset her, and she became truculent as a result. Her electricity needed to be earthed in something solid—such as the Jewish family life that she idealized. "It's a good thing to marry a Jew," says one of her fictional characters. "They don't look on their wives and children as something they let themselves in for when they were silly, like a lot of Christians do." She had tried to marry a Jew, she told John Gunther, "until the veins stood out on my forehead"—but always drew back in the end. She sent yet another "Jew boof" away a couple of weeks after the Election Dinner, as she reported to Winnie: "I must say that nevertheless I loathe being without a boof. . . . Lord knows why I can't get a really good boof, I've got so good-looking lately. But I never see a boof I fancy. I suppose they've all been killed in the war. The contrast with America is great—where there is a plenitude of booves but all too coarse for the refined palate."

When she met Beaverbrook by chance in the park—"another wrench"—she "smashed everything up" by arguing with him. "I feel that I shall never get out of the black magic of this relationship and get on with my life." The "frustrated love" she felt for him was like the way "people who've had arms cut off feel pain in the arm that isn't there." She took a holiday with Gladys Stern and Anthony—"the cub has been as good as gold"—in Austria; her passport photo shows her with bobbed and waved hair. When Lettie took the same radical step in the modern world, her experienced youngest sister sent advice: "For the first few weeks it helps if you roll up your side-pieces on hairpins after damping them in the morning and before you go out in the evening. It's also a good thing to wear side-combs under your hat—it trains the hair to cling to the head and keep in the wave."

4

Emma Goldman, the anarchist and feminist, had been brought up in Russia and emigrated to the United States, where she was imprisoned for her political activities and for her advocacy of birth con-

trol. In 1917 she was deported to Russia, but left five years later disgusted
by the authoritarianism of the revolutionary regime. She was befriended
by the literary adventurer Frank Harris in France before coming to England in September 1924; her aim was to mobilize British anarchists—
who turned out to be disappointingly sparse and unorganized—and to
rally the radical left in support of the political victims of what she now
saw as the Russian dictatorship.

Rebecca West had met Emma Goldman's niece in New York, and it
was to Rebecca that Emma turned on her arrival in London. Frank Harris
was sceptical, since Rebecca had written a condescending review of one
of his books, "as if she were the spouse of God and I a blackbeetle who
had happened to cross her path—silly bitch!" But Rebecca was good to
Emma and became her heroine. "Is there anything that generous creature is unwilling to do for her friends?" Rebecca reminded Emma of "the
early Russian revolutionists who would give their last shirt for their
friends."

Rebecca had to explain to Emma, who was ingenuously optimistic,
that it was no good just hiring a hall for a meeting and expecting people
to turn up. In England, Rebecca told her, there had to be "some organization or party back of it. . . . In fact I would despair utterly if it were
not for Rebecca who is such a generous spirit."

Rebecca provided the necessary backing for Emma Goldman. She
contacted Shaw, Wells, and Lady Rhondda, the owner and editor of *Time
and Tide,* a feminist-socialist weekly. She introduced Emma to Lettie and
her friends. Emma's only other active supporter was the philanthropic
Colonel Josiah Wedgwood, of the pottery firm; he was in the chair at the
dinner for 250 people that Rebecca organized to launch Emma's crusade
at Anderton's Hotel on 12 November 1924. Other speakers at the dinner
included Bertrand Russell and Rebecca herself. Wells sent "a beautiful
card" but did not come. Rebecca reported to Winnie that Emma "is magnificent, and speaks marvellously. . . . I made a magnificent 8-minute
speech of which one sentence has travelled far and wide: 'For the next
four years we are going to be governed by our inferiors.'" (This was a
reference to the recent Conservative election victory.) She had already
scotched a press campaign to have Emma expelled from the country. "I
wrote Max a letter of such unparalleled venom that he has not replied,

but he shut down the campaign and gave her dinner a good show [in the *Express*]."

Rebecca gave lunch parties, tea parties, and presided at Emma's lectures, but Emma's crusade never really got off the ground. To the people who might have sympathized with her anti-Soviet line she was "Red Emma," suspected of a connection with political assassinations in America; to the radical left, she seemed to be betraying the Russian Revolution. Tired and no longer young, she had lost the personal charisma which might have won her a cult following. Emma was naïvely astonished at her lack of success, and her disillusionment in England was nearly as great as her disillusionment in Russia. Rebecca was to remember her as "a solid thickset woman with heavy glasses" and "no vestige of sexual attraction," but great warmth and charm. She had "a rollicking sense of fun but for the most part she was sad because she had no outlet for her gifts."

"Rebecca continues to be my joy," Emma Goldman wrote after she had been in England for nine months. "I always feel rested when I am with her." She had the reverse effect on Rebecca. Emma's single-mindedness was overpowering, and the loving commitment she exacted was time-consuming and exhausting. By early 1925 Rebecca was protecting herself: Greta Mortimer wrote to Emma explaining that Rebecca could do no more at the moment since she had "rather a bad nervous breakdown." But she continued to offer hospitality. At dinner at Queen's Gate Terrace, Emma Goldman met Anthony, "a lanky chap," "affectionate and unspoiled," though Rebecca told her he was not good at school. Emma thought the boy's voice was badly nasal and his speech "barely audible," and took it upon herself to suggest he should have his adenoids out.

Emma Goldman's secondary passion was for the modern European drama, and Rebecca wrote a publicity paragraph advertising a series of her lectures on Shaw, Strindberg, Ibsen, and Chekhov. She also wrote the introduction to Goldman's *My Disillusionment in Russia* (1925), which began on a note of humorous personal appreciation: "Emma Goldman is one of the great people of the world. She is a mountain of integrity. I do not know how one would set about destroying Emma, except by frequent charges of high explosive. . . ." But the introduction, as it proceeded into

seriousness, provides an indication of how Rebecca's own political thinking was evolving.

She wrote that uncritical admiration of Soviet Russia would "rot the
Socialist Movement and give over our unhappy country to the Conservatives for a generation." Those who were sentimental about the British
Empire became "intellectually impotent" and "tedious liars about life."
The same was true of those who were sentimental about the new Russia,
which denied basic human freedoms; such people pretended that it was
"a conscientious experiment in Communism, which it is not." It was
impossible to imagine how these self-deceivers were going to face "the
problems of British influence in India or Egypt in any way that is con-
sistent with the traditions of the Socialist Movement." As in her suffragist youth, Rebecca could toe no party line that cut across her ideas of
truth, common sense, and the deeper human values.

The last time that Rebecca West became involved with Emma Goldman was on film. In 1981, two years before Rebecca died, the movie *Reds*
was released. This was the story of John Reed, the American communist
who was in Petrograd with his lover, Louise Bryant, during the Russian
Revolution of 1917; subsequently he wrote the bestseller *Ten Days That
Shook the World* about his experiences. Emma Goldman, a friend of
Reed's, played a prominent part in the film, portrayed by Maureen Sta-
pleton; Reed himself was played by Warren Beatty, who also co-wrote and
directed the film.

Rebecca West, in her late eighties, appeared in *Reds* among the
"witnesses" from the past. She was filmed sitting on a sofa with her contemporary Dora Russell, once the wife of Bertrand Russell and a cham-
pion of pacifist and feminist causes. The two aged sibyls traded acerbic,
eccentric, but good-humoured memories of Reed, Bryant, and the long-
ago days of their youth. The editors of *Who's Who* suggested to Rebecca
that her appearance in *Reds* should be mentioned in her entry in their
next edition. She agreed with alacrity, confiding to that impersonal repository of achievement the story of her unhappy experiences at drama
school, and saying that "to end up in *Who's Who* as having acted heals a
wound that has hurt for seventy-four years." She had appeared as herself;
if indeed she had "acted," she had put on a fine performance of Rebecca
West being Rebecca West.

Back in 1924, young John Gunther was in London, and attended

the Emma Goldman dinner to report on it for the Chicago *Evening News.*
Rebecca wrote him a note afterwards, and until his departure some
months later they met frequently. Gunther wrote diary-letters to Helen
Hahn,* his girlfriend at home. Rebecca's flat, he told Helen, was "beautifully furnished, of course, in exquisite taste. I was the only guest at
dinner, though people kept dropping in later. The dinner itself was just
the kind one might expect Rebecca West to have; almost nonchalantly
prepared, salt forgotten and such. . . . I like her. I am also a little afraid
of her." Sometimes he was a little shocked by her too—as when she referred to Anthony as "H.G.'s brat," or when he asked the boy whether he
had seen his mother and Anthony in reply referred to her as "my aunt."

Rebecca entertained John Gunther, mothered him, introduced him
to writers, and loved him dearly in a carefree way. The young man took
her out to lunch at the Ritz—which was way beyond his means—and
they sat and talked over the "dreamlike food" for two and a half hours,
"and Rebecca was very brilliant." She repaid him with a star-studded
luncheon party at Claridge's. Before he left England in March 1925, he
and Rebecca went on a last rampage down Bond Street and through May-
fair: "We went into dress shops and saw mannequin parades, we tried on
hats. . . . I fingered a huge elephant gun in an army store, we tried
perfume shops . . . everything in the world, bubbling with laughter most
of the time. It *was* fun!" All they actually bought was flowers—armfuls
of daffodils from the barrows on the street corners, which they piled into
a cab and took back to Queen's Gate Terrace. "A mad afternoon . . ." At
the flat, Gunther told Helen Hahn, they talked "seriously, very seriously,
for an hour or more. . . . And all the time, in Rebecca's white-panelled
room, the radiance of bunches of brilliant yellow flowers . . ." They were
lovers in London.

* Sister of the *New Yorker* writer Emily Hahn, who was to be a close friend of Rebecca's
later.

5

Rebecca spent part of the summer of 1925 at Diano Marina in Italy with Gladys Stern, slipping over to Villefranche on the French Riviera to see Paul Robeson, whom she admired as a person and as an artist—though it took some nerve, she said, to take "a 6'4" negro to lunch at the Hôtel de Paris in Monte Carlo." She needed to be out of London in order to work; apart from journalism, she had undertaken nothing substantial since finishing *The Judge*. The break with Wells, and her unhappiness over Beaverbrook, had thrown her off balance. She was planning a novel based on these events, in the hope that she could write Beaverbrook out of her system. She already had a title for it: *Sunflower*. But this novel was never to be finished, and what she did write of it was only published after her death.

She spent much of the winter in New York, returning only for Anthony's Christmas holidays and Beaverbrook's Christmas party, where Rudolph Valentino was the star guest. There was a plan to produce a stage adaptation of *The Return of the Soldier* in New York; there was even a possibility that Rebecca herself might act in it, but she backed out since ridicule was being poured on "various amateurs who had emerged in leading parts this season—particularly Mrs John Barrymore." She had a good time in New York, returning from a party at Carl Van Vechten's "in a taxi with five coons" at 4:00 a.m., and feeling that "this was lil old New York indeed." Van Vechten's tastes were making Harlem fashionable. Black was beautiful, if it danced or played jazz or sang the blues. She sailed home on the *Olympic*, having on board "a very pleasant time with Noel Coward who is a really nice person, and Mrs Somerset Maugham." (Rebecca always took Syrie Maugham's side in her disputes with her estranged husband.) She had been pressing on with *Sunflower*, she wrote to Lettie, "but it is going to be a very long book."

Lettie, as she reproachfully impressed on Rebecca, had been visiting

Anthony at St. Piran's in his mother's absence. Rebecca deflected her eldest sister's implied criticism with a four-page letter telling her, "I know that you are quite unconscious of it, but you very often don't behave as if you were a woman among your equals, but as if you had some sort of authority, like a prefect, and people do not like this." Later in the year, Rebecca, Anthony, and a governess, Miss Ludlow, drove south in a hired car to the Mediterranean coast.

That summer of 1926 was the first of several that Rebecca and Anthony spent on the Riviera, with stops in Paris at both ends. In those days the coast was unspoilt, and the cost of living less than in either England or America. France was deep in recession; these were the golden days for expatriates on the coast. Two summers later, Somerset Maugham moved into the Villa Mauresque, where his lover Gerald Haxton, as Rebecca ironically reported, "taunted me with the sight of his nudity in the swimming tank." The Armenian novelist Michael Arlen—"every other inch a gentleman," as Rebecca said—was in Cannes, Frank Harris in Nice, Alexander Woollcott and Harpo Marx in Antibes, Edith Wharton in Hyères. Wells himself was near Grasse, in the house he shared for part of each year with his current mistress, Odette Keun. Anthony, who found very little to remember that was good about his childhood, acknowledged the delight of those long, sunlit summers in the south; he found very little to praise in his mother's character, but allowed that it was she who taught him to see and appreciate beauty, and the sensuousness not only of sun and sea but of porcelain and fine fabrics, and the light on flowers and leaves.

That first French summer they stayed at the small Hôtel Josse between Juan-les-Pins and Antibes—Rebecca stealing a few days with John Gunther in Marseilles. In the Hôtel Josse and the hotels and villas around, they found a ready-made community of friends. Most people spent all day on the beach, though Rebecca, struggling with *Sunflower* and an outbreak of facial herpes, worked in her room, unkempt and slatternly, until evening; then she emerged, splendid in one of her couture dresses from Nicole Groult in Paris, to join whatever parties the night offered. She seemed to Yvonne Kapp, an impressed young journalist staying in the Hôtel Josse with her little daughter, to be generous, friendly, but oddly unsure of herself, and vicariously involved in the private lives of others.

If she was particularly inquisitive about the affairs of Dudley Malone, a handsome New York lawyer, it was because he was the husband of her American feminist friend Doris Stevens, and the marriage was breaking up. In her own hotel was Lloyd Morris, the young critic and academic, with his mother, and the aspiring writer Glenway Wescott. Everyone swam off the rocks from the Lloyd Osbornes' villa, at midnight. The Scott Fitzgeralds, with whom Rebecca was reconciled, held court on the beach. (This was *Tender Is the Night* territory.) Gerald and Sarah Murphy, wealthy and beautiful, entertained on a lavish scale at the Villa America, overlooking the Garoupe lighthouse. Maurice Sachs, in his extravagantly Catholic period, trailed around in a soutane; Trotsky's friend Max Eastman, whom Rebecca disliked, was at the Grand Hotel of Cap Ferrat; Anita Loos was at St. Paul. More significant for Rebecca than any of these was William Gerhardie.

Gerhardie's second novel, *The Polyglots,* had so impressed Beaverbrook when it appeared the previous year that he had taken the young writer up socially and professionally, and commissioned from him a serial novel for the *Daily Express.* In order to get it written, Gerhardie fled to France to escape the Beaverbrook regime of nightclubs and country weekends. *Doom,** the novel he was writing, contained, with his patron's permission, a portrait of Beaverbrook in the guise of Lord Ottercove.

Their separate accounts suggest that the meeting between Rebecca and Gerhardie was not a success. Gerhardie reported to Beaverbrook, who was on his yacht in the Mediterranean: "I have just spent a fortnight at Antibes in the company of Rebecca West and her satellites, and you were the theme of our discussion. Curiously enough she is also writing a novel about you. . . . The first day or two we were very pleased and charmed with each other, but towards the end got thoroughly bored with one another. . . ." Beaverbrook, displeased to hear about Rebecca's novel, sent a disagreeable message. This was the first check on *Sunflower.*

In her turn, she reported to Lettie that Gerhardie had turned out to be "a most unpleasant sort of lunatic, who had come over because he thought he ought to have a love affair with me because of our literary eminence, but on seeing me decided I was too sarcastic and too old." But

* *Doom* was published under several different titles: *Jazz and Jasper, My Sinful Earth, Eve's Apples.*

he caused some innocent amusement to the regulars at the Hôtel Josse; Anthony, coming in from a midnight bathe, caught him in the office checking out the residents' bills. By day he rode around on a gaunt horse like the White Knight, his typewriter dangling from his left hand.

Rebecca was perhaps unwise enough to confide in him something of her experiences with Beaverbrook, including her theory about his incapability. In 1931, when he published his *Memoirs of a Polyglot,* he described Rebecca at Antibes as having "a strange worried look in her eye" and seeming "distracted by something"—as well as being "a witty woman" with a beautiful voice. Four pages later, he wrote what might have been a covert comment on her judgement of Beaverbrook. Even intelligent women, he wrote, "seem not to understand that, for physiological reasons, a man's impotence to satisfy the passion of a woman who loves him, but whose body does not excite him, is not a sign of ill-will or lack of affection, or proof of his emasculation, or a slur on her sex attraction. . . ." Men understood the definition of an impotent male to be "one deemed unable to seduce a woman who, lacking attraction to him, has really failed to seduce him."

6

Anthony, twelve years old, was unhappy at St. Piran's. He was bullied, and suffered agonies on being asked the usual schoolboy questions about who his father was and what his father did. He resorted to lies and fantasies, which were inevitably detected as such when he got his stories mixed up—upon which he would be surrounded by "mocking rings of tormenters." Like Rebecca, he found most of his friends among other sensitive outsiders, the Jewish pupils. Even Lettie, the stable, kindly aunt, made him feel that his mysterious origins were something shameful that no one would wish to hear discussed. Anthony was trapped in a nightmare of stale morality.

More was wrong at St. Piran's than Anthony's difficult position there. At the end of the summer term of 1926, Rebecca had gone down to the Speech Day, and came away feeling "more and more sure that there was something wrong with the school." She had already contacted Wells about moving Anthony when she read in the *Evening Standard* that the headmaster had been convicted for drunken driving.

The new school Rebecca chose was an improvement. It had been recommended to her by the socialist author and Africa-expert Naomi Mitchison, and was "much better than the average prep school which teaches the young to think like the *Daily Mail*." The Hall, in Hampstead, was run by Gerard Wathen, "a real fine liberal" according to Rebecca and "a saintly man" in Anthony's opinion. There was no bullying. The necessary liaison with Wells over the change was also beneficial; Anthony treasured a letter from him written around this time in which he told the boy he was proud to be his father. The fiction that Panther was his aunt was unofficially dissolved as well. Rebecca's relationship with Anthony during the holiday at the Hôtel Josse seemed to one close observer, Yvonne Kapp, to be "easy and normal," and he himself said that it was "bliss" to be with Panther when she was in a good mood. She could illuminate and enlarge life for him as she could for everyone else, and at those times he adored her.

But he said in later life that he felt he was on an emotional switchback with her as a child; when she was anxious, ill, or depressed the charm was switched off. He felt she was like an actress, moving in and out of roles with unnerving rapidity: dispirited and sharp-tongued at one moment, brilliant and affectionate at the next. It was as an actress that he was to depict her in his own novel *Heritage*, and it was to an actress that she was ascribing her own experiences in *Sunflower*. "If I could I would never write another line," she had told Winnie in late 1924. "I wish to Heaven I had succeeded in getting on the stage. I believe it would have suited me far better."

Rebecca loved Anthony, the only person in the world who really belonged to her. But she was not fundamentally "good with cubs," as she put it. Winnie's daughter and son felt easier with Aunt Lettie than with Rebecca, whom they called Aunt Cissie. But Aunt Cissie was the exciting aunt, who sometimes provided wonderful treats; and her glamorous clothes first showed her niece, Alison, the difference between "good clothes" and those worn by her mother; Winnie had neither the means nor the skill to dress well.

7

Rebecca felt "desperately, fundamentally ill" as she sailed for America on the *Pennland* in the autumn of 1926, after settling Anthony at The Hall. She found that the projected dramatization of *The Return of the Soldier* had been abandoned, and that her New York circle seemed permanently and alarmingly drunk. Short of money, she agreed to ghost someone else's story for a serial in *Cosmopolitan,* to appear under her own name, in return for a healthy $10,000. The material was the recorded memoirs of a young nurse in the Great War; when *War Nurse*— "The True Story of a Woman Who Lived, Loved and Suffered on the Western Front"—was later republished in book form, Rebecca shared the profits with the nurse and had her own name removed from the title page. Later the movie rights were sold for another $10,000, and came to Rebecca; she gave a third of this to John N. Wheeler, the friend who had recommended her for the original job to Ray Long, the editor of *Cosmopolitan.*

She had to work very fast on *War Nurse,* at the same time as her *Herald Tribune* reviews, which was a strain: the reviews had to be long, and she often had only thirty-six hours between receiving the book and handing in her article, "and they get great publicity, so it is like working under a spotlight." *Sunflower* had temporarily to be put to one side, "but my God the difference to my nerves and health now I see in front of me enough money to keep me more than a year!" She was shrewd, and made another $2,500 on Wall Street, which she reinvested: "If I do not do sensible things about investments I shall spend my old age in a work-house, where nobody will understand my jokes."

But she was still emotionally uneasy; John Gunther was engaged in a serious love affair with someone else, and she was annoyed by a rumour that she herself had been in love with Ralph Barton of *Vanity Fair,* the illustrator of *Gentlemen Prefer Blondes,* and that his sudden marriage had been a blow to her. She made it clear to gossipping American friends that she thought Barton was "an amusing little male strumpet and as such has his uses." She was in love with someone else, "and while I don't mind really if people say that I've slept with everybody from Nicholas Murray Butler* to Jazzbo it revolts me if they say I've loved anybody."

Aboard the *Berengaria* on the way home, she met the writer John Van Druten, who had shot to fame with his play *Young Woodley;* he read her *Return of the Soldier* their first day out "and fell in love with it, and is dramatizing it. And whether it'll be done or not I have had a very amusing time with van Druten." In order to re-establish herself on a new basis with John Gunther, who was shortly to marry Frances Fineman, she confessed to him from the *Berengaria* that she was involved with a California banker who had been her lover for her last three weeks in New York. "It isn't what I feel for Max," and she did not want to marry him. "I do want you to say you'll come back to me and be my nice sweet friend you've always been. I truly love you, John, and I'm enormously grateful to you for all the dearness you've shown me. You really did fill my flat with yellow flowers."

John Gunther remained her "nice sweet friend" for the rest of his life. In 1975, after a researcher had visited her seeking information about Gunther, she wrote in her diary: "I could remember nothing about his intellectual performances, and could only think of his heavenly kindness. How *good* he was."

Rebecca's capacity to enjoy her friends and the good things of life was at least as developed as her capacity for unhappiness. She gave pleasure a very high value. But her unhappiness is easier to document, because it outraged and frightened her, and she recorded it. As she wrote, "the bad is more easily perceived than the good. A fresh lobster does not give such pleasure to the consumer as a stale one will give him pain."

Rebecca had lots of fresh lobster, figuratively and literally, in her long life. She had the satisfaction of her work; celebrity; rooms full of books and flowers; summers in the sun; the best parties in London, in Paris, in New York; the deep pleasure she found in landscapes, paintings, ideas, pretty clothes, good food, music; a vast range of interesting acquaintances, a sufficient number of intimate friends; and, in the end,

* President of Columbia University.

money. Life does not offer much more. She adored all these things and
she communicated and shared her pleasure in them.

But on her thirty-fourth birthday, celebrated on the *Berengaria*, it
seemed to Rebecca that although she was doing better professionally, her
private life was just a sequence of disasters. "Fannie, it is preternatural,"
she wrote, citing "my awful childhood, my worse girlhood, . . . my life
with that insane sadist H.G., and then Max." She "watched everything
with terror to see it won't grow into something monstrous. I even watch
Anthony with terror in case some tragedy cuts in on us. I suppose it must
be something in myself that invites these things but I don't know what
it is."

Bringing Anthony into the chain of disasters was a self-fulfilling
prophecy. She expressed this perverse, quasi-artistic impulse in print,
but with reference to someone else. She was writing about Ernst Toller,
the left-wing German writer, whom she knew, and who was to commit
suicide, when she described "a theory I have long held that to authors of
more than a certain power events present themselves according to their
own style. They begin by inventing certain incidents . . . and then life
says, 'Oh, that is how he likes things to happen, is it? Well, then, they
shall happen to him like that!'"

The "something in myself" that seemed to invite tragedy worried
her, as did her feeling of isolation. Both were, paradoxically, an effect of
her celebrity and personal dynamism. She wanted to be liked by ordinary
men in an ordinary way, and was hurt when, as she told Winnie, "booves
sit and gaze at me with adoration at parties and go away and talk about
me rapturously as the most marvellous woman on earth—but they refrain
from taking any steps about it whatsoever. . . . It's obvious that men are
terrified of me. I can't imagine why. I loathe life without a boof." She felt
she had had the bad luck to have found two men "who could have satisfied
me absolutely," but "H.G. was possessed by a devil and Max by one of
another sort (see the Apocrypha, the Book of Tobit*)."

She wrote that letter soon after the Beaverbrook episode; but even
on the *Berengaria* she felt that the other passengers "gawked" at her, and

---

*In the Book of Tobit, the seven successive husbands of Sarah are killed by a demon on
the wedding night. Through the intervention of an angel, the eighth husband, Tobias,
survives.

had "this inexorable sense that I'm outside their world. I can't bear to feel that I will presently have to build up a position in the world simply by dominance, when I could have done it if anybody had let me simply by being a human being." It was only Anthony, she told Fannie Hurst, who "commits me to humanity."

Feeling excluded from the highest circles, "on the outskirts of an attractive world in which one has no foothold," Rebecca felt the additional exclusion from ordinary humanity all the more keenly. She exaggerated these feelings melodramatically; more genuinely frightening was the "something in myself" which, she thought, made the men she liked reject her physically. In order to discover what that something was, she decided to be psychoanalysed—a far more unusual and radical step to take in the 1920s than it has since become.

8

Rebecca's unwillingness to stay in England was in the nature of a fugue. In the spring of 1927 she, Anthony, his governess Miss Ludlow, and her analyst Mrs. Wilshere (a Freudian from Los Angeles) were established outside Florence at the Villa le Rose, Strada Vecchio Fesolane 24. Doris Stevens, now separated from her husband, came to stay with her in Fiesole, and she saw old Reggie Turner, but work and her analysis precluded much social life. Mrs. Wilshere, she explained to Lettie, was "the only person I've ever talked to who had any plausible explanations of various experiences that have happened to me in recent years, and I feel it's rather urgent it should be done soon, if my life isn't to be greatly interfered with."

Since her relationship with Beaverbrook was also the subject of her novel in progress, *Sunflower* and her analysis became mixed up together. The heroine in her novel, Sunflower herself, is an actress famous for her beauty rather than for her talent, who longs to leave the stage and be comfortably married. Essington, Sunflower's elderly married lover of ten years' standing, is a portrait of Wells: in his scenes with Sunflower, Rebecca demonstrated both his bullying manipulation of her and his love-ableness. In her portrait of Beaverbrook as the fictional Francis Pitt, she conveyed not only his magnetism but her own obsession; *Sunflower* is a study in thwarted desire, all the more compelling since Rebecca abandoned her story without reaching either climax or anti-climax.

In the back of the manuscript book in which she was writing the novel, she made notes in her small, neat handwriting on the process of her analysis and recorded her dreams. Much of the vivid material uncovered during her sessions with Mrs. Wilshere related to Rebecca's original and inconclusive romance with her father. When it came to her difficulties with Beaverbrook, the analysis centred, inevitably for the period, on her masochism and penis-envy. Both she and Max, she noted, had "Jehovah complexes"; her masochism was "expiation for guilt due to transfer of libido to father." With Max she wanted "a bond as between me and my father—purely sexual." ("Purely" is an ambiguous word here. The memories uncovered about her father, if they were not in fact fantasies, would constitute a mild sort of child-abuse.) She noted with some satisfaction Max's "inferiority intellectually and morally," and the fact that her "gifts and power" attracted him.

They also, perhaps, put him off. Star quality like Rebecca's did fascinate men but, as she had found, it did not make them want to spend their lives with her. Clever, achieving women pose a threat to even a successful man's supremacy—perhaps particularly to a successful man's supremacy. The concept of femininity has included a measure of subjection and service. Rebecca was in her own person fighting a battle for parity which is still not altogether resolved; she drew up the battle lines simply by being as she was.

Her emotional forces were as formidable as her witty tongue, her vitality, and her talent, and as alarming to the average male in the 1920s as was her capacity for terror and worship. As the Beaverbrook-figure in the novel says (quoting from the Song of Solomon), "You are so terrible as an army with banners, Sunflower." Even female desire can seem threatening, in a patriarchal society; Rebecca made a joke about this in another context, describing a woman descending on a man "like a fold on the wolf."*

Sunflower is longing for an uncompromisingly male mate, a primitive "hunter," a non-civilized man who will be strong enough to satisfy her "thirst for passivity." Sunflower's creator, tired of fending for herself and her "cub," often shared these feelings. But the Rebecca who longed to be overwhelmed, possessed, and protected was at odds with the stellar Rebecca West that the world saw. She had become a role-model for radical independent women. A paragraph under a photograph of her in *London Calling* named her as "the owner of the wittiest tongue in London, and the most gentle brown eyes . . . a woman deeply imaginative enough to have discarded more black and vivid fears than most people in this life. Therefore today she stands more cleanly and shiningly free of them than anyone I have ever met."

After three weeks in Fiesole, her analyst's husband fell ill in America; she had to leave, and Rebecca, who had expected to continue for another three months, was left stranded. But, as she told Lettie, the retrieval of early memories seemed to have made "an extreme difference to my life already. I can even contemplate coming back to London." But she did not return. She went to Paris, and acquired "a Callot sports-suit in orange and yellow in which I look gorgeous. I couldn't afford it, and nobody will see it at Agay." Agay is a village near Cannes, where she and Anthony spent the summer. Rebecca rented a villa overlooking the sea called Fri-Fri Palace: "It has a palm avenue, a spiral living-room, twenty statuettes each enough to get the artist ten years in Sing-Sing, four balconies and a centenarian gardener." There was also a cook, a cat, and two kittens, and Rebecca felt "in a state which was more beautifully near pure living than anything I had known for many years."

She worked on a balcony overhung by roses and mimosa. Mrs. Wilshere returned, and the analysis was continued—"a terribly intricate and complex business, based on an inconceivably disguised father fixation," she explained to Lettie. "I wish you would tell me one or two things. What was the family doing during the first twelve months of my life? . . . When did we have a servant called Kate?" The seeds of her autobiographical novel of childhood, *The Fountain Overflows*, written

---

*A variant of Byron's "The Assyrian came down like the wolf on the fold. . . ."

thirty years later, were sown during this excavation of the half-forgotten past. Mrs. Wilshere also spent some time with Anthony; predictably, she told Rebecca that he had a mother-fixation.

9

In London in the autumn of 1927, Rebecca made a new start. She left the flat with its unhappy memories of Wells and Beaverbrook and moved a short distance into a leafier area of South Kensington: 80 Onslow Gardens. In Paris, on her way home, she had a brief affair with Prince Antoine Bibesco (who wore black *crêpe de chine* in bed), a Romanian diplomat married to Elizabeth Asquith, daughter of the Liberal leader. In the 1930s she was to lunch at the French Embassy in London and find that the principal guest was Elizabeth Bibesco and that every other woman guest was a former mistress of Antoine Bibesco: "I suppose some attaché's little joke." She was to remember her own affair with him as "rapturous," but at its close felt that some blight still affected her personal life. The evidence suggests that Bibesco's sophisticated sexual inventiveness frightened Rebecca, and that she interpreted it as a further manifestation of male hostility and aggression; and she continued in analysis when she returned to London, this time with Sylvia Payne, another early Freudian. Nevertheless, the elation of the first days of her time with Bibesco coloured the writing of *The Strange Necessity,* in which her meditations on art and literature are embedded in an account of a "sun-gilded autumn day" wandering through a magically illuminated Paris.

Her new London home, large and airy, consisted of two upper floors with a wide roof-terrace over communal private gardens. Today the houses in Onslow Gardens are elegant, gleaming with fresh cream-coloured stucco; in the 1920s they were equally charming but less chic, the stucco peeling and "the colour of a hippopotamus." Rebecca and Anthony shared their flat with a new Sealyham puppy, a present from one of her more lighthearted "boofs," the young publisher Hamish Hamilton.

Rebecca had a new and "incredible arrangement" with *T. P.'s Weekly* "by which I write whenever I like on whatever I like for vast sums." She was also contributing to *Time and Tide* and *John O'London's Weekly.* She was back on form. In Beaverbrook's *Express,* in a series of "Open Letters to Celebrities," she attacked the outspoken Tory churchman, Dean Inge of St. Paul's, for his attitude to Ireland, for his "morbid" views on eugenics and the working-classes, for his anti–trade unionism, and for his "pathological" and antidemocratic hatreds.

Wells's wife, Jane, and Beaverbrook's wife, Gladys, died within two months of each other, in October and December 1927. Rebecca was affected by Lady Beaverbrook's death, ostensibly because "I did deeply like her" and because "I am still fool enough to hate Max being hurt." But she told Beaverbrook's biographer A. J. P. Taylor that when his wife died Beaverbrook wrote her a letter which upset her so much that she destroyed it at once. She had no mercy for Jane Wells, who died of cancer, finding it intolerable to hear it said "how sad it was that such a sweet and kind little person as Mrs Wells should have died."

On Jane's death Wells made a financial settlement on Anthony, who was to receive the income from one trust at eighteen, from another at twenty, and the capital at thirty. The original sum in trust was increased after pressure was brought to bear on Wells by his mistress Odette Keun, an act of kindness on Odette's part for which Rebecca (for whom no provision was made) was grateful.

Wells was keen now for Anthony to meet his half-brothers, Gip and Frank, and asked him to Easton Glebe for Christmas—something that would have been unthinkable while Jane was alive. Anthony was thrilled, and Rebecca, knowing how he idolized his father and feeling threatened, made difficulties. She and Wells exchanged angry letters; but Anthony went to Easton. The same conflict blew up the following Christmas, but on that occasion Rebecca stood firm. Wells accused her of behaving maliciously; they were in any case on bad terms at that point, on account of Wells's reaction to Rebecca's latest book.

Rebecca's extended essay *The Strange Necessity* was published in a book of the same name along with a selection of her *Herald Tribune* reviews in the summer of 1928. She had every intention of completing

Sunflower, but realized that its autobiographical content, and its immediately recognizable portrait of Beaverbrook, would lead to trouble. "I am scared to death that people will identify the persons in *Sunflower* and that he will wreak some awful vengeance on me." She would finish it, "in full knowledge that I may have to suppress it for years." Gladys Stern, who had read the manuscript in its incomplete state, approved her decision as "absolutely right." "I've been terrified for years over what might fall on you, when you published it." Her literary reputation, as Gladys Stern said, would be sustained by *The Strange Necessity.* "People won't bother you, after that, with friendly enquiries as to what *work* you've been doing lately."

The Strange Necessity begins with a meditation on James Joyce and *Ulysses.* Rebecca West's attitude to Joyce was like her attitude to Lawrence: she did not always like what he wrote, but she upheld it. Her opinion was among those cited in the successful defence of *Ulysses* when it was prosecuted for obscenity in New York in 1933; and it was she who had persuaded an unwilling Wells to review it in the *Nation* when it was first published. She paid Joyce the compliment of structuring her essay round a day in Paris, as *Ulysses* is structured round Bloom's day in Dublin. She thought Joyce was sentimental, narcissistic, and incompetent— but a genius. He "pushes his pen about noisily and aimlessly as if it were a carpet-sweeper," yet Marion Bloom's soliloquy was "one of the most tremendous summations of life that have ever been caught in the net of art."

Joyce was irritated by the manner of her essay. In particular he minded having criticism of his writing mixed up with Rebecca's accounts of buying herself a black lace dress and trying on Paris hats. There was nothing disrespectful, in Rebecca's view, about such juxtapositions. She wrote extravagantly in *Sunflower* of "the beauty of tragedy, and the beauty of good clothes, which is one and the same beauty," and consistently wrote of *haute couture* both as a serious minor art-form and as an example of women's doomed, deflected aspiration to excellence.

Rebecca wrote about Joyce's *Finnegans Wake* (when it was still called *Work in Progress*) with cheerful open-mindedness: the word-play was a "pâté de langue gras," and though "it cannot be read as quickly as ordinary English" it could nevertheless be read. But Joyce's supposed revenge on Rebecca was to allude to her throughout *Finnegans Wake* with reference to bonnets. Rebecca believed the work was full of spiteful references to her, in the guise of Biddy Doran and in phrases such as "robecca or worse" in the Anna Livia Plurabelle chapter.

Perhaps because she herself used real people in her novels, and because Wells had used her, often punitively, in his—he had done it again only recently in *The World of William Clissold* (1926)—Rebecca was always ready to identify herself in the pages of other writers' novels. This went on all her life. She believed she was Stella Salt in Wyndham Lewis's *The Roaring Queen,* and that Hugh Walpole's *The Young Enchanted* contained "a vicious portrait" of her as Jane Ross; she believed she was Retta Spencer-Savage in Storm Jameson's *A Cup of Tea for Mr Thorgill,* and Charmian in Muriel Spark's *Memento Mori;* she believed that Iris Murdoch's *The Sacred and Profane Love Machine* was based on herself, Jane Wells, and Wells. As for the novelist Phyllis Paul, she had "in every book some sentences which have actually been spoken by me at some critical moment of my life, and her books are haunted by Anthony in all his manifestations."

The Strange Necessity got her into trouble with Wells as well as with Joyce. She reprinted in the book the review she wrote in America of Arnold Bennett's *Lord Raingo,* which began with her much-quoted remarks about the literary Uncles: "All our youth they hung about the houses of our minds like Uncles, the Big Four: H. G. Wells, George Bernard Shaw, John Galsworthy and Arnold Bennett." She then proceeded to assess the strengths and weaknesses of each Uncle. Shaw, to whom she sent the book, did not mind a bit, and sent her a cheery postcard signed "your too affectionate uncle" with a photograph of himself on the back: "This is my most avuncular postcard."

Wells, however, took umbrage. Rebecca had written flatteringly that she had been lucky to be young "just as the most bubbling creative mind that the sun and the moon have shone upon since the days of Leonardo da Vinci was showing its form." She spoilt this effect by examining "the only thing against Uncle Wells," with a mocking characterization of the feebleness of his love scenes, where his prose "suddenly loses its firmness and begins to shake like blanc-mange." She provided a parody of such a passage, and referred to Uncle Wells's having once "sent out into the world a large blond novelette with a heaving bosom called *The Passionate Friends.*" Even if she was motivated by revenge for the way she had sometimes been portrayed, her parody was justified in literary terms—and anyway, "take him all in all, Uncle Wells was as magnificent an uncle as one could hope to have."

Wells's first reaction was irritated but resigned. Rebecca was playing her ancient role of "Pert but Charming Niece. . . . You win—so far as you are read." His next letter, in response to her self-defence, chided her for inventing a heroine "with a silly name" in her parody, instead of quoting directly from his books to make her points. Anthony West, when he came to write about his father, diagnosed as the major and unforgivable insult the fact that Rebecca had, in her parody, not only given the archetypal Wells heroine a "silly name"—Queenie—but a menial name, suitable at that time only for "a sweatshop seamstress, a laundry hand, a popular barmaid, or a boarding-house slavey." In other words, Rebecca was implying Wells had "a cockney imagination." This would suggest on Anthony's part a sensitivity to social-class distinctions more sore and raw than that of either of his parents.

As the correspondence between Wells and Rebecca grew more heated, Wells told her that "*The Strange Necessity* only does for your critical side what *The Judge* did for your pretensions as a novelist. You have a most elaborate, intricate and elusive style which is admirably suited for a personal humorous novel. . . . You are ambitious and pretentious and you do not know the measure and quality of your power." Parts of *The Judge,* he told her, had been magnificent, but "As a whole it is a sham. It is a beautiful voice and a keen and sensitive mind doing 'Big Thinks' to the utmost of her ability—which is nil." And she lacked humility. "There my dear Pussy is some more stuff for your little behind. You sit down on it and think." This is all in keeping with what he wrote to Arnold Bennett about the latter's novel *Imperial Palace:* "I agree with the thesis of the increasing 'secondariness' of women"; he himself had in his novels tried to make the point that women were able to support, but not share in, the serious work of men. "The women won't like you," he warned Bennett.

Rebecca's essay set out to discover why art mattered. "Art is not a luxury, but a necessity," she wrote, and there was "a fundamental unity between all art and all experience," in that the individual is always examining his environment to see what chances of spiritual survival it offers him. Only art brings about an equilibrium between the will to live and the will to die; art is a way of "making joys perpetual." Art is not enjoyed only with the mind: *King Lear* "overflows the confines of the mind and becomes an important physical event." She suggests that there may be a continuum between minor art (such as *haute couture*) and major art, as between animal life and human life, as between affection and passion.

She was to make this point about the unity of experience again in *Black Lamb and Grey Falcon,* writing that when one makes a cake for guests one likes and respects, "one is striking a low note on a scale that is struck higher up by Beethoven and Mozart." The effect of a Mozart aria is to propose a world "where man is no longer the harassed victim of time but accepts its discipline and establishes a harmony with it." In *The Strange Necessity* she wrote that art showed her that "within me I held some assurance regarding the value of life, which makes my fate different from what it appears. . . ." Art, at whatever point on the continuum, reconciled the mud with the stars for Rebecca West—salvation not through suffering, but through pleasure.

Arnold Bennett, like Wells, put her down. His review in the *Evening Standard,* under the heading "My Brilliant but Bewildering 'Niece,'" was condescending. He praised her acrobatic, disorderly mind, "which ranges like a tigress over the whole spectacle of mankind"; but "she must, at all costs, 'perform'. She must be odd." Her essay, he wrote, was infested with "mere irresponsible silliness." She had not learned to use her gifts. "In other words, she does not know how to live." A less prejudiced observer might judge that her essay showed precisely that she did know how to live.

Rebecca was shown Bennett's review by a *Standard* journalist who had come to interview her about the book. "I said a few things, just the things one would say." When the interview appeared, she found that the journalist had written "a tissue of lies simply beyond belief, representing me as having covered Bennett with the lowest form of insult." Readers' letters came in to the *Standard* criticizing Rebecca for her alleged remarks. She brought a libel action against the *Standard,* and won, in that the case was settled out of court with Rebecca being awarded an apology and costs.

Rebecca had been in contact with Beaverbrook, who owned the *Standard,* throughout this trouble, although Beaverbrook was one of the public figures featured in *Lions and Lambs,* a collection of portrait caricatures by David Low with uncharacteristically bland commentaries by

Rebecca under the pseudonym "Lynx."* Rebecca had not recovered from her obsession. The young secretary whom she took to France with her later in the year overheard her calling out "Max!" in the night from her adjacent room in their Paris hotel.

10

America, which had spelled fun and freedom, lost its charm for Rebecca. Her California banker had died. Prohibition New York now seemed seedy and dangerous. "I loathed all the crime," she wrote after her visit in late 1928. "I hated nightclubs where policemen came in with clubs and cleared the place because the proprietor had struck a chorus-girl two days before and she had just died. I hated always lunching in speakeasies with the blinds down. I hated the liquor-trucks going down through New Jersey with armed guards. It's got too bad to be funny and nobody sees it."

She had been exhausted when she set out, not only by troubles over *The Strange Necessity,* and her lawsuit, but on account of "a summer of anxieties over Anthony." There had been an emergency about the fourteen-year-old's health. What made it worse was that he had seemed "more exultantly happy" since they had moved to Onslow Gardens than Rebecca had ever seen him, "and we have never been so much to each other." He had done well at The Hall, Hampstead, and was all set to go to a public school, Stowe. But his doctors, after an X-ray, diagnosed tuberculosis of the right lung. Tuberculosis was still a potentially fatal disease.

---

* The caricatures and commentaries had originally appeared in the *New Statesman* and were published in book form in 1928, the year of *The Strange Necessity.* She collaborated with Low again on *The Modern Rake's Progress,* but without enjoyment, since he did the drawings at the last minute, giving her almost no time to compose her commentaries. *The Modern Rake's Progress* first appeared serially in Nash's *Cosmopolitan,* and was published in book form in 1934.

Anthony went to be treated at Sellbrigg Sanatorium at Kelling in
Norfolk, a place they knew well from holiday visits. Rebecca herself
immediately fell ill—her customary, involuntary response to the illness
of anyone close to her—with flu, colitis, gallstones, ear-ache, in rapid
succession. In between bouts of illness and getting her work done, she
visited Anthony, staying for a few days at a time at the Royal Links Hotel
in nearby Cromer. John Gunther, briefly in London, found her just setting off for Cromer and made time to accompany her on the journey. She
wrote to him: "Never, never, shall I forget the sweetness of your visit to
me. . . . There is something between us that is very real and will never
be broken." She had come to terms with Gunther the married man, and
apologized for being "mistaken" in her earlier attitude to his wife,
Frances, who was now pregnant: "I hope everything will be wonderful."

Two letters survive from Anthony in the sanatorium to "Dear Panther" in London.

> I hope your back pain is gone the dog is in perfect health it
> roams about the garden most of the day. I am (I am told) much
> better. I feel just the same wich is to say I am feeling much
> the same. I recieved your lovely meccano, you have given me
> to much. I meant at most no:5 wich is much cheaper and all
> that I wanted. I thank you very much indeed. my fellow cap-
> tives are awfully nice.

And:

> I am very sorry to hear that you have had "flu", I am equally
> sorry to hear that you have had to stay in bed.
>   I am very sorry to miss you for a whole week more.
>   I am getting on very well and Doc Morris says that latest
> X-ray photographs show great improvement. Dr Morris is now
> on holiday.
>   I enclose a radio advt. it looks good.

Anthony recovered very quickly. He had what he later called a "life-
changing experience" at the sanatorium. He caught sight of a corpse
through the open door of the mortuary, recognized it for what it was, and

thought: "Oh yes, of course. But I'm not going to die." The doctors decided he did not have TB after all, but only "a most vile and poisonous infection of pneumonia," as Rebecca told S. K. Ratcliffe with relief, "which it will take him six months to get over." (But Anthony in later life said that X-rays always revealed the scars of tuberculosis on his lung.) His father was supportive of Rebecca over the "cub's" illness. "I feel like your dear brother and your best friend and your once (and not quite forgetting it) lover. . . . I'm still very hopeful about the case, for what comes suddenly may go as suddenly."

Wells went to John Van Druten's dramatized version of *The Return of the Soldier,* which was produced in London that summer, and told her how glad he was to see her having "that blaze of success." He went down once to visit Anthony in the sanatorium, and took him out to the little resort of Wells-next-the-Sea. Here Anthony took a photograph of Wells with the Kodak he had given him for his birthday—a picture of "Wells-next-the-sea at Wells-next-the-Sea," as Wells said—"so beguilingly the father of my dreams," that day and always.

This rare treat only tipped Anthony's longings more sharply in the direction of his elusive father. Once, visiting Wells and the exotic, scandalously outspoken Odette Keun in the south of France, the boy asked if he could stay with them permanently. He was sent back to his mother as arranged. As an elderly man, Anthony West still spoke sarcastically about the fact that Rebecca, while making much of her anxiety over his condition, had stayed in London most of the time he was in the sanatorium; and he maintained that she had lied for some melodramatic purpose of her own when she said that the original diagnosis of tuberculosis was mistaken. It is hard to see what this purpose can have been; and hard not to feel that his mother was being blamed for something different—in fact, for absolutely everything.

11

Christmas 1928 was enlivened for Rebecca, who always dreaded Christmas, by the presence in London of Carl Van Vechten and his wife, Fania. Carl fell ill, and received visitors in bed at the Carlton Hotel wearing a jade-green Spanish shawl over cerise pyjamas. In the new year, Anthony started at Stowe, the school chosen for him by Wells, who was taking an increased interest in that "charming and worthwhile young man," as he described him to Rebecca. He wanted Anthony to be known at Stowe as the son of H. G. Wells.

This was a tremendous gain for Anthony, who had not only an official father now but one whose name and fame were enviably familiar to the other boys. Wells's visits caused a flattering stir. It was unnerving for Rebecca, knowing how Anthony adored Wells; she was irrationally afraid that Wells would, after allowing her to see the boy through the difficult childhood years, try to take him from her. In early 1929 she decided to adopt him legally (which would remove the stigma of illegitimacy from his personal records), and consulted the solicitors Charles Russell and Co., who put her in the hands of Theobald Mathew. He had acted for the *Evening Standard* against her in the libel case, but on this occasion they got on well and he became "the nearest thing to a brother that I've ever had in my life." Wells opposed the adoption, casting aspersions on Rebecca's way of life and choice of friends, when the case came before a judge in June 1929. But the adoption was granted, under certain reasonable conditions: that Rebecca should consult Wells over Anthony's education, allow him to spend part of his holidays with Wells, and designate Wells as his guardian in the event of her death.

Rebecca complied with all this. But she wrote a long letter to Bertrand Russell, whom she had known slightly for years, setting out her doubts and grievances and asking him to stand as co-guardian with Wells. Russell wrote a long, kind, prevaricating letter: "I shall not shrink from this if I am convinced it is useful. . . ." He did not care for Wells, and suggested that Wells's hostility might have begun when he learned that Jane had cancer: "This would cause his remorse, inducing hostility towards any woman who had formerly, but not now, attracted him sexually. . . .WOMAN tempts him to acts which are ill thought of, not which he thinks ill of." Wells, Russell said, would have liked public honours and burial in Westminster Abbey; "if he had been a 'moral' man both would probably have happened." In the end Russell, a "dreary womanizer" himself in Rebecca's later opinion, decided not to take on the co-guardianship of Anthony West. Theo Mathew accepted the office in his stead.

The day after Bertrand Russell posted his letter to Rebecca in France, she was writing to Lettie: "What it means to send Anthony off to Easton you can guess—it depresses me to death, and of course the way he adores H.G. is ghastly. . . . The month Anthony was here was a great success. I had Pamela Frankau here and she was an ideal companion for him. She's just 21 but very young for her age." Pamela Frankau was the brilliant, erratic daughter of the popular novelist Gilbert Frankau; she had published her own first novel at the age of eighteen. Rebecca had met her at the house of Mrs. Eliza Aria, Pamela's great-aunt and the last attachment of the actor Henry Irving. Rebecca was fifteen years older than Pamela, who worshipped her, never having met before such a "glamorous, overshadowing personality."

In the summer of 1928 and the following two summers, Rebecca took the Villa Mysto—one of half a dozen Edwardian villas on an offshore island between Cannes and Saint-Raphaël, "a heaven on earth, with rocks at the bottom of the garden from which one steps into fifteen feet of nicely warmed Mediterranean." In 1929 she and Anthony rolled south in a hired car through country whose signposts, Rebecca said, read like a wine-list: Chablis, Beaune, Nuits-Saint-Georges, Meursault, Macon. Before they left England, Rebecca had attended the party of the year: the all-night General Election Party given by Gordon Selfridge in his great department store in Oxford Street. Rebecca went with Michael Arlen and the two Dolly Sisters, the musical-comedy stars; but the jewelled gathering was overwhelmingly Conservative. The results, as they came in, proclaimed a Labour victory. Inside, the rich commiserated with one another; outside, the crowds cheered. Rebecca, walking in Selfridge's roof-garden, cheered inwardly herself. She went home and wrote a brilliant article about the party, and about the English political psyche, for the American *Bookman*. "English perpetualism," she wrote, "(which the foreigner is apt to mistake for Conservatism) will not fight Socialism, it will permeate it and mitigate it."

She had had her enjoyable summer at the Villa Mysto before the financial crash in America put a stop to the ambitious Labour programme. The Villa Mysto was an entirely female world, though male friends such as John Van Druten paid visits, as did the journalist and novelist Beverley Nichols, who fifty years later recalled Gladys Stern "clambering out of the sea looking like a pregnant lobster just after the poor thing has been plunged into the pot." Gladys Stern brought her pretty young secretary-companion with her; Rebecca had a new young secretary too, an attractive blonde called June Head. Everyone had nicknames. Gladys Stern was not only Peter, or Tynx, but Lady Mary Pussinger (Rebecca upheld a Fairfield family custom of dividing the human race into Pussingers and Puppingers). June Head was "Ça," from a line in a French play: *"On appelle ça une secretaire."*

The atmosphere and talk were playful, and suggestive in a sub-Colette, schoolgirlish way. An assumption of innocence, the absence of male companionship, Rebecca's liking for fun and fantasy and for games of dominance, all contributed to the flirtatious innuendo of the way she and the Mysto habituées behaved with one another. Pamela Frankau was to remember weeks of hot sun and blue sea, "of the white villa with its Empire ornaments, mosquito-nets and unimagineable meals, of wearing only a bathing suit and cotton trousers; of swimming with Anthony to small rock-islands." And above all, "listening to Rebecca, talking to Rebecca, besieging Rebecca with fundamental questions . . . laughing until one ached about the middle."

When Rebecca read and praised her novel in progress, Pamela felt "like a Ford being patted on the back by a Hispano-Suiza." Rebecca, in her turn, liked being idolized by someone of the younger generation, to whom H. G. Wells was just "a tired mole with blue eyes and large whiskers." In old age, ruminating on the loyalty of women and the iniquities of men towards women, Rebecca wrote: "If I were young again, I would deliberately (and against my nature) choose to be a lesbian."

The teen-age Anthony, dazzled by "the beautiful bodies of young women baking in the sun," felt the strength of this female republic, and it did nothing for his own sense of worth as a non-female. But he had an ally in Pamela Frankau, whom Rebecca described as being "beautiful in the manner of Disney's Bambi." "I fell head over heels in love with her at fifteen without looking closer," wrote Anthony. She recognized his unhappiness, treated him as an adult, and listened and talked to him for hours. "The confusions that she helped me with most were about my sexual being. The way I had been brought up had given me the idea that a woman was the thing to be, and that I had somehow done wrong by being a male."

Rebecca, aware of the peculiarity of Anthony's position, formulated the problem a little differently. A working mother, she wrote in the *Daily Mail* that autumn, put a strain on the future of society: "When a boy has seen his mother acting as both father and mother, supporting the house as well as managing it, where is he to get his idea of fatherhood?" When he grows up, he may "take it for granted that some woman will do two people's work and father his children as well as mother them."

In retrospect, Anthony felt that the relationship between Pamela, Rebecca, and himself was, emotionally, a triangular one, "and that Pamela was consciously attempting to mediate between us with a clearer idea of what its realities were than either I or my mother possessed." If this was so, Pamela was not so "young for her age," as Rebecca believed. Pamela kept up the contact, visiting Anthony at Stowe and taking him out to long lunches at The Spread Eagle at Thame; she took up issues that were bothering him with Rebecca—which, since this constituted an unspoken criticism of Rebecca's regime, marked the beginnings of a lessening of intimacy between the older woman and the younger.

12

In the autumn of 1929, Rebecca's novel *Harriet Hume* was published. All through the 1920s she had been wanting to write a short non-fiction book about feminism. She never got round to it—

though she gave a lecture on the position of women to the Fabian Society
in the autumn of 1928—and her feelings about the relations between the
sexes worked their way into her fiction instead.

She had begun *Harriet Hume* as a short story, and it had grown.
"However it has turned out rather odd and pretty. . . . It is a fantasy, not
a novel." She dedicated it to Robert and Sylvia Lynd: "I hope you will like
it in its unpretentious way—it's only an hour's crazy entertainment."
Somebody who liked it very much was H. G. Wells, and his praise half-
healed the breach over *The Strange Necessity* and the adoption. She had,
he wrote to her, got her "distinctive fantasy and humour" into the novel,
and her "peculiar intricate wittiness." There was a mild sting in the tail
of his praise; it was as if she had come alive, he wrote, "after years in a
sort of intellectual trance." His correspondence with Bennett makes it
clear that he saw the novel's very theme as proving, unintentionally, their
shared belief in the essential "secondariness" of women.

Other critics liked it less than Wells did. St. John Ervine's review,
in Beaverbrook's *Daily Express,* was headed "Rebecca's Worst Book." Subsequent critics of Rebecca West's work have tended to pass over *Harriet
Hume* rapidly, labelling it mannered and insubstantial. In its lightness it
clashes with most people's idea of Rebecca West's writing; it is a product
of her private rather than her public self.

She based her heroine on a visual memory of her friend Harriet
Cohen waving to her from the balcony of a house in Regent's Park Terrace, looking "exquisitely in accord with Nash's London. . . . I had
a sense that time was being spun about her which I tried to express in a
book named *Harriet Hume.*" Like the real-life Harriet, her heroine is a
pianist; she seems her creator's idea of undiluted femininity—flexible,
unaggressive, passive, anarchic—just as her lover, a "great man" on the
Wells/Beaverbrook model, seems a distillation of masculinity—dynamic,
ambitious, egotistic, ultimately unscrupulous. The two represent opposite poles: "There is the North, and there is the South, and there is no
war between them." But war breaks out between these lovers, the man
seeing Harriet's oppositeness as opposition, and therefore malign. The
ideas behind *Sunflower* are here, but deployed in a stylized, fanciful manner, like light opera. Harriet has access to supernatural powers, and the
story is weighted in favour of her values and attitudes. But the masculine

principle is also justified; the conclusion is that neither sex can achieve much in the world without harnessing the complementary attributes of the other.

Very few women possess undiluted femininity, and certainly not Rebecca West. She may have longed for a simple world where men were men and women were women, but her own experience had taught her how common role-reversal was. *Harriet Hume,* which was to be her own favourite among her novels, seems like an act of faith that these matters are negotiable, and that synthesis is both desirable and possible, both between couples and within individuals. Ever since she was a girl, she had seen the world in terms of opposing dualities of all kinds, and the dialectics of gender were so central to her thinking that it is unlikely she planned the novel in any formal, schematic way; she told Sylvia Lynd that "It never seemed at all relevant to myself, and in fact most of it was very 'automatic' writing."

The novel was written during a phase of hopefulness and new insight. Shortly before she began it, she wrote to Hugh Walpole, whom she had flattened by her reviews in the past, explaining that the near-cruelty of her criticism had its roots in her own insecurities. "But I'm willing to admit it was an unnatural attitude, and I imagine it made everything I wrote up to a very few weeks ago apt to strike people as highly unsympathetic." Unfortunately for her, but fortunately for the future of English literature, this vision of serenity was interrupted by the storm over her adoption of Anthony—though even then, "since I've realized that nothing pleasant or easy is ever going to happen to me I have found that one has marvellous strength and that the things one would have judged certain to crush one don't."

London's streets and squares and parks, in changing lights and seasons, are central to the mood of *Harriet Hume.* The green garden in Kensington, the scene of Harriet's magical experiences, is the garden overlooked by Rebecca's terrace at 80 Onslow Gardens. She said she wrote the book to find out why she loved London; she was at last reconciled to the city which had for so long "just hopelessly, finally, heartrendingly meant Max to me." Around this time she contacted Beaverbrook and asked him to return all her letters. He came to the flat, and together they burned both sides of their correspondence. She told this to Beaverbrook's biographer forty years later, when he came across a surviving few of her letters: "and I would be grateful if I were not associated with Max in any way."

The reason for her new confidence and calmness became clear when, on 1 November 1930, Rebecca married. Fannie Hurst, among others, received the news by telegram: "Sorry darling but am becoming Mrs Henry Maxwell Andrews Saturday love Rebecca."

PART FOUR

Mrs.
Henry
Andrews

1

Rebecca West met Henry Andrews in late 1928 at a party in Earls Court, West London, where the pacifist writer Vera Brittain was living with her husband, George Catlin, and her close friend Winifred Holtby. Rebecca and both her hostesses were involved in the independent weekly *Time and Tide;* among the directors of the paper, Winifred Holtby found Rebecca "both the most fascinating and the most alarming." It was Vera Brittain who made the introduction: Henry Andrews had been a friend of George Catlin—an academic political scientist—since Oxford days, and had particularly asked to meet Rebecca West. Henry Andrews spent the evening on a cushion at her feet, and saw her home after the party.

Rebecca's first impression of him, she recalled, was of someone "gentle, very odd to look at though tall and beautifully dressed, rather like a dull giraffe, sweet, kind and loving." He was an admirer of her work, and had been to see the play of *The Return of the Soldier* six times. A departmental head at Schroders, the merchant bank, he appeared to be a typical Englishman, diffident, well-mannered, and even then a little deaf. In fact his background was complex, and not at all English.

Two years younger than Rebecca, he was born in Rangoon, Burma, in 1894. According to her, his first known ancestor was a horse-dealer from the lowlands of Scotland who, on a business trip to Denmark, met and married a Jewish girl. Also according to Rebecca, Henry's grandfather Max kept a livery stable in Schleswig-Holstein, and both he and his wife were German subjects. Henry's father, whose name was Lewis (or Louis) Henry John Andrews, and Lewis's brother Ernest both joined the British East India merchant company of Wallace Brothers, and were posted to Rangoon. (There was a third brother, Willy, who stayed in Germany.) To complicate matters further, Henry's father married a girl he had met in Hamburg, Mary Wordsworth Myres Chavatsky, who had been brought up in Lithuania and had mixed French, English, and Lithuanian origins. That, at least, was Rebecca's usual account of her mother-in-law; but in the year Henry died she wrote to friends that her mother-in-law's maiden name had been Charbert (perhaps a Gallicized version of Chavatsky?) and that her origins had been Polish and Estonian rather than Lithuanian. She spoke several European languages, including English, but none of them without an accent. Henry's genetic inheritance could hardly have been more widely European.

In Rangoon the two Andrews brothers became re-Anglicized; his uncle Ernest was naturalized British in 1910. (The certificate, surviving among Henry's papers, is signed by Winston Churchill as Secretary of State.) Both became rich, and Uncle Ernest settled in London, in charge of Wallace Brothers' timber imports from the Far East. Around the turn of the century, Henry's parents were living in Hamburg, where Henry and his elder brother, another Ernest, attended the Wilhelm-Gymnasium. Later they were sent to Uppingham, an English public school, though their parents stayed in Hamburg—where in 1909 their father died, apparently beset by failed investments.

Henry went up to New College, Oxford, in 1913, but when the Great War broke out he was caught in Germany, where he and his mother were selling the Hamburg house and negotiating for her to become a British subject, as her sons already were. Mrs. Andrews was finally allowed to leave for England, but Henry was interned in Germany for the duration of the war. He was sent to Ruhleben, where four thousand Britishers were held in prison-camp conditions. He was a serious boy, and from Ruhleben he sent his mother essays on Plato and Shelley to be forwarded to his tutor at New College; he took an active part in the informal camp "university." After three years of internment, he was in the camp hospital suffering from "nerves"; as he wrote to his mother, "it is clear that anyone saying that I am conspicuous for mental balance lacks all discernment." A blow on the head from one of the Ruhleben guards—Henry insisted it was accidental—was responsible, it was later thought, for the headaches and depressions from which he was to suffer afterwards.

A fellow-inmate wrote to Mrs. Andrews that Henry "tells me that in the Camp he had 'found himself,'" and that he was "full of devotion and unselfishness to others." What was worrying Henry, the friend said, was the knowledge that his mother and his uncle Ernest, "the two people for whom he cares most," had quarrelled (about money). Henry wrote introspective, descriptive letters about camp life to his mother, which she had published during the war under the pseudonym "Richard Roe."* The letters from his cell, "a box for four people," reveal him as an emotional intellectual—a hero-worshipper, he analysed his intense camp relations, was inspired by the life of Joan of Arc, enjoyed reading H. G. Wells and the philosophy of history, and missed the companionship of women.

After the war he picked up his undergraduate life at Oxford with difficulty, obtaining a pass degree in 1921. Where he starred was as a speaker at the Oxford Union, becoming "one of our ablest performers," according to *Oxford Magazine*. If he could have cultivated "a more assertive manner," his speech on the languages of Greece, India, China, Germany, and Britain would have been "more effective"; nevertheless, it would "bear reprinting."

Henry Andrews became a scholarly and formidably well-informed man, and something of a pedant, but he did not become an academic, which is what he would have liked. He never found work for which he was really fitted, or which fulfilled his aspirations. Though he seemed the perfect English gentleman, his hybrid origins and his fragmented youthful experience made him insecure. Familiarity with several cultures and countries might have been exploited with confidence and pride, as it was by the Heinemann family who had befriended the Fairfields. But Rebecca always felt that Henry, like herself, was somehow a displaced person:

> The grim fact is that . . . he was not a gentleman, what does that mean, except that owing to historical accident and his forebears' lack of prudence he did not fit into any class, and had to move among people who did not understand him and whom he could not understand; of necessity errors abounded. There was a bewilderment through which he blundered. Mine was much the same predicament, it is a misfortune which evokes no sympathy, only derision.

* *In Ruhleben*, Hutchinson 1917. Reviewed in The *Times Literary Supplement*, February 1917.

2

When Rebecca first knew Henry Andrews she was hardheadedly contemplating marriage with a friend of John Van Druten's called Jack Cohen, who dealt in butter and eggs. It was only after she had broken with Cohen that she focussed properly on Henry. They had always talked about places: "He spoke of Chartres and the Pyrenees, and I spoke of the South of France and Spain." But there was a relationship between them, she found with surprise; they became lovers. Writing later to a friend with personal problems, Rebecca told her: "Don't worry about your physical limitation. After I left H.G. I had a bad crash of a love affair. . . . For years I was like you—but it came back with the right person."

She wrote in old age that when Henry began to explain that he could not marry her, though he would like to, she felt "as if I had been cast to act the star role opposite him in some important play. . . . It did not matter whether I loved him or what sort of man he was, the contract could not be cancelled." She had to ask him, "as an actress might enquire of a playwright," what the impediment to their marriage was. Thus the Sunflower in Rebecca West prepared for her next role.

Henry's problem was money. He had made himself a small fortune at Schroders, buying and selling stock on margin. Though he seemed cautious he was, like Charles Fairfield, a gambler. When the crash came, shortly after he had met Rebecca, Henry not only lost all he had made but found himself heavily in debt, with only his salary and no capital.

Henry's mother was living in Queen's Gate, Kensington, very near Rebecca, while he himself lived with his rich uncle Ernest in Cavendish Square. His mother had inherited from her husband what remained of his half of the family money, but had joyously spent it, according to Rebecca, "on the last feather boas and picture hats to be seen in London." Uncle Ernest had paid the Uppingham school fees; Henry was his uncle's executor, and had expectations of being his heir. He did not want to tell his authoritarian uncle about his present predicament, especially since his brother, who had emigrated to Australia, was already proving unlucky or unreliable about money.

Rebecca's reaction to this tale of misfortune was to suggest that they marry and pool their resources. She was not deeply in love with Henry. He was nicknamed "the Elk" among her intimate circle, and his mother "the Elk's dam." Rebecca had written to her secretary, June Head, from the Hôtel Raphaël in Paris, where she and Henry had stayed together, that "your Elk was beyond price—but I don't want to marry it after all. It's too slow in its movements about the house. *Mais comme l'elque qui visite* it's perfect." Her sister Winnie later destroyed the letters Rebecca wrote to her in the months preceding the marriage, presumably because her references to the Elk were not quite what might be expected from a woman writing about her future husband.

It was the revelation of his anxieties and his need for her, plus her need for marriage, that precipitated her decision. A fortnight before the ceremony she sent her agent a short story called "Sensible Folks," which was an indirect farewell to the past, and perhaps to Wells and Beaverbrook. It was about the meeting of a divorced couple who still love each other; they wept "for the love that something incurably naughty and childish in them made them destroy; and they looked into the grey years ahead of them, which they must spend imprisoned in their freedom from each other."*

The past two years, Rebecca told S. K. Ratcliffe, had been the worst of her life, and "if I had no happiness to look forward to I would want the wedding as a sign of gratitude to Henry for what his feeling for me during the last year has done to build me up." The marriage, by special license, was arranged at short notice, and there was no public announcement. Rebecca had spent the summer at the Villa Mysto as usual, and had even talked of buying it, noticing the "amazing effect" these summers had on Anthony. She had a great deal of work on hand, which she was trying to get out of the way right up to the day before the wedding.

---

* This theme was replayed with variations in "Life Sentence" in *The Harsh Voice*. "Sensible Folks" appeared in *Saturday Evening Post* 25 Oct and 1 Nov 1930.

They were married by the Reverend Sir Henry Denny, a cousin of the Fairfields, from the house of Amy St. Loe Strachey, widow of the editor of the *Spectator* and a family friend, at Abinger in Surrey. Sappho Dawson Scott was co-hostess at the reception. June Head collected Rebecca's honey-beige velvet dress from the Knightsbridge dressmaker and rushed down to Surrey with it on the wedding morning. Henry's best man was Douglas Woodruff, then on the staff of the *Times,* who had been at Oxford with him. Henry's mother and uncle were there, and Rebecca's sisters, and Lady Rhondda of *Time and Tide.* As the couple left the reception, June Head said, "At last she is going away with someone who will buy her railway ticket. Hitherto, she has bought everyone else's."

But, as Rebecca remarked in her widowhood, "I would rather have been married to Henry than to anybody else in the world, and he gave me a certain sense of security, but not the sort of security that is evoked by the word 'banker.'" Her friends clung to the belief that Rebecca was marrying for financial security, since some of them could see no other justification for it when they met Henry. Others felt betrayed that she was marrying at all. "You can't do this to me," Madge Garland said when Rebecca told her the news at a Hampstead party. Madge Garland was assistant to Dorothy Todd, editor of *Vogue,* and one of the many younger women who idolized Rebecca for her independence. Their friendship was unimpaired: in 1977 Rebecca inscribed a copy of her *Celebration* to Madge Garland, "my dear friend for years, who is still as exciting to meet as if she were the lovely stranger."

Rebecca, on her Italian honeymoon, wrote to Lettie that the newspaper writers reporting on the wedding were "illiterate idiots." One headline had been: "Rebecca West Married: Word 'OBEY' Omitted from Her Altar Vow." "Had they never heard of the Revised Version of the marriage service? I suppose they just had to look for some aggressive aspect of the situation until they found it!" Lettie had given her sister away, in the absence of any close male relation. "Blessings on you," Rebecca wrote, "for everything you have done for the wedding. . . . Boof is so sweet to travel with you'd hardly believe! So altogether it's lovely."

Rebecca West did nothing halfheartedly, and she intended to make her marriage a success. If she was not *in* love with Henry, she would love him; he was her husband for better for worse, for richer for poorer. "In fact it was the job I was born to do, and I did it."

3

The new Mr. and Mrs. Henry Andrews came home to her flat, which was not big enough. Then they stayed with Henry's large and jovial mother while their own home was being arranged. "I am growing hysterical with horror at living in this horrible flat of my mother-in-law's." She and Henry moved into 15 Orchard Court, "as lovely a flat as I have ever seen," in a luxury modern block on Portman Square,* "just on the other side of Wigmore Street from Selfridges"; Rebecca was paying the rent.

Henry's work for Schroders took him to Berlin and Vienna, and he was a keen winter sportsman; it was chiefly to Germany, Austria, and Switzerland that they travelled in the early 1930s, with spells in Paris. Before they set out for a holiday in Switzerland the summer after their marriage, Henry wrote a letter "to be handed unopened to my wife in the event of my death." Since it was not possible "to safeguard against all accidents in Switzerland," he wanted her to know that he had made a new will in her favour and—rather more relevantly—that "no words can express what I owe to you":

> All the best that life gave me until I met you, all generous thoughts and efforts, seemed to find their true value in whatever ability they gave me to understand you and to love you. If ever you should feel lonely and disheartened I hope you will recall how when I was lonely your work recalled me to the ideals and enthusiasms of my youth and gave me strength not to compromise. In the same way, many whom you will never know are surrounding you with their blessings.

* The actress heroine of Rebecca West's unfinished novel *Sunflower* had dreamed of living in wedded bliss on Portman Square.

He addressed her as "My darling Cicely," "Rebecca" being her name as a
writer, not as his wife, though he used both names or either in public.
He signed himself "Ric." Their private names for each other were Rac
and Ric, after two dogs in a French cartoon strip. They were a loving
couple.

Rebecca, describing her husband to Fannie Hurst after three years
of marriage, said, "I like him more and more." He was "a queer creature,
naive in some ways and full of genius in others"; he was "full of unusual
knowledge and understanding," and partly Jewish. "You know I always
wanted to marry a Jew, nobody knows better than I do that you are the
chosen people." Domestic life was "the only kind I'm adapted to, the
perfect routine in which my brain works with a spring." Henry's business
life was "a progressive death dance," but "we carry on and we don't worry.
Anthony was a trial for a time. . . ."

Rebecca felt she had come home at last, though there were problems. She took Henry to the Villa Mysto—just the two of them alone—
in the summer of 1932, since he was "so tired he is beginning to forget
things all the time." The following summer she gave Anthony, in his turn,
a holiday alone with her on the Riviera, touring the coast that still seemed
to her "the nearest place to heaven I know."

What had been happening to Anthony? He had been away at school
when the wedding took place; Rebecca had visited him twice in the preceding month. His feelings about himself belied the optimistic modern
view set forth by Vera Brittain in *Time and Tide* just a couple of weeks
before Rebecca's marriage: "The courage and initiative which leads a
woman deliberately to undertake motherhood outside marriage is likely
more than to atone in her child's upbringing for any disadvantage that it
may suffer from initial lack of status." The father of such a child may be
so anxious to compensate for possible handicap that illegitimacy may turn
out to be "a positive advantage." It did not seem like that to the adolescent
Anthony; and it may have been Vera Brittain's ingenuousness on such
topics that provoked Rebecca into referring to her privately as "a trumpeting ass."

Announcing to Reggie Turner her marriage to a "tall and slender
and silent (in all points unlike me, you see) angel," Rebecca wrote stoutly
that "Anthony approves the match." He did not. On first being introduced
to Henry Andrews as his future stepfather in the familiar Onslow Gar-

dens flat, the sixteen-year-old boy was incredulous and appalled. Henry seemed the opposite of Wells in all possible ways. Anthony may never have had enough of his mother's time and attention, but at least he had had no rival in the house. He was jealous of this tall, thin man, who was kind "in a bang-on way" but whom he could not accept. He did not believe that his quick-witted mother wholly accepted Henry either; he sensed that she "writhed with impatience" at Henry's slow, deliberate utterances.

Nor did Anthony enjoy the formal elegance of the flat at Orchard Court. A journalist who came to interview an "incredibly young-looking" Rebecca West there a year after her marriage described the uniformed hall porters downstairs, and the velvet seats in the lift. In Rebecca's "sublimated entrance hall" she noted the sea-green carpet, the circular mahogany table with its vase of flowers, the apple-green walls, silver bookshelves, the silver-green silk curtains. The dining-room, which had a view of London from Piccadilly to St. Paul's, had pink-grey walls, brocade curtains, gilt wall-lights. There was a butler.

Anthony slept at Orchard Court in half of a bed that had been his mother's. It had been seven feet wide, with a bedhead of Spanish leather, made to order at Heal's. After the break with Wells she had it divided into two. Visitors to the new flat remembered Anthony as sullen beyond what was normal for an adolescent boy. He was unhappy. He was unhappy at Stowe as well, except in so far as its beautiful buildings and wooded parkland were a "sensuous experience." Being the son of H. G. Wells did not, it turned out, make any difference when it came to being bullied. He was further disturbed by a school scandal in which he was not directly involved but which resulted in wholesale expulsions of boys he knew well.

He was making little academic progress. Rebecca had told Winnie that "so long as I can drag him into Oxford or Cambridge I don't care." That turned out to be something she could not do, though it took her some time to face the fact. He failed Latin, an essential entry qualification, in his school certificate, and left Stowe. Wells intervened at this point, suggesting to Rebecca that Lettie was undermining the boy's self-confidence by making him feel that he was an "unfortunate accident." Although Rebecca did in private blame Lettie for much, she answered Wells sharply, saying that Anthony and Lettie rarely met these days. She went on: "I don't think I quite like your tone. 'I've interfered very little in his education so far because I have trusted in your love and pride in him.' This is nonsense. You interfered very little because you couldn't be bothered." However, "though I know you are a great humbug I also know you're a great man."

Henry wrote to his old New College friend Roy Harrod, now an economics don at Christ Church, Oxford, to pull strings, asking advice about how to get Anthony into New College or any other college. He also found Anthony a private tutor, but Anthony again failed to meet the Oxford entry requirements and was thrown into such "hysteria and depression" by the examinations that Rebecca arranged for him to have a "six weeks diagnostic course under Dr Hanns Sachs, who is supposed to be the best practising psychoanalyst in Europe." Sachs, an affable Viennese who had been one of the original "secret committee" established by Freud, advised seven or eight months' analysis. Anthony's depression was deepened by the fact that he had quarrelled with his father, which, as Rebecca saw it, left "no normal outlet for the boy's desire to please him."

Anthony had been to see Wells at Lou Pidou, the house in Provence where he was still spending part of each year with Odette Keun. The visit had not been a success. Wells wrote to Anthony afterwards that "when you came down there and made an appeal for my interest and sympathy I was quite ready and willing to concern myself with your affairs." But apparently Anthony now wanted "to be left to your mother (with whom you have temperamentally much in common) and Pamela [Frankau]. Very well. So be it." Without further comment, he informed Anthony of the trusts set up in his favour.

Wells wrote to Rebecca too: "Our relations continue friendly I hope. But Anthony is very *young* and extremely silly in certain ways. (He writes me a letter 'Dear Mr Wells'.) I gather he takes offence at the imperfections of his host and hostess at Lou Pidou. It doesn't matter very much. Let him take his offence and be off with it. He's very likeable, but I'm not going to run after him." Anthony knew his father was disappointed in him. "I don't think he liked me very much because I was so like Rebecca and because I was arty." Anthony did not want to go to Oxford. He wanted to paint.

Anthony resented Rebecca's new life, and the pressures she put on him. Rebecca found it hard to let him write his own script, and resented his recalcitrance. Her pet name for him was "Comus," which could have been a reference to the dionysiac pagan god in Milton's poem. Anthony chose to identify instead with the beautiful doomed adolescent of the same name in Saki's story "The Unbearable Bassington," whose mother's love of possessions and gracious living is such that she will sacrifice her son rather than part with a painting. When Hanns Sachs went to work at Harvard in late 1932, it seemed good sense for Anthony to go too, so as not to interrupt his analysis. He sailed on the *Bremen,* preceded by letters of introduction to Rebecca's American friends.

Rebecca was pregnant (at forty); it was an ectopic pregnancy, and she had a therapeutic abortion. Some time later she had a hysterectomy. ("Have you had one? I've had one. Well, you can't have *two.*") When Henry was dying Rebecca wrote that she was sure he had resented their not having had children, "but how could I"—she did not have enough faith in the genetic inheritance of either herself or Henry to make another attempt at motherhood. After the operation she convalesced at a German spa, and while she was there she received a suicidal letter from Anthony in America. Henry contacted him by telephone; he was safe and well, staying with Rebecca's friend Emanie. Rebecca's reaction was not so much relief as fury at the panic that Anthony had caused.

After another crisis which concerned a customary bone of contention—Anthony's attitude to money—he wrote to "Dear Panther" from America: "So happy again. I wish you had told me about your sanitarium expenses before or would not have been so unreasonable about finance. We are adept at misunderstanding but I feel so much improved since this last month that I don't think I shall find it so easy to misunderstand you again. You're a greatly loved Pussinger though in the past I have sometimes seen you through a glass darkly."

The separation helped both mother and son. Alexander Woollcott, who always looked up "the incomparable Rebecca" when he was in London, took her out to the theatre that Christmas. "Seeing Rebecca again is my great delight. She is now extraordinarily beautiful, having gone over to some doctor near Vienna or Dresden and lost eleven and a half pounds."

Anthony, on his return to England, became an art student, and his next few years were happier. "Anthony is painting very nicely, and everybody seems to be satisfied with his work, and he certainly is very nice and amiable." A few months after Rebecca sent this report to Reggie Turner, Anthony became twenty-one, and in March 1936 astonished everybody by getting married. His bride was Katharine (Kitty) Church, a few years older than he, already an established artist with exhibitions to her credit, a pretty, fair-haired young woman. The young couple took a lease on a house at Tisbury in Wiltshire, and there was peace and normal relations between mother and son.

4

Rebecca's considerable income in the 1930s came chiefly from journalism on both sides of the Atlantic. In Britain she had a new arrangement to review exclusively for the *Daily Telegraph*, at 15 guineas a time—no easy option, since she had to shape a weekly article of twelve hundred words around four or five unrelated books. She was a frequent contributor to the column "Notes on the Way" in *Time and Tide*, a prestigious space filled on other occasions by writers of the calibre of G. B. Shaw, T. S. Eliot, E. M. Forster, and Aldous Huxley. She continued to write reviews, feature articles, and short stories for the Hearst Press in the United States, and contributed a regular personal column headed "I Said to Me . . ." to the New York *American* at the equivalent of £20 a time. She arranged with A. D. Peters, her London agent, for $40 a week from her American earnings to be paid to Anthony.

By now she had been writing about books and authors for over twenty years, and her tastes were formed. The pedigree of English literature, for Rebecca, was passed down through Shakespeare, Blake, Defoe, Fielding, Sterne, Jane Austen, Scott, Dickens, Thackeray, and Trollope to her four literary "Uncles"—Wells, Shaw, Bennett, and Galsworthy—and on to the modernists: Joyce, Lawrence, and Virginia Woolf, "the poet whose imagination is so sternly controlled by the critic that she also is." In a hostile review of Queenie Leavis's *Fiction and the Reading Public*, she berated Mrs. Leavis for underrating Defoe ("a fatal self-betrayal") and for showing contempt for Dickens, which was "unpardonable in an adult."

Her preferences were for muscular, ambitious, demanding writers who, like Proust (whom she admired most among the moderns), were not afraid of committing themselves to "the large, simple, classic emotion." The three Sitwells delighted her by being "among the few illuminants England possesses who are strong enough to light up post-war England." She liked authors who lit up the world, and made fun of Thomas Hardy's poetic gloom, which she had experienced at first hand on her visit to him. "One is apt to be discouraged by the frequency with which Mr Hardy has persuaded himself that a macabre subject is a poem in itself: that, if there be enough of death and the tomb in one's theme, it needs no translation into art. . . . Really, the thing is prodigious. One of Mr Hardy's ancestors must have married a weeping willow."

Rebecca liked to laugh, and enjoyed the comedic fiction of Nancy Mitford, Stella Gibbons's *Cold Comfort Farm,* and the early novels of Evelyn Waugh. After reading *Vile Bodies* in 1930, she wrote that "this young man is, I fancy, to be the dazzling figure of the age as Max Beerbohm was of his," and shrewdly advised collectors to invest in Waugh manuscripts right away.

She wrote a funny account of the inability of Max Beerbohm, that *fin de siècle* dandy, to relate to modern woman as represented by herself, G. B. Stern, Elizabeth von Arnim, Clemence Dane, and Marie Belloc-Lowndes, who were among the women writers asked to a party to meet him in 1929. A woman, for Beerbohm, had to have a lot of emollient, old-world Edwardian charm if he were not to be terrified. "Minute, perilously fragile, enormously precious," he could not cope with this group of outspoken, expansive, "liberated" women: "our nearest equivalent to charm was, perhaps, a group of factory chimneys in a northern dawn; or an assembly of Fords at a parking place." Rebecca rebelled against too much refinement, just as she rejected any form of censorship: "God forbid that any book should be banned. The practice is as indefensible as infanticide." She nevertheless disliked obscenity, and therefore the work of Henry Miller, whose influence on her friend Anaïs Nin (whom she considered "a real genius") she deplored.

Her judgements are instructive in suggesting both the kind of person she admired and the kind of fiction to which she herself aspired. She first saw Colette at the railway station at St.-Raphaël, waiting "with the stance of a Spanish fighting bull" and holding her bulldog by a wine-coloured *crêpe de chine* scarf twisted through its lead. She admired Colette as a writer for putting "into infallible artistic form her gross, wise, limited, eternal views about life." Reviewing *Death Comes to the Archbishop* (1927), she praised Willa Cather for the way her writing combined sensuality and sensitivity with a "mountain-pony sturdiness." ("Packhorse" was one of the Fairfield family nicknames for Rebecca, on account of both her build and her determination.)

In the mid-1930s Rebecca's longer short stories were commanding between $2,000 and $3,000 apiece. Four of these came out in book form under the title *The Harsh Voice* in 1935, dedicated to George T. Bye, her appreciative New York agent: "I adore you and am entirely at your service," as he wrote. These stories, which are about love, hate, and money, are the best she ever wrote; and the three lines of verse on the title page, allegedly by "Richard Wynne Errington," were actually by Rebecca West herself.

One of her English publishers, Jonathan Cape, attempted to make a contract with her for several books, with the intention of building her up as an author "rather than as a writer of scattered books." This was always her problem, in so far as it was a problem, right up to the end; if her reputation was unclear, it was because her work was impossible to categorize. She had submitted to Bye a play, "Goodbye Nicholas," under her poetic alias of Richard Wynne Errington, but, like all her attempts to write for the theatre, it came to nothing. Still, the lure of the stage never left her, and over the years she came to count among her favourite friends many stage and film people—especially the theatre critic James Agate, Joyce Redmond, the Lunts, Dulcie Gray, and Michael Denison. John Gunther and his second wife, Jane, introduced her to Greta Garbo ("who is a darling," she said), and with the New York theatrical attorney L. Arnold Weissburger she met Rex Harrison and Yul Brynner. She was always at least as keen to meet actors and actresses as she was to meet writers and intellectuals.

5

The first book by Rebecca West after her marriage was a short life of the early Church Father St. Augustine. She had first been introduced to his writings as a girl by a Jesuit, Fr. Matthew Prior, a friend of her mother's in Edinburgh. She saw Augustine as working "in the same introspective field as the moderns," and likened him to Proust. He was for her an egotist, a self-dramatizer, and a "great romantic artist" whose theology was set in order eight hundred years later by a "great classical artist," St. Thomas Aquinas.

Rebecca read extremely fast; she worked through quantities of scholarly works on Augustine before what amounted to a lively paraphrase of and commentary on his autobiographical *Confessions*. She acknowledged that she had given an incomplete account of his theology; all she attempted was "a simple account of Augustine's personal life and background." She told her brother-in-law, Norman Macleod, that "the only departure I have made from strict historical accuracy is that I have soft-pedalled on his innate lack of decorum—also I have omitted some examples of his curious callousness." She replied to a reader who complained she had made Augustine unsympathetic that "if I had told all I know about the old blackguard he would have been asked to resign from all his clubs."

St Augustine came out in February 1933. She had been writing it when Anthony—his relations with herself, Henry, and Wells, and her hopes and fears for his future—were uppermost in her mind. Augustine as a young man was alienated from his father and emotionally bound to his mother, the devout and dominating St. Monica. If a child comes to regard his father as hostile, Rebecca wrote, "the result is desperation, which may either paralyse it or move it to efforts so great as to be greatness." Augustine's love for his mother was so strong that "he was bound to hate anyone who had a competing claim on her."

She returned to St. Augustine in the course of *Black Lamb and Grey Falcon* a few years later. Here she wrote that Augustine, "so curiously called a saint," was a great man but a cruel one. His mother and he "were like dam and cub in the strength of their natural relationship, but his appetite for nastiness made him sully it. Throughout their lives they achieved from time to time an extreme sweetness, but the putrescence gained, and at her death he felt an exaltation as mean as anything recorded in literature. . . ."

When Rebecca West died in 1983, Anthony West, in the United States, received the news by telephone. He did not come over for the funeral; he was recovering from an operation, and knew that it would be a fraught occasion. The following year, at the age of seventy, he published his *H. G. Wells: Aspects of a Life.* A secondary purpose of this book about his father was to vent the resentments of a lifetime. In it he effectively demolished the reputation of his mother both as a writer and as a human being.

6

In the same year as *St Augustine,* Rebecca contributed to the Hogarth Letters series published by Leonard and Virginia Woolf. These were personal statements in pamphlet form about art, literature, religion, or politics, by leading authors. Rebecca's *Letters to a Grandfather* created a fictional self with a family history steeped in tradition and historical significance, using this as a parable of the English way of life, now threatened by events in Europe. She emphasized that the truths of history have always been cruel, and that only by facing up to fear, and by trusting in the survival of the human spirit, can one find happiness. It is a religious essay, into which is woven a surreal image of Christ as a Negro at a fair; it adds up to a diffuse, discursive literary firework which Virginia Woolf failed to understand, though she published it.

Rebecca had first met Virginia Woolf in 1928 at lunch with Dorothy

Todd and Madge Garland at their flat in Chelsea. Mrs. Woolf reported to her sister, Vanessa Bell, that "Rebecca was much the most interesting, though as hard as nails, very distrustful, and no beauty. She is a cross between a charwoman and a gipsy, but as tenacious as a terrier, with flashing eyes, very shabby, rather dirty nails, immense vitality, bad taste, suspicion of intellectuals, and great intelligence." She looked, Virginia Woolf thought on their second meeting, as if she "has some bone she chews in secret, perhaps about having a child by Wells." A few months later Rebecca praised Virginia Woolf's *Orlando* in the New York *Herald Tribune* as "a poetic masterpiece of the first rank," and Mrs. Woolf wrote her a grateful, happy letter.

If Rebecca West's shabbiness struck Virginia Woolf, Virginia Woolf's untidiness struck Rebecca West. She was untidy herself at the time, she said, "being overworked and rather ill, but I always used to gain confidence from the sight of Virginia"—though Virginia's face and body "could not have belonged to a person not of rare gifts." Virginia Woolf, in return, marvelled at Rebecca's animal energy and her fierce, outspoken talk: "R's great point is her tenacious and muscular mind, and all her difficulty comes from the wheals [*sic*] and scars left by the hoofmarks of Wells."

Rebecca West did not fit into Bloomsbury, or want to. She found the whole group "physically peculiar." She made friends with Raymond Mortimer and Clive Bell, but thought E. M. Forster nothing more than a "nice old cosy" who had made a minor talent go a very long way. Vanessa Bell's painted plates were "not good enough to feed a dog off." Lytton Strachey's beard was "an extension of his personality in the direction of doubt." She did not think that they liked her much either.

It was a question of style. After Rebecca married she no longer dressed so shabbily, and her nails were less often dirty. She had only ever been bohemian as part of youthful protest, or from necessity, or misery. All her instincts were towards consolidation and the sort of conventional respectability that had evaded the Fairfields. "Respectable" literally means "fit or able to be seen": for too long her domestic scene had been pushed away into the margins of social life, into the wings, first by Wells, and then on account of her irregular household. She and Henry were at one on what they wanted their ménage to be like. Neither wanted to limit their circle to writers: "The literary world gets fuller and fuller of bitter-

ness." Rebecca gave what June Head called "straight" dinner parties for
Henry's business friends; many Christmas cards were sent out, conven-
tionally overprinted with greetings from Mr. and Mrs. Henry Andrews.

Occasionally Rebecca, in this new role, made a misjudgement.
After a Christmas spent in New York with Henry, she left instructions
with her temporary secretary there to write farewell letters to her American friends: "Dear Mr and Mrs Van Vechten, Miss Rebecca West has
asked me to write to you explaining that she deeply regrets her inability
to write to you personally. . . ." The secretary mistakenly addressed this
letter to Fannie Hurst, who, remembering the informal and intimate Rebecca of the old days, wrote to Carl Van Vechten: "The enclosed scarcely
indicates the stuff of which warm human relations are made. . . . However, I am die-hard where friends are concerned, and I shall struggle a
little longer to care about this mutual one of ours."

Virginia Woolf referred with mild irritation to Rebecca's "careening
society voice," though John Gunther, at the same period, found her talk
as always "a golden dusky flow, flawless in wit and rhythm." Mrs. Woolf
could not see the point of Henry either—"such dead, though excellent,
mutton." In her diary she described the atmosphere of the flat at Orchard
Court,

> with the view, with the £750 book case, & the fish carved out
> of a yew branch,* & the modern pictures,† period furni-
> ture. . . . Of course it's admirable in its way—impersonal,
> breezy, yes, go ahead, facing life, eating dinner at the Savoy,
> meeting millionaires, woman & man of the worldly; but—no,
> I must add the kindness intelligence & erudition of the admi-
> rable effete spectacled swollen eyed Andrews—the cultivated
> don turned banker, with his devotion to R.—Cecily he calls
> her, for whom he buys these fish & bookcases. What's wrong
> then?

What was wrong, for Virginia Woolf, was "the formality, the social strata
they live on—appearances." Which was, of course the object of the ex-

---

* *Shoal of Fish* by Maurice Lambert, acquired that year (1933).
† During the 1930s Rebecca and Henry bought French pictures: in July 1937, for example, Dufy's *Langres* and *Les Moissons à Langres;* a Bonnard; and Vuillard's *Le Sentier.*

ercise for Mr. and Mrs. Andrews. Mrs. Woolf, socially and intellectually secure with friends and family, could afford to disregard appearances. Neither Rebecca nor Henry felt that they could, though the style of their life was predominantly Henry's. Mrs. Woolf saw Rebecca as "a buffeter & battler" to whom she could never get close; she had a sense of Rebecca being, like Orchard Court itself, "a lit up modern block, floodlit by electricity."

Rebecca still had reason to buffet and battle. In the first years of her married life she received a series of malicious anonymous letters, clearly composed by someone who knew her circumstances, and Henry's, in considerable detail. By a meaningless coincidence, they read like a vulgar parody of Virginia Woolf's elliptic diary notes:

> With your grandiose ideas you hated your poor father—poor little clerk who was able to afford you only that shabby poverty house on the Edinburgh tramlines, 3 greedy daughters—poor man! Dr Letitia another pusher OK. The other left her post office job, but not for a lunatic asylum?? You sing well for the supper (Shroder) of the very very odd Henry of the hen-toed walk specks and furtive air your peculiar dud Oxford hubby— no honours degree here, ye gods, no!! Apes well the accent of the "English ruling class. . . ."

And so on. Rebecca and Henry, in their different ways, needed the up- holstered fortress they were building against the world. Rebecca could not get closer to people like Virginia Woolf now without in some way betraying her alliance with Henry; she always signed herself "Cicely An- drews" to Mrs. Woolf, and they remained mere acquaintances. During the 1930s Rebecca and Henry used to rent houses in the country for the summer; just before the Second World War broke out they took Old Pos- singworth Manor at Blackboys in Sussex (the house where Vita Sackville- West had lingered with a previous tenant, Violet Trefusis), and invited friends to stay for the opera season at nearby Glyndebourne. From Black- boys, Rebecca went to see Virginia Woolf at Rodmell, taking with her one of her guests, Emanie Sachs, thinking that Mrs. Woolf and she would appreciate each other. But Mrs. Woolf was not interested in the Ameri- can visitor, and Rebecca felt let down. The disappointment was mutual.

"Why this dilly-dallying with the world and the flesh?" wrote Virginia Woolf afterwards. "No, I don't think one makes much headway. . . ."

7

"I liked doing *St Augustine,* and I'm now doing a novel, *The Thinking Reed,* which ought to be finished early in the New Year," Rebecca wrote to Fannie Hurst in the autumn of 1933—and then, with reference to political events in Germany: "Don't think that we don't weep the tears of blood that all decent human beings must weep just now (but this must be secret, Henry must go back and forwards there all the time) but we ourselves are happy." It was not only Henry's job now that took him to Germany but also his anxiety about friends and relatives there. Rebecca accompanied "my Boof" on some of these trips, and hated the atmosphere. It was "a pity that they should happily look forward to a Hitlerite government, which will shoot all the Jews."

The Thinking Reed took much longer than she planned. In 1935 she went to the United States for the first time since her marriage to report on the New Deal policies in a series of articles. (She waxed much more optimistic about "the radiance of the most hopeful administration to be found in the whole world today" in *The New York Times* than she did for *Time and Tide* in London.) By the time the new novel came out in 1936, Rebecca had embarked on her second visit to Yugoslavia—a country that was to become a major focus of her political and literary life. She did not published another novel for two decades.

The Thinking Reed was a critical and commercial success. It is the only funny novel she wrote; it is her "French novel," in which she exploited her fond familiarity with Paris, French landscape, and the leisurely life of the *côte d'azur.* She wrote many more lyrical descriptive passages than appeared in the final version, and her manuscript is spattered with her own notes to herself: "Condense," "cut," "Get into 300 words." She had been watchful during those French summers and, as always, had taken notes of conversational exchanges, gestures, turns of phrase. She was effortlessly funny at the expense of the bored and mindless expatriate playboys, crooks, phonies, and spoilt women—English, American, and Russian—who colonized the coast, and even more deadly in her humour about arrogant upper-class Englishwomen of the type who had infuriated her since childhood. They were women such as she had seen in New York in a room full of talented and lively people—two English peeresses who "sat down together on a sofa and turned their backs on the rest of us and talked to each other." *The Thinking Reed*—and Orchard Court—were a sort of revenge on both the slender, brainless girls whose gabbling chatter excluded her, and the complacent aristocrats for whom she had not even existed.

The Thinking Reed had a serious intention as well. It is the story of a marriage and of the bonding of an apparently incompatible pair. Rebecca West said that the two themes of the book were "the effect of riches on people, and the effect of men on women, both forms of slavery." She wanted too to find out what would happen to two modern people who had abandoned the religion-based ethical code yet wanted to make their marriage "as noble an association as possible." She invented a controlled, intelligent American woman with money, married to an ebullient French Jew, a compulsive gambler. Marriage, the heroine states, diminishes a woman and is "never very satisfactory." "Forced adaptation" is the price the woman must pay for the sanctuary of intimacy.

> It struck her that the difference between men and women is
> the rock on which civilization will split before it can reach any
> goal that could justify its expenditure of effort. She also knew
> that her life would not be tolerable if he were not always there
> to crush gently her smooth hands with his strong short fingers.

The novel was dedicated to Henry Maxwell Andrews. Rebecca said in her old age that the first five years of her married life—the years in which this novel was taking shape—were the happiest of her life. *The Thinking Reed* was, among much else, her wry, appreciative assessment of those years.

8

"Money is poison," wrote Rebecca in *The Thinking Reed*. It was for her; money became the battle-ground in all her difficulties with her near and dear. In 1936 Henry's uncle Ernest died, and Henry came into his inheritance—about £170,000. It was just as well, since he had lost his job at Schroders in 1935.

As head of their European division, Henry had been in charge of reorganizing the finances of Berlin. The city utilities were running at a loss; the companies were refloated, and the debts rolled back. The local man Henry put in charge of the operation was a Jew. After the Nazis came to power, this man disappeared and the Nazis took over the organization.

Schroders as a bank was not pro-Nazi, but when Henry declined to work with the new regime he was told there was no place for him. His subsequent professional career was free-lance and occasionally disastrous. He joined a group planning to mine chromium on a Turkish island; Rebecca was appalled by his new associates, and not surprised when he lost his investment. Henry himself was philosophical. He kept an office in the City for a while, became a "name" at Lloyds, and developed his business interests in his own idiosyncratic way.

He put £50,000 into Pascal's film of Shaw's *Caesar and Cleopatra* when it was running out of money at a late stage, and told A. J. P. Taylor that he was "very proud that he had insisted on being repaid before anyone else, even before Bernard Shaw himself. I said he presumably collected a good interest as well, 10% or so. Henry looked at me with his innocent blue eyes and said, 'Far more than that. You see, the knife was at their throats.'" Henry had also insured Pascal's *Pygmalion,* and made another satisfactory profit. But what really interested him was European industry and the European transport network, on which he was an expert. He could—and frequently did—recite the timetables of any railroad on the Continent, including the stations where it was necessary to change trains, and even for countries which he had never visited.

As a private citizen Henry was able to do more for friends and relatives caught in Nazi Germany and Eastern Europe than he had as a bank official. Because of his contacts, he and Rebecca understood the nature of the Nazi threat before most people in Britain. From Austria, where she accompanied the overstrained Henry for a cure at Bad Gastein, Rebecca wrote to Winnie: "If only we had put every man woman and child of that abominable nation [Germany] to the sword in 1919. The insane mercy and charity of the Treaty of Versailles makes me gnash my teeth. I hope you realize . . . the Huns will go down into Austria, and civilization will be over."

After the Russian-German pact in 1939 her hostility was extended to the Soviet Union as well; she found it "disgusting" that a state "based on the Gospel" of a Jew, Marx, had joined hands with anti-communist, anti-Semitic Germany. She never trusted the Soviet Union again, and in 1940 resigned her vice-presidency of the National Council for Civil Liberties, since she felt it was being infiltrated by communists. The German action which forced Russia into the war on the Allies' side the following year did little to soften her attitude.

Whatever her earlier reservations about the Soviet experiment, Rebecca had not up to this time been anti-communist. She wrote in support of the republican government cause during the Spanish Civil War, and described herself as "passionately anti-Franco." She signed a petition organized by the Lynds' daughter Maire (a Communist Party member) in protest against the expulsion of an American communist from the London School of Economics. In 1936 she was among the British delegates at the conference of the left-wing International Association of Writers for the Defence of Culture; she was a sponsor of a short-lived organization called Writers Against Fascism and War.

But to be anti-fascist is not the same as being pro-communist. Nor was Rebecca West ever a pacifist. She was violently opposed to the policy of appeasement of Germany, and against the Peace Pledge Union: "Do you believe that you are going to abolish cancer if you get 100,000 people to sign a pledge that they do not intend to have cancer?" She sat on the platform of an anti-appeasement rally with her friend the historian Philip Guedalla, who was also an old Oxford friend of Henry's.

It was not merely Henry's special knowledge and her own instincts
that made her so sure that Nazi Germany would have to be confronted.
One of her American friends was the journalist Dorothy Thompson, two
years younger than herself, who was a primary force in alerting the
United States to the dangers of Nazism and the necessity for intervention—a necessity which was not recognized until the bombing of Pearl
Harbor.

Dorothy Thompson had become the second wife of Rebecca's one-
time admirer Sinclair Lewis in 1928, and she was a friend of the Gun-
thers. A European correspondent, she was expelled from Germany by the
secret police on account of an interview with Hitler which made her
famous and earned her a regular political column on the New York *Herald
Tribune*. She and Rebecca were two of a kind, both born communicators:
"I might have done it myself if I had been clever enough," she said of
Rebecca's journalism.

Dorothy Thompson was a German expert but had a special interest
in the small Eastern European nations and peoples who had been crushed
and bartered between empires and armies throughout recorded history.
Many well-informed people, especially women, in administration and the
media in the West had a special field of interest and concern among these
nations in the 1930s and 1940s. Another of Rebecca's American acquaintances, the writer Marcia Davenport, had left her heart in Czechoslovakia with the man she loved, the doomed Czechoslovakian Prime
Minister Jan Masaryk.

But the tradition was older, and more literary, than this. As Rebecca
put it, English travellers "of humanitarian and reformist disposition . . .
all came back with a pet Balkan people established in their hearts as
suffering and innocent, eternally the massacree and never the massacrer."
She was thinking particularly of adventurous women travel writers such
as M. Edith Durham, who had been producing books on the Balkans
(*Twenty Years of Balkan Tangle*, *Through the Lands of the Serb*, etc.) since
before the First World War. Rebecca professed contempt for Miss Durham's brand of romantic ethnology; but she was herself, in *Black Lamb
and Grey Falcon*, to produce the apotheosis of the genre. Rebecca West
fell in love with Yugoslavia—the country, its people, and its myths.

9

In the autumn of 1935 Rebecca, without Henry, went on a lecture tour for the British Council to Scandinavia and the Baltic provinces. Fascinated by Finland, she began to learn Finnish on her return. The following spring the British Council sent her to the Balkans—Greece, Bulgaria, and Yugoslavia. As all British Council lecturers were asked to do, she wrote a report on her return; given the political situation in Europe, she slanted her report towards personal and political assessments of the various government officials she had met, with special reference to their attitudes to Germany and to Britain. This information was passed from the British Council to the Foreign Office.

Though her lecture was, she told the Council, "in great part a waste of your money and my time" because of bad organization, she came away knowing that it was Yugoslavia rather than Finland that she wanted to write about, even though she found Serbian just as hard as Finnish and "have never got further than to be able to speak to peasants with a dictionary open on my lap," as she confessed to Marcia Davenport. To embark, as she did, on the anatomy of such a complex nation seemed "senseless," especially since the position of the Balkans did not then seem so significant as the position of Scandinavia in relation to its powerful neighbours; "but the thing just got hold of me and made me do it," even though for months it seemed "a complete folly."

It may have seemed folly to her publishers too. Her London agent could only secure an agreement from Macmillan for £200 on publication in advance of royalties for "a book on Yugo Slavia." George Bye in New York arranged with Viking for 15 percent royalties on sales between four and six thousand copies, and 25 percent on sales over six thousand; below four thousand, Rebecca would receive no royalties at all.

Rebecca West made three trips to Yugoslavia: the British Council visit, during which she was ill for some of the time; a second in the spring of 1937, with Henry, after covering the inauguration of President Roosevelt's second term in Washington; and a third early in the summer of 1938. The book that came out of it all, *Black Lamb and Grey Falcon,* was written as if based on a single extensive visit. It was much more than a travel book. It turned out to be the central book of her life: a two-volume, five-hundred-thousand-word work that not only encompassed history, archaeology, politics, conversation, folklore, prophecy, and the evocation of landscape, but was also the work in which Rebecca West formulated her views on religion, ethics, art, myth, and gender. John Gunther was right when he told her he saw its main theme as the conflict between love of life and love of death, applied to every sort of human problem, and encapsulated in a now famous passage:

> Only part of us is sane: only part of us loves pleasure and the longer day of happiness, wants to live to our nineties and die in peace, in a house that we built, that shall shelter those who come after us. The other half of us is nearly mad. It prefers the disagreeable to the agreeable, loves pain and its darker night despair, and wants to die in a catastrophe that will set back life to its beginnings and leave nothing of our house save its blackened foundations.

This fight between the love of life and the love of death, she continued, "can be observed constantly in our personal lives." This world-vision, which is like a reflection of the Freudian *eros* and *thanatos,* of the pleasure principle and the death-wish, was compatible with her own personality and her own perception of experience. As Gunther recognized, *Black Lamb and Grey Falcon* became "not so much a book about Yugoslavia as a book about Rebecca West," and as such it is required reading for any understanding of her.

Yugoslavia, the South Slav state put together after the Great War of 1914–18, was in the 1930s a constitutional monarchy under the regency of Prince Paul. It was not so much a nation as a federation of Serbs, Croats, and Slovenes, plus Bosnian Macedonians, Montenegrins, and a scatter of diverse minorities. In her book, Rebecca described the impossibly complex relations between the two major groupings thus: "A Croat is a Catholic member and a Serb an Orthodox member of a Slav people that lies widely distributed south of the Danube. . . . A Serbian is a subject of the kingdom of Serbia, and might be a Croat, just as a Croatian-born inhabitant of the old Austrian province of Croatia might be a Serb." The Serbs and the Croats did not meld: in 1939 the province of Croatia was being granted home rule. Rebecca was not keen on the Croats, because they reminded her of the Catholic Irish. She identified passionately with the Serbs.

The chief of her official guides in Yugoslavia was a plump, emotional, curly-haired Serbian Jew whom, in her book, she called Constantine. His real name was Stanislav Vinaver, a writer and scholar and, at the time of her visits, press officer to the Yugoslav Council of Ministers. He had a German wife, but it is doubtful whether she was as terrible as Constantine's wife, Gerda, in the book, where she becomes a hate-figure, personifying insensitivity, stupidity, and everything Rebecca feared and disliked about the German mentality in the late 1930s.

Vinaver's German wife had, in her turn, reason to dislike the dynamic foreigner who took up so much of her husband's time, for Vinaver fell romantically in love with Rebecca, as he made clear in an eloquent letter in French written after her final departure from Belgrade. Their parting had been formal, he wrote, only because she was a woman who protected herself by observing the conventions rigidly. She was, he felt, a character seemingly out of Proust, actually out of Stendhal; she was delicious, adorable, obstinate, unattainable. (Rebecca's romantic evenings in Belgrade were spent not with Vinaver but with her former lover Antoine Bibesco—a surprise encounter not recorded in *Black Lamb and Grey Falcon.*)

When World War II broke out, Rebecca and Henry offered Vinaver asylum in England, but he preferred to stay in his own ravaged country; he ended up as a prisoner of war in Germany. Rebecca sent him food parcels through the Red Cross, but they did not meet again. In happier days, on her last research trip, there had been a bus journey to Bitola "through fields of wild narcissus and hedges of wild roses"; and the hospitality she was shown verged on the excessive. She was driven to Prizren, and "6 hard-boiled eggs and ½ kilo of cherries were put in the car as *refreshers,* as *elevenses,* so you can gather the strain my digestion has been put to of late." On a postcard she told Henry, "I think I have found out what is wrong with the end of the book, and I believe I could finish it as well at home."

The declaration that Britain was at war with Germany in September 1939 changed not only the proposed end of the book but its whole spirit and intention, and *Black Lamb and Grey Falcon* was not published until the autumn of 1941 in New York, early 1942 in London.

In Yugoslavia the Regent, Prince Paul, had pursued a policy which has been interpreted first as positively pro-German and later as appeasement. In the spring of 1941 a coup in Belgrade abolished the Regency, put the under-age King Peter on the throne, and set up a pro-Allied government initially under General Simović. The Germans invaded ten days later, starting with a massive air raid on Belgrade which killed tens of thousands. The new Royal Yugoslav Government and its young King were forced into exile, and set up their headquarters in London.

The plight of occupied Yugoslavia, and the gallantry of its resistance movements against the occupying forces, gave the final version of Rebecca's book a heightened emotional tone. Pre-war Dalmatia, for example, now seemed another lost paradise, where the people "had found some way to moderate the flow of life so that it did not run to waste, and there was neither excess nor famine, but a prolongation of delight." Even the ambivalences of gender were absent in the islands off the Dalmatian coast, where the men were "very handsome," with that "air of unashamed satisfaction with their own good looks which one finds only where there is very little homosexuality." It was strange, it was heartrending, she recalled, "to stray into a world where men are still men and women still women." There is an uncomfortable echo in this sentiment of the words of the British Fascist leader Sir Oswald Mosley, who in his manifesto *The Greater Britain* (1932) had written that "we want men who are men and women who are women"—with women consigned to a domestic role. Ideas and catch-phrases circled like bats in the 1930s, settling in unexpected places. But it was the poetry and courage of the Serbian character which chiefly caught Rebecca West's infatuated imagination. "Often, when I have thought of invasion, or when a bomb has dropped nearby, I have prayed, 'Let me behave like a Serb.'"

10

When war broke out Rebecca decided to buy a house in the country. "It doesn't need to be a particularly large house—anything from 6 or 7 bedrooms to up to 12 or 14," she airily told her friend Ruth Lowinsky, who with her artist husband, Thomas, was living at Lady Ottoline Morrell's former house, Garsington Manor.

The surveyor's report on Ibstone House—with its farm, cottages, walled vegetable garden, tennis court, and seventy acres, on the edge of Ibstone village in a valley of the Chiltern Hills in Buckinghamshire—was not encouraging. The fences and farm buildings were in poor repair, there was rising damp in the house, and the roof needed attention. There had been a Tudor house on the site, but the present building was the single remaining long wing of a large eighteenth-century house originally built round a quadrangle.

The property was bought in Henry's name, but he made it over to Rebecca legally almost at once—not as a gift, she wanted it understood, but as repayment to her for having subsidized the marriage in early years. (Sometimes she said that it had been bought with her savings.) The house was "horribly wallpapered but clean, we can move in without a lick of paint and we will do our pretties after the war, provided we and the farm still exist."

Rebecca wrote one of her first pieces for *The New Yorker*—for which she began to write regularly, brilliantly, and profitably from the beginning of the war—about her first days at Ibstone House. "I write sitting in a room, forty-five miles from London, which is furnished with magnificent yellow taffeta curtains trimmed with bottle-green ruching, the kitchen chair which supports me, an electric fire, and nothing else. My husband left me this morning to return to bombed London. . . ." Most of their four thousand books came down to Ibstone, and their best pictures, but they kept the Orchard Court flat for most of the war years.

Henry, at the beginning of the war, was working for the Ministry of Economic Warfare on a committee that made practical plans for the postwar economic recovery of the Balkans. An economic federation was envisaged, with new roads, railways, and industries, to be financed by British investment. Representatives of Poland, Czechoslovakia, Yugoslavia, and Greece sat on the committee. The project, in the eyes of Henry and of the Foreign Office, was more than legitimate. To Rebecca too it seemed a doubly worthy enterprise: good for Yugoslavia and its neighbour countries, and good for Britain.

Rebecca, as fiercely individualist for nations as for persons, held no brief for empires nor for empire-building: "Empires live by violation of the law." But opposing factions saw the schemes of Henry's committee as blatant financial-political imperialism, and, indeed, it would be naïve to think its members were not concerned to build up Western influence and a dependence on Western institutions in territories susceptible to Soviet control. (For related reasons, it has been Western policy ever since 1948 to lavish economic aid on Yugoslavia.)

Jan Masaryk, a member of the committee, warned Henry Andrews that Czechoslovakian left-wingers were claiming that Yugoslav concessions were being granted to Henry himself, to be profitably resold in the United States after the war. Croatian and pro-communist members of the Yugoslav government-in-exile proved increasingly uncooperative. In 1943, with the Russians—now Britain's allies—expressing their distaste for the committee, it was disbanded and, in factional publications, discredited.* This, as Rebecca knew at the time, was all part of a wider shift in Allied policy towards Yugoslavia.

Her involvement with Yugoslav affairs did not end with the writing of her book, or with Henry's committee. The Royal Yugoslav Government in London was composed of representatives of all the main parties. The Minister for Justice of the government-in-exile was a Serb, Milan Gavrilović, leader of the Serbian Peasant Party, a member of the Orthodox Church, and an upholder of constitutional monarchy. Sir Orme Sergeant, Assistant Under-Secretary of State for the Foreign Office, asked

---

* See the vitriolic article by Louis Adamić in *Today and Tomorrow* (Milford, New Jersey), Jan/Feb 1945. Adamić also wrote critically about RW's *Black Lamb and Grey Falcon* in the *Saturday Review*.

Rebecca to take Gavrilović under her wing, along with Father Cukar of the Slovene Catholic Democrats.

Gavrilović, who sat on Henry's economics committee while it lasted, became a particular friend, involving Rebecca deeper in the internal dissensions of Yugoslavia. The Yugoslav government information service operated from an apartment in Kingston House, Kensington (where Rebecca herself was to live in her widowhood), and she was inundated with their reports, pamphlets, manifestos, speeches, abstracts, offprints, minutes, appeals, and confidential memos. There were two rival Yugoslav relief organizations in Britain; Rebecca spoke only at the meetings of the one supported by the royalists, the Yugoslav Relief Society. She was in Eastern Europe up to the neck. The British Air Ministry enquired whether she had "notes or illustrations of industrial objectives" dating from her research visits, and she sent what she had.

There was a demanding personal dimension to her political involvement. Milan Gavrilović had a wife and children; to this family and to many other refugees and exiles Rebecca and Henry offered friendship, hospitality, financial help, and—most valuable and difficult of all—time. Her papers contain letters from exiles as prominent as General Simović, and from unknown and obscure Eastern Europeans, all giving testimony to what this meant to them. Lela Gavrilović, wife of the Yugoslav minister, unhappy in London, wrote in poetic bad English to thank Rebecca for bringing her flowers: "It is nice to get flover when you expect thorn, it is nice to get them when you expect nothing, but the nicest is to be sure that somewhere somebody exists who will always find a bunch of flover for you."

Rebecca, under pressure, was candid about the unlikeableness of some of the strangers who were landed on her at Ibstone, especially those sent to her by Lettie, who was equally active and generous. Some of the refugees were "time-bombs in themselves," not so much lame dogs as "lame wart-hogs, lame cobras." But her commitment continued even after the war. She and Henry sponsored refugees and stateless persons, helping them with both cash and influence to find jobs or educational opportunities in England and America. The Gavrilovićs, who ended their days in Washington, like other Yugoslav families remained friends always, and Rebecca and Henry continued to help their grown-up children.

They fulfilled similar obligations to members of Henry's European family, scattered post-war over three continents, many of them unable to find work, or settle down, or make stable marriages. A cousin, Louis Andrews, had flirted with the Nazi Party in spite of his Jewish blood, and sustained an erratic career as an agricultural economist in Germany, Hungary, Yugoslavia, Italy, and Australia before the war. Henry, who had sent money for the care of Louis's dying first wife, went to great trouble to provide documentation for his unsuccessful re-entry application to Australia after the war. Louis's second wife ended up in England, where Henry helped her as best he could. Both he and Rebecca took commitments of this kind, and there were many, extremely seriously, even though Rebecca railed fluently against the gross misfortunes, and the improvidence, of some of these connections.

In his will, Henry requested that "in so far as she is able to do so" his wife should "continue to assist those friends of ours whom I have been able to assist during my lifetime," and she did. Henry had always to subsidize his unlucky elder brother, Ernest—which was fair enough, since their uncle had left Henry everything and Ernest nothing. Their mother, Rebecca's mother-in-law, visited Ernest in Australia the year after the war ended, and died there. By coincidence, Ernest Andrews's home in Australia was in St. Kilda, Melbourne, where Rebecca's own parents had started their married life.

11

The political conflict over Yugoslavia, on which Rebecca West took up such definite positions that the consequences dogged her for the rest of her life, was twofold. One issue was the British conduct of the war in relation to Yugoslavia, and the choice made as to which of two rival resistance leaders to support militarily against the Germans; related to this was the dissension between Serbs and Croats, as disruptive among the Yugoslavs in exile as it was, more lethally, on their home ground. A second main issue was the British attitude to the deposed Regent, Prince Paul.

Rebecca handed in *Black Lamb and Grey Falcon* to her publishers only shortly after the Axis forces invaded Yugoslavia; it is dedicated to her friends there, "all now dead or enslaved." At this point the British propaganda machine was presenting Prince Paul as pro-Hitler, and it is thus that Rebecca describes him in the emotional epilogue to her book.

Prince Paul was an art-loving Anglophile, and brother-in-law to the Duke of Kent. As Rebecca conceded in her book, "those who really knew him believed him to be inspired by British sympathies." Such people have violently contested her account of his politics ever since, among them Kyril FitzLyon, Alastair Forbes, Cecil Parrott (who had been young King Peter's tutor), and Neil Balfour, co-author of *Paul of Yugoslavia*, published in 1980, which reopened the controversy. Balfour, the former husband of Prince Paul's daughter, described Rebecca's epilogue as "astonishingly misinformed": Prince Paul's aim in signing a pact with the Axis powers in March 1941 had been to keep his country out of the war—a policy of appeasement, not unlike Britain's in 1938. The treaty, it has since emerged, was relatively favourable to Yugoslavia in that it deprived German troops of the right to use Yugoslavia as a corridor, a fact not publicized at the time at the request of the Germans—who might not have honoured the pact, even if it had not been made void by the anti-appeasement coup which toppled Prince Paul.

When she was finishing her book, Rebecca had only official sources to work from. As she wrote to her solicitor during the attacks on her in 1980, how, in 1941, "could I possibly know what was going on except through the Foreign Office? Who do they think suggested I wrote a final chapter to my book except the Ministry of Information?" She defended herself in the letters page of *The Times Literary Supplement*, and won an action against the *Spectator*, sending the £2,500 she received in damages to the Serbian Orthodox Church in London, where Father Miloye Nikolić was her valued friend.

By then Rebecca was in her late eighties; Cecil Parrott acknowledged that when she first published her book only partial truths were available, and expressed a hope that she would now "take into account all that has been authoritatively published since, and above all Prince Paul's shameful treatment by the British authorities." (It is probable that the putsch against him had been facilitated by British undercover activists in Yugoslavia.) *Black Lamb and Grey Falcon* was reissued in 1982. Rebecca did not change a word of it.

Its republication brought her a letter from King Peter's younger brother Prince Androj, in exile in California. He praised her book, which he had read as an undergraduate when it first came out, and added reassuringly that "your references to Uncle Paul are really very mild." He added a family footnote which is not without interest. His mother, Queen Marie, had told him that when Prince Paul and his wife, Olga, returned from visiting Hitler in Germany, Prince Paul was "pale with anxiety from what he had just seen and heard, frightened for the future and of the capability of Hitler." It was Princess Olga, "or so it seemed to my mother," who had been "so well impressed with Hitler as a man and who spoke so glowingly of him." *Cherchez la femme.* Rebecca had, as so often, been half-right.

In 1941 the Foreign Office told Rebecca that internal resistance to the Axis occupation of Yugoslavia was being led by a Serb staff officer, Colonel (later General) Draza Mihailović, who was officially named as Minister for War by the Royal Yugoslav Government in London. She had never met him, but had heard him spoken of in Yugoslavia as strongly anti-Nazi.

But it was not only with the Axis invaders that Mihailović and his guerrillas (called Chetniks) had to contend. The horrific casualty figures emerging from Yugoslavia were the result of a multi-faceted civil war. Hitler's local führer, Ante Pavelić, and his Ustashas were pursuing their own Catholic Croatian separatist aims by massacring Orthodox Serbs by the thousand. It sometimes seemed to Mihailović more important to fight the Ustashas, and save Serb lives, than to attack the occupying forces.

Mihailović also had to reckon with a rival resistance group, the Partisans, led by Josip Broz, a communist known by his Central Committee codename, Tito. Tito wanted to dismantle everything that Mihailović was fighting to preserve. He was working not for the monarchy (which had, under King Peter's father, the murdered Alexander, been a repressive dictatorship) but for a communist Yugoslavia. He had been in Russia, and was known to Stalin; he aimed to eliminate both the Ustashas and Mihailović's Chetniks, as well as to get rid of the Axis occupation.

The Special Operations Executive (SOE) was set up in England,

ABOVE LEFT: Winnie aged seven,
Cissie (Rebecca) aged one, and Lettie
aged nine at Streatham Place
ABOVE AND LEFT: Rebecca's parents,
Charles and Isabella Fairfield, c. 1890

RIGHT: Winnie feeding blackberries
to Cissie, watched by Lettie (right)
and cousin Jessie Bidgood. BELOW:
No. 2 Hope Park Square, Edinburgh,
the house in *The Judge*

LEFT: No. 24 Buccleuch Place, Edinburgh, where Mrs. Fairfield and the girls had a flat. BELOW: Winnie Fairfield. BOTTOM: Cissie (back row, fifth from right) at George Watson's Ladies' College, Edinburgh

LEFT: George Bernard Shaw photographed by Rebecca at a Fabian summer school. ABOVE: Dr. Letitia Fairfield in World War I uniform. BELOW: Fairliehope, Chatham Close, Hampstead Garden Suburb

ABOVE: Rebecca in her late teens
RIGHT: H. G. Wells in 1920

LEFT: Rebecca and Anthony at Quinbury.
BELOW: Quinbury and the path across the
fields to Braughing. BOTTOM: H. G. Wells
outside Quinbury

LEFT: Southcliffe, Marine Parade, Leigh-on-Sea. BELOW: Anthony and Rebecca in 1916

LEFT: Rebecca. BELOW: Lord Beaver-brook in 1921

OPPOSITE: Friends Sylvia Lynd (above left), G. B. Stern (above right), and Fannie Hurst (below left), and Rebecca herself

LEFT: *Rebecca West,* by Wyndham Lewis. BELOW: John Gunther, by a young artist named Simkovitch

OPPOSITE: Anthony and Rebecca with their dog (above left), and on holiday in the south of France: Pamela Frankau (above right), Rebecca with her secretary June Head (below left), and Anthony and Rebecca (below right)

ABOVE: Henry Andrews as
a child in Rangoon. ABOVE
RIGHT: Henry's mother in
her youth. RIGHT: Rebecca
and Henry on their wedding
day, 1 November 1930

RIGHT: Rebecca soon after her marriage. BELOW: Ibstone House

LEFT: Rebecca in her prime.
BELOW: The drawing-room at Ibstone.
OPPOSITE: Henry and Rebecca with their labrador, Albert, and cat, Ginger Pounce, on the terrace at Ibstone, 1957 (above), and Rebecca after Henry had died (below)

Rebecca West, 1982

originally under the auspices of the Ministry of Economic Warfare, for the purpose of "subversion and sabotage against the enemy overseas." Its headquarters were in Baker Street, over the head office of Marks and Spencer; the section which liaised with Yugoslavian resistance was based in Cairo. Officials there were exasperated that Mihailović and Tito spent more time fighting each other than fighting the Germans. SOE was largely staffed by steady establishment types, but it had its quota—necessarily, given the nature of its operations—of professional agitators, communists, and fellow-travellers.

Some of the personnel in Cairo were more sympathetic to Tito's claims for Allied support than to Mihailović's. When Russia entered the war on the Allied side, such sympathies became more open, because more legitimate. Though many British politicians perceived Russia as the major threat to be faced post-war, the intelligentsia (the people whom Rebecca called "the left-wing carriage-trade") saw communists simply as the more committed members of the wider socialist fraternity; and for those disillusioned by capitalism and already disaffected there was no apparent problem: how could it be treason to facilitate an ally?

Thus it was chiefly SOE Cairo, during 1943–44, that brought about a complete turnaround in British policy. Churchill was soon backing Tito and ignoring, and finally repudiating, Mihailović. Captain William Deakin and Brigadier Fitzroy Maclean were sent out to liaise with Tito; dazzled by his personality and impressed by his Partisans' courage, they confirmed SOE's reports. Tito became an honoured and popular ally, awarded not only political recognition but also military assistance, some of which he deployed against Mihailović. The British became officially and openly critical of Mihailović, stimulated by reports that he was collaborating with the Germans. It was Guy Burgess who came up to Rebecca in a London restaurant asking if she had heard the news: Mihailović was a traitor.

Rebecca understood the political machinations as nearly as anyone not in the inner circle of intelligence could. The British organizer of her lectures for the Yugoslav Relief Society was suddenly unenthusiastic about her. There was the suppression of Henry's committee. Sir Orme Sergeant took her out to lunch at the Ritz and explained that the new policy of supporting Tito was a matter of military necessity: he was killing more Germans than Mihailović was.

Rebecca wrote to her sister Winnie about the "appalling" news from
Yugoslavia: eight thousand Slovenes, she said, had joined Mihailović in
the belief that Allied troops were on the point of joining them, only to be
butchered by Tito's Partisans. "The relatives of these unhappy boys now
listen to the BBC praising Tito's heroism." The sort of Conservative who
had supported the Munich agreement "is now absolutely infatuated with
the idea of offering the whole of Eastern Europe to Russia."

Churchill, while he put top priority on beating the Germans, did
not intend to leave the Balkans to Russia. He meant Yugoslavia to choose
her own form of government when the war was over. But by enabling Tito
to wipe out the opposition he made that choice unrealistic. He did not
believe, apparently, that Tito would force communism on Yugoslavia, and
even envisaged a union between King Peter and Tito (who had already
repudiated the monarchy). "I am at a loss to know what it all means,"
wrote Rebecca in a long letter to Philip Guedalla in which she told all
she knew, which was a lot. One of the things she knew was that some
groups and individuals were fighting fascism not for the preservation of
democracy and the rule of law (and the capitalist West's markets and
investments in Europe) but for international socialism.

Passionately loyal both to the romantic Yugoslavia of memory and
imagination and to her bewildered Yugoslav friends in London, monarch-
ists to a man, Rebecca never believed that Mihailović had discussed a
deal with the Germans. He had. So had Tito, in November 1942; both
were turned down. The politics of survival dictated day-to-day events in
Yugoslavia, and the last details of their dreadful, complex war can never
be known.

Rebecca, though under strong pressure from the Foreign Office and
her friends in political life, continued to argue the case for Mihailović,
refusing to suppress her own moral judgements and critical faculties even
for the furtherance of a common purpose—in this case, as she was told,
beating the Germans. All she saw was that Mihailović had been betrayed,
and with him many thousands of pro-Allied Yugoslavs. She published a
stream of articles and letters making her points. After the war, when
Mihailović was tried and executed by Tito's regime, Rebecca attended his
memorial service in London, and preserved a photograph of his dead body
among her papers.

She was baffled by Tito's breach with Stalin in 1948. She happened

Mrs. Henry Andrews 175

to be in Italy at the time, staying with the art historian Bernard Berenson. "The best informed opinion here" agreed with her that "Tito is opposed by the open Communist party but supported by the important underground members, and that the breach with Moscow is only a breach with some particular section in Moscow and that Tito will back his successor to Stalin by swinging away from the West to his side at the right moment." She was again half-right; Tito was reconciled to Moscow in 1956 with Khrushchev at the helm. Yet she underrated Tito's independence from Moscow, just as she underrated his overwhelming popular support in the first post-war elections in Yugoslavia; she saw Tito simply as a tyrant imposed on the people against their will.

The Mihailović controversy, like the Prince Paul controversy, rumbled on down the years, in books and articles and letters to the press, and Rebecca West never changed her ground or detached herself from Yugoslav issues. In 1978 she associated herself with the memorial in London to the Victims of Yalta—who included by extension thousands of pro-British, anti-Tito Yugoslav refugees who were repatriated against their will at the end of the war only to be massacred. She never declined to speak out when it would have been expedient to be silent. In 1945, when King Peter's future was in the balance and she was making representations to the British government on his behalf, she wrote in her diary, "This week I feel a growing fear of what the Communists may do to me personally."

She was not in physical danger; fear fed her paranoia. But because she spoke out against communist imperialism and ruthlessness, she was labelled a reactionary. Yet on polling day, 5 January 1945, when the first post-war general election dismissed Churchill with a resounding Labour victory, she recorded: "Voted Labour." She was a democratic socialist. As she saw it, it was communism, and not she, that was betraying the ideals of socialism. She had little regard for Churchill. She recognized that she owed him her life and freedom, "but there is nobody to whom I would not rather owe that particular debt." She wrote him a personal letter asking him to subscribe to a fund for Yugoslav refugees, and later scribbled on top of her draft: "The old meanie didn't send me a farthing."

Only in extreme old age did Rebecca West detach herself from Yugoslav affairs, and then not for her own sake. The year before she died she was asked to support an appeal for the return of the passport of Milovan Djilas, Tito's disillusioned vice-president. She replied that, since she was "considered an arch-villainess and ally of the press of reaction" by the Yugoslav government, she had best keep silent.

The arguments about Yugoslavia during and since the war continue over Rebecca West's grave, recurring with customary animosity on both sides of the Atlantic on the publication of books such as Nora Beloff's *Tito's Flawed Legacy* (1985). As survivors, experts, and interested parties continue to exchange conflicting memories, facts, fantasies, opinions, and interpretations, the outsider comes to understand how intimately all writing of history relates to ideology and propaganda, no matter how precisely documented; or, as Rebecca West wrote in *Black Lamb and Grey Falcon,* "It is sometimes very hard to tell the difference between history and the smell of skunk."

12

B*lack Lamb and Grey Falcon* was greeted in 1941 with some awe. The *New Yorker* review, headed "Magnum Opus," said it was "as astounding as it was brilliant," and compared it with T. E. Lawrence's *The Seven Pillars of Wisdom*. It was "one of the great books of spiritual revolt against the twentieth century"—even though "it must candidly be confessed that not many readers will want to read its every page." *The New York Times Book Review* praised it as a "monumental chronicle," the apotheosis of the travel book. The San Francisco *Chronicle* commended it as "a treasury of all that is worth treasuring in humanity and a self-portrait of one of the richest minds of our modern world."

Those critics who explored the "self-portrait" aspect of Rebecca's magnum opus wrote the most perceptively, if less eulogistically. A syndicated piece by Malcolm Cowley saw, as John Gunther had done, that *Black Lamb and Grey Falcon* was "her own story." He, like the *New York Times* reviewer, remarked on her "excessively" pro-Serbian stance, and the over-interpreting quality of some of her writing. The New York *Her-*

ald Tribune identified her relation with Yugoslavia as "a love affair," like Hemingway's with Spain.

Black Lamb and Grey Falcon is a great work of romantic art constructed over a framework of research and scholarship. Judged by the stiff criteria of this framework, it is excessive, unbalanced, sometimes wrong, sometimes silly. In *St Augustine* Rebecca West had written: "Augustine's errors were the result of his position in time, and so are not disgraceful. It was for him to be the great romantic artist, leaning far out to the apprehension of yet unformulated truths, and bringing in the false mingled with the true in an immense mass of material. . . ." The same is true of her own major work.

She was in *Black Lamb* uninhibitedly judgemental, sweepingly certain about things about which no one on earth can be certain; and she spun vague, mystifying, lovely webs of words around ideas that could have been expressed simply. Some passages sound like self-parody. Her sense of scale was distorted, perhaps deliberately. Significant people or events were deflated by images drawn from kitchen or nursery, to comic effect, while the gesture of a stranger glimpsed for a second might be drenched in an intense, apocalyptic significance not always accessible to the reader. These epiphanies are part of the equipment of a mystic or a poet; they were also a feature of the disturbed mental states which sometimes frightened her. Either she exploited these abnormal perceptions in her writing, or they flooded her mind spontaneously as she wrote. This is the balancing act of art. She took risks with the equilibrium of something that had started out as a travel book, and she achieved her work of art. If man has a talent, she was to write in the last sentence of *The Meaning of Treason,* it is for tightrope walking.

Some readers felt she had fallen off the tightrope. Nigel Dennis saw in her book the quest of "the frustrated Western intellectual for a Nirvana of vitality and self-expression," and "prejudice in the grand and foolish manner." One of the most critical, and the wittiest, of the commentators on Rebecca West's presentation of her material and of herself has been Mary Ellmann. The polarization of male and female qualities is one of the subtexts of *Black Lamb and Grey Falcon;* Ellmann, writing as a 1960s feminist, found this anachronistic and the reverse of radical. Rebecca, as every reader must remark, brings Henry Andrews into the book at every turn. "My husband" is constantly consulted, and "my husband"

provides long factual statements, generally in support of the author's intuitive judgements. Rebecca West, in Ellmann's analysis, is a "Balloon,"
the woman's mind being represented as "light, fragile, drifting and buoy-
ant," a complement to the "masculine Ballast":

> The Ballast thinks round, careful, solid thoughts. Wherever
> he goes, his mind carries a knapsack full of precise and irre-
> futable facts—the Serbian soybean crop yields of 1932 and
> 1933, that sort of thing. . . . Meanwhile the Balloon *appre-
> ciates*, her working day is given to piercing perceptions and
> lightning intuitions.

The Balloon's acknowledgement of the Ballast's virtues "is like the com-
pulsory modesty of astronauts who must always attribute their personal
glory to desk work on the ground."

Although the Balloon and Ballast image does to some extent reflect
the complementary qualities of Rebecca and Henry in real life, and although she consulted the reference-library of his mind constantly and
with gratitude, Rebecca was in fact both Balloon and Ballast, her thirst
for information being equal to her capacity for intuitive insights; and she
knew quite well that she was capable of conscripting reality "into the
service of a private dream." The division of labour between the author
and "my husband" in the book is in part a structural device; if it also
reflects a "private dream," and a desire for men to be men and women to
be women, that was because she had reason to feel that the qualities
traditionally ascribed to women were manifested in her own world by
men, and vice versa. Nor does Ellmann point out that the Balloon cheerfully and knowingly allows the Ballast to puncture her superior sensibil-
ity: "As for your other demands," says "my husband," "that from now
on every day will be an apocalyptic revelation, I should drop that, if I
were you!"

But this is only the surface tension of an extraordinary book which
in its intensity, its scope and scale, pageantry, comedy, descriptive virtuosity, and narrative drive was, as a contemporary critic said, "the most
remarkable book to come out of the war thus far." Rebecca West was one
of nature's Balkans as a chronicler as well as in her own person. Those
people who were less interested in *Black Lamb and Grey Falcon* as a per-

sonal statement on a grand scale, or as literature, than in their own brand of single-issue politics—military men, political journalists, Titoists—were to use the book as an area of the battlefield. In 1956 the book was even attacked from the extreme right—by Diana Mosley, wife of the leader of the British Fascists, who objected to Rebecca's "tribal" values, particularly her overt hostility to the Germans. Britain had no "natural enemies" in Europe, wrote Lady Mosley. In 1941 Rebecca West, like most other people in Britain, felt she had sufficient reason to disagree. And *Black Lamb and Grey Falcon* survives as a classic among travel books, a monument not only to its author's love of Yugoslavia but to the protean virtuosity of her writing talent as well.

13

In 1940 and 1941 Rebecca had operations, one of them for a fibroid tumour on her breast. Her surgeon, she said, "leaned over me saying 'She loves me, she loves me not', plucking out organ after organ." Apart from these major crises, she suffered as always from a sequence of infections, sinus trouble, fibrositis, bronchitis, and chronic colic and gastritis. These episodes of physical and sometimes emotional breakdown, which would have laid another woman low, had astonishingly little effect on Rebecca. As she said of Proust, who had chronic asthma and produced a masterpiece, "Let us all pray for that kind of ill-health." The violence of her symptoms seems to have been a safety-valve relieving stress and fear and liberating her energies for further effort.

She was well aware of the functional aspects of illness, even though she extracted the maximum dramatic effect from her collapses. "Behaving badly," she wrote, was a wholesome reaction to, say, fear of a German invasion, just as colic was a wholesome reaction to an irritant in the gut. "The outward and visible signs give onlookers an exaggerated impression of what the person who is ill or afraid is suffering. Anyone who has undergone pain so severe that it has to show itself in cries and movements knows that these often overstate the degree of discomfort that is actually felt." The body, calling for help, "makes the appeal as strongly as possible"; experienced nurses realized that most patients who claimed they longed to die (as Rebecca often did) want "nothing so much as the longest possible enjoyment of life."

Rebecca did enjoy life, even during the worst times of the war. "I wish I could write you a really candid letter about the extraordinary liveliness of England, but I couldn't do it without indiscretion," she told John Gunther. Apart from her own chosen writing, she was producing morale-raising articles for the provincial press and for journals such as *Farmer's Weekly*, commissioned by the Ministry of Information.

In the early part of the war, before she fell foul of government policy, she made propaganda broadcasts to Yugoslavia. For these, and for the meetings of the consultative committee of the Scenario Institute (which reported on scripts and treatments for the Rank Organization), she went to London. The claustrophobia that had always prevented her from travelling by Underground lifted, "which shows either that psychoanalysis has cured my claustrophobia, or that claustrophobia is caused by fear of death, and that I no longer fear death."

The New York Times commissioned an article from her about Princess Elizabeth, the young heir to the throne. Rebecca, who also reported the Princess's wedding in 1947, took the British monarchy seriously. Her attitude to the abdication of Edward VIII in 1936 had been uncompromising: "I should have made him stay even with a bayonet in his ribs." She had nothing against Mrs. Simpson, on whose account the King had abdicated; she had met her with American friends in the south of France, and liked her. It was the King's "paucity of being" that appalled her; his mind seemed to her like "a telephone exchange with not enough subscribers."

Rebecca had been a republican as a girl. Now she felt that monarchy was "an essential symbol" without which mankind—or at least the British—could not maintain law and order. She prepared for her afternoon visit to Buckingham Palace to meet the Princess by buying a new hat, having a facial, and hiring a Daimler. She met King George VI, Queen Elizabeth, and both the Princesses. The Queen was like "a fat wild flower," she wrote in her diary; the girls very short, not particularly well dressed, and seventeen-year-old Elizabeth "sweetly dutiful, possibly with her father's obstinacy." She felt there was a "shrewd egotism" about the younger sister, Princess Margaret: "When she grows up people will fall in love with her as if she were not royal. The other one is too good, too sexless, she may be the one who falls in love and is too innocent to be loved."

She felt that although the Palace atmosphere was one of "really beautiful innocence" it was also one of "intellectual poverty," and the Queen's sincerity reminded her of one of her own epigrams, about Mrs. Baker Eddy: "She tried to think without the power of thought." Nevertheless, in wartime these "symbols of a natural life" took on for Rebecca a value that transcended criticism, and her published article was entirely positive.

Ibstone was now the centre of Rebecca's life. It was not a literary village, and to most people there she was just Mrs. Andrews, who was some sort of a writer. Living in a big house on the outskirts, she and Henry were not part of ordinary village life, though they both took on local responsibilities: Henry became a manager of the village school, and a member of the Rural District Council. Ibstone House itself was always full of people. The Orchard Court domestic staff had been called up for war service, but Rebecca had a housemaid and a parlourmaid—the first because she was under-age, the second because she was too delicate for war-work—and an erratic sequence of refugee cooks.

She also had a living-in secretary, who became like a daughter to both herself and Henry. Margaret Hodges had worked for Henry in the City in the 1930s; she took on the monumental task of typing *Black Lamb and Grey Falcon,* and came to Ibstone on a temporary basis after the first of Rebecca's operations in 1940. Margaret's husband was away in the army; no one mentioned her leaving Ibstone, and she stayed until after the war, working for both Rebecca and Henry—not that working for Henry amounted to very much, after the demise of his economics committee. Another blow to him was that the part of his income which still came from Burma was cut off by the Japanese.

As in Villa Mysto days, no secretary of Rebecca's was just a secretary. Margaret Hodges was a confidante and a fellow-conspirator. The house was full of jokes and laughter, as well as of impossible refugees, sad Yugoslavs, and interesting, important visitors. Farmers could get petrol, so they retained the pre-war Rolls, in which they all three went to market to buy their first Jersey calves, Primrose and Patience, who rode home in the back seat "fluttering their eyelashes to the manner born," as Rebecca said. (Later they built up a pedigree herd: the Jersey bull's registered name was Ricrac Mr. Rochester.)

Rebecca became a good cook, excelling at pastry, scones, ice-cream, jam, marmalade, and ingenious soups. (She always left a mess in the kitchen.) She inaugurated a branch of the Women's Institute in the village, with herself as chairman and Margaret Hodges as secretary; she wrote a play, "Our Village," full of local allusions, which won third prize at the Women's Institute Drama Festival and in which she and Margaret took parts. She hired a canning machine and ran canning sessions in her kitchen, to which all the village brought their garden produce. They kept hens, and planted whole fields of peas and beans; Rebecca's voracious reading expanded to include manuals on poultry-farming, tomato-growing, cattle-breeding, butter-making. They had a bull-terrier, and a ginger tom cat called Pounce. Fantasies were woven around Pounce, who was credited with the characteristics of a London clubman and immortalized in Rebecca's war-time articles in *The New Yorker.* The cat-loving author Paul Gallico addressed to Pounce his thank-you letters for visits to Ibstone.

The role of countrywoman was one that Rebecca enjoyed very much. Some of her old friends felt that there was a contest going on between Cicely Andrews, the mistress of Ibstone House, and the real Rebecca West, and regretted the fact that Cicely Andrews seemed too often to get the upper hand. Henry adapted less wholeheartedly to country life, even retaining his formal three-piece city suits (with the addition of Wellington boots). Rebecca wanted to do everything, having a flair for everything. She took over the management of the greenhouses and the kitchen and flower gardens from Henry, who in theory retained control over the farm. This was a job to which he was not really suited, though he achieved a triumph with the design of new cow-houses. Rebecca complained that Henry could not even take a dog for a walk, and could only just distinguish a tulip from a rose.

But she loved exercising her new skills, and running everything. She furnished the house with the best things from Orchard Court (though a good Empire table that had stood in the drawing-room window in the flat was destroyed by blast) and from local sales: "The Mrs Brownlee who was the mistress of the beautiful old Lord Shrewsbury . . . sold her house on the river and I reflected that she would know something about beds if anybody did, and I bought several, they are superb."

She wrote to G. B. Stern: "I am also organizing a Warship Savings Week in the village—I have arranged a smoker concert . . . and I am also organizing the house as a Casualty Clearing Station in case of invasion." The patients' beds were to be lined up in the drawing-room; Rebecca was in charge of supplies and equipment, and she and Margaret Hodges, in white aprons, held Red Cross classes—occasions of much comedy, since neither of them had any training.

Rebecca, said Margaret Hodges, "made everything fun." She extracted surreal and sometimes ribald humour from the most unlikely situations. Christmas at Ibstone was a great event, with musicians playing on the landing that ran like a gallery above the large stone-flagged hall. Margaret's name for Rebecca was Simpkin (from Beatrix Potter's *The Tailor of Gloucester*) because of her endless knitting. It is hard to know how Rebecca found the time to knit. Margaret, who watched over Rebecca, if only from a distance, for ever afterwards, thought that in many ways the war years at Ibstone, in which her dominance, energy, and generosity found practical outlets, were Rebecca's "best time."

"The best way to appreciate Rebecca was to surrender to her. Throw up your arms and go under." Margaret Hodges, a surrogate daughter with a circle of her own to go back to, could surrender to Rebecca without danger, in love and gratitude for such heightening and enhancing of life. Anthony was not sufficiently sure of himself to do that, and survive. The "best time" ended for Rebecca with the first of the tragic rows with Anthony which were to punctuate and poison the rest of their lives.

14

In 1941 Rebecca, in her late forties, became a grandmother. Anthony and Kitty had a daughter, Caroline, and two years later a son, Edmund. The family often came to Ibstone, and Rebecca adored the children. This was an important aspect of her "best time."

When war broke out Anthony, a pacifist by conviction, used money from Wells's trust fund to buy Chapel Farm at Ecchinswell, near Newbury in Berkshire, where he and Kitty inaugurated the "Panther Herd" of pedigree Guernsey cattle. Anthony was not called up for war service; like many pacifists in the south of England, he was temporarily under surveillance as potentially pro-German. His house was visited by the police, who took away books and papers and even the collection of toy soldiers that Wells had given him as a child. He asked Rebecca not to intervene with the authorities (though she did): "I must look after myself and you can only help me by being calm and sane outside the whirlpool of hysteria that has been pulling at me."

Rebecca was proud of Anthony: "He is running a 68-acre farm, and gets up at 4.30 every morning, and sends 40 gallons of milk into the nearest town, and is ploughing up derelict land in his spare time," she told Margaret Rhondda. Later in the war he worked part-time as a sub-editor in the news room at the BBC, staying in the mews flat behind Wells's house in Hanover Terrace, Regent's Park, and seeing his father regularly.

In March 1944 Anthony told Rebecca that Wells, now seventy-nine, was dying of cancer of the liver. She was sad, remembering only the happy times and the easy affection of recent years. She was appalled, on visiting the old man, to find that his sons had told him he was terminally ill, and that they had quarrelled with Lord Horder, Wells's doctor and friend, who had not wanted to tell him the probable truth. When Rebecca argued the case for recalling Horder, Anthony hurt and irritated her by reminding her that she was no longer at the centre of Wells's life, and had no right to behave as if she were. This small spat was soon over, but it was an omen.

Two months later Rebecca heard from Kitty that Anthony wanted to divorce her in order to marry a girl he had met at the BBC. Rebecca assured Kitty that it would blow over; they had been so young when they married, she wrote, there were bound to be temporary aberrations, and "I don't suppose you realize—it took me till the forties to realize it—how immensely less staying power men have than women." She blamed Anthony's unstable childhood: Kitty must "reckon him as shell-shocked. . . . I am deeply sorry my failure should have given you such a thorny problem to solve."

But, brooding about this situation, Rebecca began connecting Anthony's behaviour with other betrayals. She wondered whether Anthony, who was so close to his own small daughter, was not "an incarnation of my own father, who with great gifts of body and mind drifted from one misadventure to another," inflicting "the deepest misery on my mother and my sisters and myself." It also struck her that "H.G., who is really only a successful version of my father, left his sweet and kind first wife when he was about Anthony's age." She felt as if Anthony "was not living his own life, but were forced to re-enact the destinies of the damned precursors."

It was partly her urge to break the chain of disasters that led Rebecca to become over-involved in the affairs of Anthony and Kitty. It was Anthony's need to live his own life—which was what she *thought* she wanted him to do—that led him, and then Kitty, to repudiate Rebecca and her involvement. Kitty decided to give Anthony a divorce. Rebecca's version of the ensuing "nightmare" was poured out in a twenty-page letter to Lettie. Rebecca displaced her violent emotions onto the subject of money; as Anthony's trustee, she became agitated about provision for Kitty and the children, and arranged that Kitty should meet herself and Henry for lunch at the Ritz in London.

Kitty trusted Anthony, and did not want to talk about money. She began to resent Rebecca's interference. Both women were under strain, and uttered raw home-truths better left unsaid. Rebecca lost her temper, and with it all self-control. She made a conspicuous exit, leaving Kitty and Henry to lunch alone. It was worse even than that sounds: an ugly, noisy, public scene which Anthony (who heard about it from Kitty) described after Rebecca's death in terms best calculated to degrade her.

Anthony and Kitty thought Rebecca was mad. Rebecca thought Anthony was mad. She was driven to despair, she told Kitty, by the implication "that I am a stranger who has somehow intruded into the family circle at an inconvenient moment." Anthony and Kitty, by bringing up unhappy incidents from the past, inflamed Rebecca's sensitivity about the fact that she seemed to have brought her son into the world only to be unhappy:

I don't hate Anthony, I wish I could, but I do see the awful
hell of his egotism, and I know that all our lives long there will
be awful crises . . . and never, *never,* NEVER any way of making
Anthony happy and NEVER any freedom from the desire to
make him happy.

It is not strange that Rebecca should feel tortured in this way, nor that
Anthony (who was in analysis with Edward Glover, an English Freudian)
felt justified in torturing her. Psychiatry has been punitive to mothers:
"Generations of psychiatrists have laid the blame for all our unhappiness
at her tired feet." Anthony's feelings about his mother were as unresolved
when he was thirty as when he was sixteen (and as they still would be
when he was seventy). That is part of his biography rather than Rebecca's,
but it was to erode the integrity of them both. After a few months he
went back to Kitty and the children, and the young couple closed ranks.
After a meal with Anthony, Rebecca wrote: "He was amiable but cold and
unfriendly. Kitty has taken him from me." This is a classic mother-in-
law's complaint; but with Rebecca, and Anthony, common situations
were enacted with uncommon intensity and a perverse inventiveness.

Before the scene at the Ritz, Rebecca had warned Anthony that "if
he had new friends who were interested in politics he should be careful."
This sounded, as Kitty remarked to Henry, like something out of a detective story. Anthony believed that "someone"—he meant his mother—had
told Wells that he, Anthony, had been "got hold of" by members of a pro-
Nazi conspiracy. He apparently never discussed this with Wells in the
two years that passed between Rebecca's warning and Wells's death in
August 1946, but it was to this alleged calumny that he ascribed the last
words his father ever spoke to him: "I just don't understand you. . . ."

Anthony blamed Rebecca for this, as he was to blame her for nearly
everything that went wrong in his life. Twenty-eight years later he wrote
that he was not sorry for anything he had done to her, since she had told
a story about his being in the hands of the Nazis "in a place where it
would do him most harm." She wrote to him that the intelligence she had
received about him had nothing to do with the Nazis and in any case "I
DID NOT MENTION IT TO HG." It grieved her that he had "let this flimsy
suspicion play such a tragic part in our lives." It was the report of a
Yugoslav in the Censor's Office, she said, that alerted her to the fact that

Titoists in Belgrade, hostile to herself, were watching Anthony closely.

His paranoia fed off hers, and hers off his. Anthony had the same problem in coming to terms with Rebecca that most males, related or not, have in coming to terms with exceptionally forceful people who are women. He dealt with it sometimes by ridiculing and denying her powers, sometimes by exaggerating them and seeing them as "evil," and building a black legend around her name. Rebecca retaliated by doing exactly the same thing to him. She could read his psychological processes as fluently as he could read hers, and each added a fabulist's gloss to every detail of every misunderstanding. As Wells had noted when Anthony was a boy, mother and son were very alike.

Rebecca and Anthony both attended Wells's cremation service. Rebecca admired the "extreme goodness of heart" of Gip Wells's wife, Marjorie, who had seen to all the old man's physical needs in his last years, and to whom she wrote: "I loved him all my life and always will." But she could not have stayed with him, "and indeed he got on pretty well without me." The Wells family invited Rebecca to the meeting which established the annual Wells Memorial Lecture in 1948, and she became a vice-president of the H. G. Wells Society. In 1949 she offered to present her letters from Wells to the British Museum, but the Museum's apparent lack of enthusiasm (as a matter of routine, they asked to inspect the material before committing themselves) dampened her own; she donated her Wells letters, along with other of her personal papers, to the Beinecke Library at Yale.

"I do not want to exaggerate the part I played in his life and I would think a great part of the pleasure he seemed to derive from seeing me in his last days was that I went back further in time than almost anybody he then knew." In 1966 she declined to take part in the H. G. Wells centenary celebrations. "It is not that I wish to dissociate myself from H.G. I am extremely proud of my association with him, and my regard for his work has grown greater every year. But I do not wish to seem to exploit that association." Rebecca never did exploit or profit from her connection with the great man, though in later life she was given every opportunity to do so.

PART FIVE

Rebecca West

1

In the summer of 1946 Rebecca applied to Sir Hartley Shawcross, the Attorney General and Chief Prosecutor for the British at the international military tribunal in Nuremberg, for permission to attend the closing sessions of the trial of Nazi war criminals; she arranged to write a series of articles on the proceedings for the *Daily Telegraph*.* The trial was by then in its eleventh month, and the courtroom had become "a citadel of boredom"—until the closing day, when twelve of the defendants were condemned to death and another seven to long prison sentences.

Rebecca approved of what was done at Nuremberg: it was necessary both to avenge the victims of Nazism and to reinstate the rule of law. But she was against capital punishment in general, and her approval of the trials was qualified ten years later "by my knowledge that the persons who were there sentenced to be hanged suffered agonies which lasted about a quarter of a hour"; moreover, the "vileness of execution" was "independent of any pain it may inflict."

Outside the courtroom, the Allied personnel—the legal and military, the journalists and observers—quartered in a ruined and grieving city, stuck together. The Russians did not fraternize, and the British, wrote Rebecca, reconstituted an Indian hill station: "anybody who wants to know what they were like in Nuremberg need only read the works of Rudyard Kipling." The best friend she made among the British delegation was the future member of Parliament Airey Neave, then twenty-nine years old and an escapee from Colditz. The Americans were the most fun, and gave "huge parties."

The American Chief Prosecutor at Nuremberg was Francis Biddle, at sixty some six years older than Rebecca. A Democrat, he was a Philadelphian, who had been Roosevelt's Attorney General during the war. He

---

* Reprinted as "Greenhouse with Cyclamens I" in *A Train of Powder* (1955).

wrote books on law and politics, and was an honorary Bencher of the Inner Temple in London. Rebecca acted as hostess for his parties during her stay in Nuremberg; she had met him before, in the United States. Now she became, briefly, his mistress.

She went with him on a military plane to Prague for four days— "the most beautiful town I have ever seen . . . with the farmlands and orchards and gardens falling down the heights right into the heart of the city, and oh, that gorgeous bridge." This episode did not make her return to Ibstone easy, as she told Dorothy Thompson: "I have had an emotional upset, which has left me horribly aware of the fact that in some ways my life has been a failure. The death of H.G., who devoured my youth and nagged and bullied me and was so much made for me that to the last he glowed when I came to see him, helped to rub that in. The worst of the life I live here is that it drives me back on the fundamentals, which are gaunt. . . . I don't want Henry to feel my terrific discontent."

Biddle was married too. He wrote to her, explaining that he could not leave his wife. She did not expect or require him to. She sent a sample of his handwriting to Winnie, who went in for graphology. "There is something odd about him I cannot understand. Is he a fantasy builder who is extremely deceitful?" He was, she told Winnie, very good-looking, a delightful companion, highly intelligent, "but notably masochistic."

The details of Rebecca's private life after her marriage are quickly told. When she said that the first five years of her marriage were the happiest of her life, she implied that the subsequent years had been less happy. She loved Henry, even though he got on her nerves and she complained about him a lot. Henry was devoted to her, transparently proud of her, and anxious to make her life easier (though he inadvertently made it more difficult). He loved her. But he stopped making love to her in the mid 1930s, which hurt her deeply. "He had appeared to find me attractive until that moment. The breach was sudden, no warning. I attempted to question him about it; he would not reply. I could not believe he was repudiating me."

Past terrors made her fear that she had somehow made him impotent, but she came to believe that "his theory was that sex was not part of marriage after the first years." She told Gordon Ray in the 1970s that Wells had asked her to go back to him, seven years after her marriage. This is perhaps confirmed by a diary entry for 22 March 1937: "Dinner

H.G. Proposal." Wells must have been one of the few people to whom at this time she confided the facts of her marriage, and her old Jaguar amiably offered his services, which were declined.

Her anxiety about her marriage may illuminate that peculiar feature of *Black Lamb and Grey Falcon,* the constant citing of "my husband." The book was written in the years immediately following the cut-off in marital relations. Rebecca, suffering then under the weight of her impotence theory, may have wanted to aggrandize "my husband" in the eyes of the world and in his own eyes, and to maximize her feminine wifeliness. There is a similarity in the eternally repeated "my husband" of *Black Lamb* to the eternally repeated "my father" of Anthony West's *H. G. Wells: Aspects of a Life.* Wells in this book is always "my father"; he is not accorded his own famous name even in contexts where his relationship to the author is of the most sublime irrelevance. The sympathetic reader, knowing the history, can feel the balm it was for Anthony to write, and to see in print, "my father," over and over. Rebecca's "my husband" and her son's "my father" both spring from insecurity and hurt; the reiteration is a public act of belonging, of claiming and reclaiming.

Unlike Henry, Rebecca did not look for romantic adventures outside her marriage. She had only one lover apart from Biddle. "I had an operation on my breasts and had fallen in love with my surgeon, who loved me, but he stayed with his wife and his profession, naturally enough, and it was brief." The surgeon—the one who had "plucked out organ after organ, saying 'She loves me, she loves me not'"—was Thomas Pomfret Kilner, two years her senior, a Lancashire man and a plastic surgeon of international reputation. "Except for my affair with the American judge at Nuremberg this was my last attempt at finding happiness in sex."

Rebecca did not accept what she saw as her "sexual deprivation" easily. She wrote to the Elizabethan scholar A. L. Rowse, of whom she was very fond, "I have never been able to write with anything more than the left hand of my mind; the right hand has always been engaged in something to do with personal relationships." But she felt that her left hand's power, "as much as it has," was due to "its knowledge of what my right hand is doing."

2

All her powers of mind and imagination were stretched by her post-war reporting of war criminals and traitors. She synthesized her gifts, combining hard investigative reportage with theatrical scene-setting and a sometimes brutal intuitive probing of personality and physical appearance. She shared Francis Biddle's view that "criminal acts are committed by individuals, not by those fictional bodies known as nations," and though the German nation as a whole did not escape her lash, it was as individuals that she pilloried the Nazi leaders in the dock at Nuremberg, often with strong but obscure allusions to sexual perversion: Streicher was pitiable, "a dirty old man of the sort that gives trouble in parks"; Goering was "like a madam in a brothel," von Schirach like "a neat and mousy governess."

The previous September (1945), she had attended the trial, at the Central Criminal Court in London, of William Joyce, better known as Lord Haw-Haw, who had broadcast Nazi propaganda to Britain, in a voice she described as "rasping but rich," through the worst months of the war. Rebecca had listened to him every evening at home at Ibstone, a fortifying glass of gin and lemon in her hand. "Cover this trial," cabled Ross of *The New Yorker*. Ross believed in Rebecca and gave her her head; she in return gave him her loyalty, and memorable copy.

Rebecca's first seven-thousand-word article on Joyce for Ross was written with intensity and at breakneck speed. Her absorption in her subject consumed her. She was among those who stood outside Wandsworth Prison on a January morning to see, and report, the "minute shred of ceremony" that accompanied the pinning up of a notice stating that Joyce had been hanged. These articles, plus her report on the trial of another British traitor, John Amery, two months later, formed the basis for a wider survey of wartime traitors and treachery, her book *The Meaning of Treason*, which she completed in less than a year. She worked obsessively, late into the night. Diary, 9 January 1947: "Have certainly written 15,000 words in last week." 10 January: "Worked and worked and worked." 16 January: "Life with Henry in hopeless disorder. Henry irritable . . ."

The Meaning of Treason was to be the book that consolidated her reputation, and the one that most people still associate with her name. Like *Black Lamb and Grey Falcon,* it was and has remained controversial. The tone of her writing about traitors distressed some people; she received letters protesting against her over-simple approach to loyalty, against her uninhibited speculations about family dynamics, against her "gloating" and "indecency," her narrow nationalism, her class-consciousness, her lack of respect for the dignity of condemned men. Others were shocked by her treatment of Alan Nunn May, the scientist who passed what he knew about atomic energy to the Russians; he was not, since the Russians were then Britain's allies, tried for treason, but was charged under the Official Secrets Act. Rebecca was equally shocked when a group of eminent intellectuals signed a protest against his sentence of ten years' imprisonment. She also got into trouble with the poet Roy Campbell, whom she described as a member of the British Union of Fascists. His letter of protest "makes my hair curl with terror."

The book came out in 1947 in the United States and in 1949 (with some emendations and corrections) in Britain, after serialization in the *Evening Standard*. These extracts brought her tragic letters—from William Joyce's son, from John Amery's mother, and a pathetic, bitter note from the mother of a "young stoker" unnamed in print: "I only hope the monetary gain that you kind of People get from these articles does them a lot of good and hope they are sleeping better at nights than I do."

But Rebecca was examining a sickness of humanity that led, as she saw it, to hell. She was investigating the Judas principle. As she wrote to Cyril Connolly, "I am consumed with pity for Joyce because it seems to me that he lived in a true hell: to have enough brains to discern that there was such a thing as political science, and to be inflamed with a passionate desire to be the instrument of political wisdom and to be such a damn fool that all you could work up was a peculiarly idiotic variety of anti-semitism; and to be puny and plain and be capable of the ardent and enduring love he showed for his wife in Berlin—there couldn't be anything worse."

Rebecca West's horror for the crime of treason grew out of her respect for the rule of law. "If a state gives a citizen protection it has a claim to his allegiance, and if it has his allegiance it is bound to give him protection." A sense of law, she wrote, "is as necessary to man as bread and water and a roof." Yet her attitude is more complex and interesting than a first reading admits. She had herself been a rebel against conventional society in her youth, and, as she stated at the end of her book, there is "a case for the traitor. . . . All men should have a drop of treason in their veins, if the nations are not to go soft like so many sleepy pears. Men must be capable of imagining and executing and insisting on social change. . . ." She, by her way of life and her combative early journalism, had been outstandingly capable of these things. And in her discussion of how the climate of treachery developed, it is her own socialist background to which, tacitly, she referred.

In the updates of *The Meaning of Treason* (1952 and 1964) she expanded her discussion to take in scientific and diplomatic espionage, with the communists now identified as the enemy. (Nazis and communists were perceived by her as equally "fascist.") She felt that progressives in England had little in their own society against which to rebel after the war. Communism, so far from being a radical break with their own or their parents' past, was the only ideology which could "truly gratify nostalgia." The Conservatives could not re-create a lost imperial past; the Liberals could not re-create the thrilling industrial expansion which had brought them to power; the Labour Party could not put itself back into "the glorious drunkenness of permanent opposition."

But the Communist Party could. Communism could carry its converts back to "the golden days when the flowering almonds along the avenues of the Hampstead Garden Suburb were saplings": there but for the grace of God, says Rebecca West without actually saying it, go I. "Communism offers a haven to the infantilist." So, in her view, did all totalitarianism. She wrote elsewhere: "When men do not put away childish things in time, they turn on their tracks and seek the sources of death, such as the Nazis unsealed for them." Since she was an individualist who had been unable to take the party whip in any organization to which she belonged, her objection to totalitarian ideology needs no explaining. When asked whether she could imagine herself having become a spy, she replied, "Of course, that's why I'm interested in them."

Events in Yugoslavia had contributed to her preoccupation with treachery, as did her perception of the way people betrayed one another in personal life. She accepted the fact that some spies were professionals—"no ideological bias, just a trade, like millinery or glovemaking." But others became spies because they were fantasists and had "no other means of establishing exceptional value," or of finding glory. Human love, which ought to give a life value, did not last; religion had lost its centrality. Political passion filled the gap.

The relation between an unacknowledged hunger for God and passionate political conviction is an undercurrent in all her writing about treachery and espionage. Was the God in whose name the law was administered a reality, or just "the dream of disappointed sons imagining a perfect Father who shall be better than all fathers?" People on either side of the law might believe that they "sacrificed themselves for an eternal principle which their contemporaries had forgotten," instead of realizing that "one of time's gables was in the way and barred their view of eternity." Uncertain herself about the nature of God (and of fathers), she was to sacrifice not herself but a great deal of her time and energy to what she grasped as "an eternal principle": the rightness of Western capitalist democracy, and the absolute wrongness of communism.

She built up her files on spies—which, in the update of *The Meaning of Treason,* included Philby, Burgess, and Maclean, among others—like a detective (or like a spy). She visited their houses and haunts, listened to their friends and relatives, and speculated fluently in print on the implications of physique, background, and education, always noting the nuances of social status. These vivid case-histories read like synopses of psychological thrillers; Rebecca West, who could turn her hand to most things, might have been an outstanding thriller-writer. She always read detective stories for relaxation—and boasted that she could devour one in an hour and a half and pass an examination on the plot.

V. S. Pritchett, in the *New Statesman,* praised *The Meaning of Treason* but detected in its voice "the tremor of the extremist." It was Rebecca's interest in the psychopathology of individuals that provoked Leon Edel, in *PM,* into criticizing her for failing to consider sufficiently the defects in a social system which threw up betrayers. But in general her book was acclaimed on both sides of the Atlantic. The Viking edition was selling a thousand copies a day on its first appearance, according to *Pub-*

lishers Weekly. It was the verve of her style, as well as the urgency and topicality of her subject matter, which attracted readers. *The New York Times Book Review's* Joseph Barnes wrote that "Rebecca West comes closer than any other living writer to the achievement of a counterpoint in prose as rich as plural melody in music. She writes, as life is lived, on many levels." Her face was on the cover of *Time,* and the story inside hailed her as "indisputably the world's No. 1 woman writer." The author of this article made a comment of great perspicacity: "Rebecca West is a Socialist by habit of mind and a conservative by cell structure."

3

In early 1947 Rebecca West, "the world's No. 1 woman writer," fifty-five years old, exhausted by the expenditure of energy on *The Meaning of Treason,* had an infected foot and a high temperature. She was at odds with Henry over staff problems at Ibstone; the farm manager was falsifying the accounts, and Henry was unwilling to exercise his authority. To relieve her feelings, Rebecca shot off a letter to Anthony about the difficulties. "Life has been perfectly hideous here, and it raises in an acute form the problem as to what I am to do about Henry. He really is not fit to run a place like this." Henry was "so strangely silly and impractical," yet "very sweet and kind and sure he is doing his best for everybody." She asked her son's advice about the possibility of selling off the farm. Her son responded by sending her letter on to Henry. It is hard to see what Anthony thought was to be gained by this.

Against her doctor's advice, Rebecca went off to the United States. One bright spot was that Anne Charles, who came to replace Margaret Hodges in late 1946, became another proxy daughter; like Mrs. Hodges, she was able to immerse herself in Ibstone life, accepting that there were no official days off, no regular working hours, no limiting of her duties to the merely secretarial. In return for her commitment she received friendship, excitement, and, as she acknowledged, an education. From Southampton, Rebecca posted last-minute instructions to Anne Charles—about planting the new gladioli, ordering clematis from Jackman's, and "mothering" Pounce.

It turned out to be a most peculiar trip. Rebecca was met in New York by affectionate friends, Emanie Sachs and Dorothy Thompson, but within two days was ill again with bronchitis and high fever. She was confined to bed in the apartment in the St. Regis Hotel which she had been lent by the literary agent Carol Brandt, cared for by shifts of nurses (paid for by *The New Yorker*), and given large experimental doses of penicillin. Lord Horder, Wells's former doctor and her old friend, who had been a fellow-passenger on the *Queen Elizabeth*, made a reassuring professional visit. She recovered, and took up her hectic New York life.

She went to a party given by Bruce and Beatrice Gould of *Good Housekeeping*, and on to dinner at Marcia Davenport's apartment on the East River, with John Gunther and Vincent Sheehan. Instead of going on with them to the theatre as planned, Rebecca collapsed, exhibiting, as she confessed to Anne Charles, "all the symptoms of advanced drunkenness." Distressed by what had happened, and unwilling to acknowledge that even a normal intake of alcohol can take a terrible toll on a person who is nervous and exhausted, Rebecca insisted on seeing Gunther's doctor, who frightened her with talk of organic disease. Yet the next evening she "ate like a horse" with Gunther at the Colony, where she was greeted rapturously by the now white-haired Charlie Chaplin, dining with the young Oona O'Neill: "My pretty wife, you know, some girls like an old man." Rebecca also coped with numerous press-interviews, shopped for herself, Anne Charles, and her sisters, and wrote instructions home about treating the fleas in Pounce's ears.

The reason for retailing this saga is that it never ended. In Rebecca's old age the events of this trip took on a terrifying resonance for her, becoming the material of nightmare. A repairman in her bathroom at the St. Regis was remembered as part of a sinister chain which linked him with a Yugoslav cook who tried to poison her and the "strange" behaviour of Carol Brandt and Marcia Davenport (were the drinks drugged?). There were strange telephone calls taken by the nurse in her sickroom and a mysterious message wrongly delivered to her apartment at the hotel. What the conspiracy was about she could not guess, and this frightened her even more. She returned to these events with anguish for the rest of

her life, and in 1975 covered forty pages of letter-paper telling and retell-
ing the nightmare of 1947. She had had hallucinations, as she had told
Anne Charles, during her high fever at the St. Regis; it was the hallucinations and not the reality which returned to haunt her.

She was, in New York, appallingly run down in health and spirits,
and obsessed with the theories of communist infiltration which had been
her subject matter for the preceding months. She stunned fellow-guests
at a dinner party given by Irita Van Doren of the *Herald Tribune* by as-
serting that the *Times* of London was now a Communist Party organ. John
Gunther, divorced from his first wife and about to marry Jane, his second
wife, looked after Rebecca devotedly during these weeks. He was himself
under severe strain, for his young son was terminally ill and died soon
afterwards—a heartbreak that Rebecca could or would not wholly share
with him. The tragedies of people on whom she depended frightened her.
Yet her very detachment could sometimes be consoling. On the evening
when Noel Coward's mother died, he had a date to dine with Rebecca. "I
didn't put her off because I felt that her clear astringent mind would be
a comfort. . . . She knew of course that I was miserable and made no
effort to cheer me, she merely talked away and we laughed a lot and she
cheered me a great deal."

Rebecca was sufficiently herself in the spring of 1947 to go directly
from New York to South Carolina, to attend the trial of a group of taxi-
drivers accused of storming the jail at Greenville, taking out a black man
who had murdered one of their colleagues, and lynching him. Rebecca
appreciated every minute of it: "It was so hot down there I dripped all day
long, but everything was favourable, I liked everyone from the dead Negro
. . . to the Judge, and I found several enchanting people in the
town. . . . I was able to do what I wanted to do in quite a fair measure."

She wrote up the town, and the trial, and its implications for race
relations, in a series of articles for *The New Yorker.** Her account of how
they were edited shows how Harold Ross provided the brakes and she the
acceleration. When she returned to New York from Greenville with her
copy, a Greenville journalist was hired "to see if my facts and my account
of the locality could be questioned; and a northern and a southern lawyer
were hired to debate together as to whether my view of the case was

*Reprinted as "Opera at Greenville" in *A Train of Powder* (1955).

sound; and then I had to sit up with Harold Ross till four in the morning while he cross-examined me on the proofs." Ross was obsessed with his craft, and "mad," Rebecca thought, in his "kindness and generosity, his sense that he was under an obligation to get anyone who worked for him out of whatever hole they might fall into." Not everyone felt the same; but for Rebecca West, he was "my marvellous editor."

4

One of the more surreal events of Rebecca's hallucinatory illness at the St. Regis had been the unexpected appearance of Lord Beaverbrook at her bedside, bearing the inevitable red roses. This was not a hallucination. It was an indication less of his sentimentality than of Rebecca West's standing and reputation that he asked her to work for him again. On her return to England she began to write for his *Evening Standard*, at the excellent rate of around £50 per article. The paper was then, as she later wrote, full of talented people, "a peculiar, amiable, self-satisfied bedlam that never sought to correct its faults. And it was a great paper." Beaverbrook treated her well: she was billed as "The Greatest Journalist of Our Time."

Her first major political assignment for the *Evening Standard* was a series of articles on the Mosleyite Fascist revival and the recrudescence of anti-Semitism in the poor Jewish areas of London, Stoke Newington and the East End. She reckoned afterwards that she had attended "38 street meetings, 10 of which ended in riots, in one of which I lost a shoe." She also sat through the court cases that arose out of the riots and demonstrations.

It seemed to her that every meeting was packed with a well-orchestrated claque from the communist opposition, and that the Fascists were in comparison a group of inadequate, uninformed "malignant simpletons": "They are quite willing to burn up the world, but God has not given them any matches." As she wrote to John Gunther, at one Fascist meeting she found only "half a dozen limp young men and half a dozen cracked old men and half a dozen wildly cracked old women," all loyal to Mosley but lacking rhetoric, ability, or funds. Such Fascists, she reported, held "pitiful meetings" which the communists exploited, sending in organized fleets of hecklers so that they could catch the Jewish vote (40 percent in some areas) at the next election.

Her interpretation caused a breach with old friends in the Labour Party, including Richard Crossman, then assistant editor of the *New Statesman*. She had a blazing row with Crossman (about one particular Fascist meeting of which Woodrow Wyatt had given a different account in the *Statesman*) on the threshold of the Dorchester Hotel, after a dinner party, and there were slurs on Rebecca's reporting in the *Statesman* the following week. Rebecca thrived on public controversy, though she was sad to lose Crossman's friendship. Henry did not thrive on public controversy, and resented the loss of Crossman's friendship since they had known each other for years.

Rebecca was in favour of the welfare state and the new National Health Service, being alarmed only by the expense, "as staggering as the cost of war." But she disliked much of the post-war Labour policy, such as fighting local Council elections on a party basis. She admitted with regret to Crossman that she was "defecting from the left"; and to Gunther, "God curse the Labour Party, these silly doctrinaires."

Her analysis of the recurrence of anti-Semitism in the *Evening Standard* elicited violent reactions, and a huge personal mail. "Let us look at anti-semitism honestly," she wrote. It was false to pretend it was a result of Fascist propaganda, it was a "strong, natural growth" which appeared wherever Jews and gentiles lived in close proximity. It was certainly "an indictment of the human animal," but it was "only natural" that it should exist. The need was not for the proscription of British fascism, which now had no teeth, but for education and better community relations in the affected areas. As for the Fascists, "Cross the road when you see them coming. Stop your ears against their clatter."

Rebecca, who had lived, loved, and worked with Jewish people all her life, was writing as an insider, but this was not apparent to readers who found her statement of the "naturalness" of anti-Semitism offensive. (She based her theory on the atavistic hatred among Christians for the people who had called for the crucifixion of Jesus Christ.) Elwyn Jones, a member of Parliament who had just been back to Nuremberg to attend the trials of SS officers, and had the horrors of the concentration camps freshly burned into his mind, wrote a furious riposte. Only a couple of years after the defeat of Hitler, it was hard to accept Rebecca's cool view that "These riots have been coldly and deliberately manufactured to persuade the electorate, quite falsely, that it is under a necessity to choose between Fascism and Communism."

Of the two, Rebecca West saw communism as the greater threat to Britain—not because it was more pernicious than fascism, but because it had more resources and an international organization behind it. These articles made her new enemies. "If I'm found 'having committed suicide' somewhere, you'll know what to think," she told Dorothy Thompson.

5

Rebecca made one of the best friends of her life on the *Evening Standard*: the lawyer Charles Curran, then features editor on the paper, a clever, witty, and ugly man ten years younger than herself. Later he stood for Parliament, against Rebecca's advice—"I don't know why you want to get into the House, which seems to me like a brown earthenware soup tureen, filled with greasy oxtail soup"—and became Conservative member of Parliament for Uxbridge.

Their friendship nearly foundered in 1949 on the rock of Curran's moral principles. He was a Roman Catholic, married, but attached to another woman, who was separated from her husband. He had no wish to commit adultery, and his scruples made Rebecca furious. "I thought his attitude so evil. It reminded me of Richard O'Sullivan and his merciless cruelty [in not making physical love] to Lettie over many years." Her own arid situation with Henry no doubt affected her reaction. She told Curran in an excoriating letter that she had been celibate for eighteen years (forgetting, for the occasion, her two brief departures from chastity) and that she had chosen "to forget about sex." She had hated

Curran, she told him, "when you talked again and again about lust. You were repudiating it, but you were so much aware of it that you practically felt it. . . . It sounds insulting and a revocation of what was good, but I don't want to see you. In the night I lay and thought of you as part of the darkness."

Then she wrote again: "What an ass I am! How rude and narrow-minded and bigoted I've been! What does it matter to me what you think about love and lust and trigonometry, and what does it matter to you what I think of them!" Curran appeared at Ibstone with a large box of chocolates, and though Rebecca threw them on the floor ("He knows I hate chocolates"), they did not quarrel again.

Curran helped her with the research for articles she wrote in the *Standard* and *The New Yorker* about the alleged spy William Martin Marshall, which became the chapter "A Better Mouse-Trap" in *A Train of Powder*. Marshall had been employed at the British Embassy in Moscow when Sir David Kelly was ambassador; while Rebecca was working on the case, Lady Kelly, an elegant and clever Belgian, became a friend. In Rebecca's last years Marie-Noële Kelly was one of the few people she was always glad to see: "Don't forget me. When a long time passes without your coming here I feel very bereft."

It was Henry who accompanied Rebecca on her visits to Marshall's parents in London (their domestic interior is described in detail in "A Better Mouse-Trap"), after which, feeling that they had been evasive, she sent a confidential memo to the Director of Public Prosecutions, now her old friend Theo Mathew. It was Curran who tramped with her across the Essex marshes to see the boatman who had fished up the dismembered body of Brian Donald Hume, when she was working on the macabre case that became "Mr Setty and Mr Hume" in *A Train of Powder*. Rebecca never learned to drive a car, and Anne Charles acted as chauffeur on this and similar expeditions, which, however grisly the circumstances, were always undertaken in a holiday spirit. The torso had been found in the Thames estuary, familiar to Rebecca from her Leigh-on-Sea days, and the suspected murderer lived near the Golders Green Underground station, another neighbourhood known to Rebecca since girlhood.

Most of her investigations in England, like her coverage of presidential conventions in the United States, provided copy for both the London *Evening Standard* and *The New Yorker* or American syndicates, and Curran was on occasion paid by *The New Yorker* for his research assistance and legal advice. Rebecca and he did not just work together, they exchanged ideas and opinions—and scandal or, as Rebecca put it at the end of a letter to him, "a few moments of abandonment to the pleasures of defamation."

She made a second new friend in the 1940s, who was to become even more important. Evelyn Hutchinson, like Curran ten years her junior, was the son of the Master of Pembroke College, Cambridge, but spent most of his adult life in the United States as Sterling Professor of Zoology at Yale. He was more than an eminent zoologist, having a connoisseur's knowledge of literature, music, and painting which suffused his scientific writing and his approach to the natural world. One of the points made in Rebecca West's *The Strange Necessity* was the fundamental unity of all experience, and the indivisibility of the aspiration that produces both art and science. Professor Hutchinson's wife, Margaret, read the book and recommended it to her husband, knowing that he would find it sympathetic and important.

After some correspondence, Rebecca spent a weekend with the Hutchinsons outside New Haven at the end of her disturbing 1947 visit to the United States. Pulling new energy out of nowhere, she enchanted them; and she was happy to be with people who were engaging seriously with her writing and her ideas. She wrote, on her return to England: "I can't tell you what you meant to me in America. . . . I will write to you about the Grandfather [*Letter to a Grandfather*] which I like myself. It was a great grief of mine that Virginia Woolf could not understand it. . . . But if you like it then nothing matters."

Evelyn Hutchinson, and by extension his wife, became not only Rebecca's close friend and most regular of correspondents; he became the curator of her literary reputation and her bibliographer. In 1953 he published an appreciation of her work* and in 1957 a *Preliminary List of the Writings of Rebecca West*. Henry Andrews kept him up to date, sending news when she was busy, and cuttings and reviews from British periodicals: Hutchinson called him "the bibliographer's ideal correspondent."

But the primary friendship was between Hutchinson and Rebecca.

---

*See G. E. Hutchinson, "The Dome," *The Itinerant Ivory Tower: Scientific and Literary Essays,* Yale University Press 1953.

It was not a sexual friendship. She wrote, fifteen years after their first meeting, "I love him dearly—and what he has done for me! I have received such generosity from people outside the sexual sphere. Within it, nothing. And the terrible thing is that I do not know if what I have compensates for what I have not had." In a letter written on board the *Queen Mary,* after reporting Wallace's presidential convention ("which was like the opening of a sewer") in 1948, she first shared with the Hutchinsons the "peculiar circumstance which deforms my life." Henry, she told them, was "complete hell to live with"—disorganized, inconsiderate, incompetent. "My life is an unspeakable chaos," and she always dreaded returning to Ibstone. (In fact, on her returns, the home world embraced and absorbed her totally.) Her confidences made it hard for the Hutchinsons to take Henry to their hearts as they had taken Rebecca, but they observed a careful and caring even-handedness.

Hutchinson's view was that Rebecca found Henry so literally eccentric—i.e., off-centre—that divagations from him were necessary if she was to preserve her own precarious equilibrium. After making that first confidence, Rebecca included the Hutchinsons among those friends to whom she poured out the continuing story not only of her intellectual and professional life but of her personal and family problems as well. It was through Hutchinson that Rebecca approached Yale in 1950 about their accepting her letters from Wells and a mass of other confidential letters and papers, on condition that access to the most personal should be prohibited for a stipulated period; the final decision was that the core of the collection should be closed until after the deaths of both Henry Andrews and Anthony West.

After her death Evelyn Hutchinson, who was one of her literary executors, added the letters that had passed between himself and Rebecca over thirty-five years, and those to and from their spouses, to the collection in the Beinecke Library at Yale, whose holdings constitute a major Rebecca West archive. It was a sorrow to Hutchinson, then in his eighties, that Yale felt unable to purchase the other half of the archive—the letters, photographs, personal papers, printed books, manuscripts, drafts, and unpublished works in Rebecca West's possession at the time of her death. These were bought in 1986 by the University of Tulsa.

6

Henry was more fascinated by post-war Germany than Rebecca was; he needed, as Rebecca wrote to Winnie, to "work out his amazing obsession with that disagreeable people." But she accompanied him on two extended visits in 1949 and 1950, out of which she wrote "Greenhouse with Cyclamens," parts II and III—some of the best, and the least read, of her post-war reporting, published in *A Train of Powder.*

Their first trip was taken in company with Dorothy Thompson ("Henry wondered if we could not have a better time if we were all there together"). In the event, Rebecca grew irritated with both her companions: "Dorothy and Henry seem to get deafer and deafer." Henry was much taken up with a German countess, a lady of great charm and, in Rebecca's opinion, Nazi sympathies, whom she referred to in her bulletins to Anne Charles as "the Fine Mind" (which was what Henry said she had).

"Daddy's" sentimental enthusiasm for ladies such as the Fine Mind was an affectionate running joke between Rebecca and Anne Charles. Rebecca was more acerbic in her remarks to Charles Curran. "I do not know why nobody puts Henry down a well, it is so obviously the natural thing to do. He couldn't be more noisily a nuisance than he is. When he plants a beetroot wrong way up he has to talk about it, when he picks a girl-friend it has to be one who would get me into an unpleasant situation." Yet Rebecca acknowledged with gratitude that "my articles would be worthless if it wasn't for Daddy," because of his "astounding knowledge of the Germans." After these trips, she escaped alone to the south of France to recover, and paid "two sad visits" to Lord Beaverbrook in his holiday villa. Henry achieved a journalistic scoop of his own with an interview with Adenauer, which the *Observer* printed on its front page.

The characteristic quality of Rebecca's reporting is best perceived by comparing it with that of Janet Flanner, her contemporary, who was

covering the same ground (for *The New Yorker*) at the same time. Both
wrote about Germany's paradoxical economic recovery, about ruins and
reconstruction, about the contrasting strategies of the four Allied zones
in Berlin, and, most vividly, about the thousands of displaced persons and
expellees from Eastern Europe, who formed a despairing sub-class, miserably housed, often starving. Flanner's brilliant reports were intensely
felt but very spare; she conveyed essential information unobtrusively; she
illustrated general points with particular cases, which stand out because
there are not many of them.

Rebecca West's method was both more novelistic and more abstract.
Her vignettes of the refugee camps are operatic, her eye picking out tragedy and comedy; she piled up her visual images of human squalor and
human dignity, branching out into sweeping generalizations, jokes, and
stories. Her language is rich, her evocations like canvases by Hieronymus
Bosch. The most striking difference between Flanner and West is the
latter's readiness to make judgements about what "we"—the British, or
the Allies—should or should not have done or be doing in Europe, and
her assumption of an absolute moral standard by which all political and
personal behaviour must be judged. She did not try to conceal her reaction to the "repellent" spectacle of the German renaissance as evidenced
by the creamcakes and well-stocked restaurants enjoyed by the entrepre-
neurs of a new laissez-faire economy: Britain was still in the grip of ra-
tioning, with a welfare state and a planned economy still in embryo. If
Rebecca West could have made an alternative career as a thriller-writer,
or as a farmer, she could also, in another age, have made a thunderingly
effective popular preacher.

During her 1949 trip to Germany, Rebecca heard that she had been
made a Companion of the British Empire. She went to Buckingham Palace to receive the honour with a high temperature: "I was so ill that the
King and the Beefeaters and the tapestries and the throne with the scar-
let canopy and the Guards band in the musicians' gallery (playing the
Valse des Fleurs of course) all swam together, and it was lovely." In 1957
she was made a member of the French Légion d'Honneur, and that was
"lovely" too: the ribbon was "pinned on my bosom by the very attractive
Pierre Brisson, editor of *Le Figaro,* in the *Figaro* offices, a view from the
window on all the tops of the chestnut trees in the Champs Elysées, and

a beautiful Aubusson carpet underfoot, and a flow of champagne. God knows how this has come about."

The previous year she had published *The Fountain Overflows*, her best-selling and best-loved novel. In 1959 she was made a Dame of the British Empire. The 1950s, which brought her not only new achievement but also public recognition of that achievement, should have been the best decade of her life. They were not. The 1950s began with self-doubt: "I can't write, I'm inaccurate," she wrote to G. B. Stern: she had made "a bad slip" in an *Evening Standard* article about the atom spy Claus Fuchs.

A diary entry explains how this could have happened. "Trial of Fuchs. Awful bungle by Charles [Curran]. Got there too late to get decent seats. . . . Wrote 3,000 word article in 2 hrs 25! Charles took me out to pub near Hatton Garden where there was marvellous ham."

Rebecca could usually be restored by "marvellous ham" or something equally simple and satisfactory, but "this last year has destroyed my wholeness, I'm frayed." She knew Curran was devoted to her, and told him that "very few people have been fond of me, or rather the people who have don't let themselves be. They have a curious feeling, which I obviously must encourage in some way, that I have got a lot out of life and am arrogant with it and should not be given any more." In one of the later sections of the novel she was then writing (unpublished in her lifetime), the character through whom the author speaks says: "I was impatient because I always feared to be overtaken by the darkness, and was not arrogant but pitiable."

7

Rebecca knew that Anthony was working on his first novel, though he was "a secretive little brute" and told her little about it. Just before her first post-war visit to Germany, in 1949, she discovered more or less by chance that Houghton Mifflin, his American publishers, were intending to announce their new author as the son of H. G. Wells. Everyone close to Anthony, and to Rebecca, and to the Wells family, was perfectly aware of this fact, as was a wider circle of knowing acquaintances. But the general public was not. Rebecca preferred it that way, and was horrified when Anthony disagreed.

Anthony wrote to Henry (to whom the novel was dedicated, "for years of understanding and friendship"), putting his point of view. Nothing would induce him, he wrote, to be ashamed of his father or to accept any suggestion that his parentage was "dishonourable." "If I do not say with pride who my father was my silence says our relationship was disgraceful. I will not do it." He felt that Henry and Rebecca, in asking him to keep silent, were conniving in the suggestion that "my origins are shameful." By this time the British publishers Eyre and Spottiswoode had announced Anthony West's *On a Dark Night,* naming both his parents. *Time* magazine followed suit in its review of the novel (called *The Vintage* in the United States).

Rebecca's reasons for hating this acknowledgement of fact were, first, that she could not honestly say that her relationship with Wells "had been anything but an utter failure and a waste of my youth." She could not subscribe to "the lie that it had been a free and exhilarating relationship." Second, she feared that the curiosity aroused would affect the way she was treated in her professional life, "and put a weapon into the hands of my political and literary enemies." She did not want her private life exposed to gossip and speculation. This instinct for reticence was not abnormal. But Anthony saw her attitude as proving conclusively that she was ashamed of him and of the circumstances of his birth. Seen from his point of view, this was not an unreasonable conclusion.

Rebecca had successfully put her foot down once already in 1947, when the cover-story on her in *Time* had included a paragraph about herself and Wells and the birth of Anthony, in terms which she had accurately foreseen the week he was born; the paragraph referred to "the age of the new freedom and the new woman and the superman." Rebecca saw the proofs and shot off letters and telegrams of furious protest and appeal; between them, John Gunther and Dorothy Thompson persuaded the Luces, owners of *Time,* to have the paragraph deleted. Rebecca saw the Wells story as a potential albatross round her neck. Now she was lumbered with it for ever. But she was impressed nevertheless with her thirty-five-year-old son's first book: "magnificently written and really rich."

The advertisements for the novel had also announced that Anthony West was working on a biography of his father. The Wells family had agreed to this, and had handed over four suitcases of Wells's letters and papers to Anthony. He was on the point of departing for the United States for an unspecified period—a fact which Rebecca learned from Pamela Frankau and mentioned, without realizing its implicatons, to the Wells family, who, not wishing uncatalogued and uninsured papers to leave England, recalled the material. Anthony went to America anyway, and began reviewing for *Time* and *The New Yorker.*

Rebecca's friends understood and loved her better than she realized. Dorothy Thompson commented to Harold Ross that "Rebecca's relations with Anthony have been, in my opinion, very queer and unfortunate from the beginning. Rebecca is a combination of the most unconventional and conventional person in the world." She saw that the conditions of Anthony's childhood must have resulted in "terrific unconscious resentment" and that, like his mother, who was "my very dear friend," he was a neurotic. "But no outsider can be of any use in a matter like this, or penetrate into it at all." And geniuses, added Dorothy, "usually have trouble with their children."

Rebecca told John Gunther that she was glad Anthony was doing so well in America, "and he deserves it." "But I wish to God he would come home on a trip, his children are fretting for him." He did not come home; in May 1952 he and Kitty were divorced, and in December 1953 he married Lily Emmet, still in her teens and a student at Radcliffe. Rebecca went to court with Kitty "to see her get her divorce." Her heart bled, she said, less for Kitty than for the judge, who "had to read a number of letters, of the sort our family occasionally produces. He could not believe his senses."

Rebecca herself was adept at such unbelievable letters; she often wrote them, or composed them inwardly, at night. She suffered from chronic insomnia, and her mind raced in the small hours. During the troubles with Anthony (which continued off and on until the end) she drafted, redrafted, and consigned to the mails thousands upon thousands of words, typed or handwritten—to Anthony himself, to Kitty, to Harold

Ross, John Gunther, Emily Hahn, Emanie Sachs, the Hutchinsons, Charles Curran, Harold Guinzberg of Viking; to Anthony's friends John and Myfanwy Piper and Raymond Mortimer; to her sister, her lawyers, her agents, and many other friends and acquaintances—thousands upon thousands of words, often obsessionally repeated, going over and over Anthony's childhood, Anthony's character, Anthony's distorted view of her, her life with Wells, her life with Henry. . . . The time and energy expended in this massive volume of communication—taking into account that she was also producing a stream of reviews and articles, writing her books, running Ibstone, travelling, lecturing, and leading a busy social life—were prodigious, beyond the normal range.

This spate of letter-writing began when she discovered that Anthony had had temporary access to some surviving early letters between herself and Wells. She wrote in her diary: "I went into a nervous breakdown and spent my time typing and retyping the same letter over and over again. I am intensely distressed that Anthony read those letters and did not end by feeling pity and gratitude for me."

Rebecca used the term "nervous breakdown" loosely. The intense agitation which was channelled into the letters was like an exaggeration of her normal way of working: it was as if a mad gremlin had got into a Rolls-Royce engine. Though she took pride in the fact that she could produce long articles for the *Standard*—on, say, the Queen's coronation— within a very short time, this was not her natural way of working. Every review she wrote, and every chapter of every book, was drafted by hand, redrafted, copied out cleanly with more minor changes, typed, retyped. Her notebooks were full of paragraphs and passages repeated almost word for word. She wrote as if her writing were music, tested over and over again for harmony, for phrasing, for dynamics, with herself as composer, performer, and critic.

This explains how in *The Fountain Overflows* and its sequels she was able to enter so authentically into the mind of a professional pianist. "Doing anything over and over again while enjoying the prestige of a musician would suit me down to the ground." Yet she called herself "a musical barbarian"—not only because she no longer played the piano, and because her sense of pitch was faulty, but also because, most characteristically, she could not imagine how composers managed to "change their personalities when writing for different instruments."

Her untutored perception of the nature of language was in terms of melody. She believed that "sentences were used by man before words and . . . are the foundations of all language." A dog, she wrote, barks and whines in sentences, and "Your cat has no words, but it has considerable feeling for the architecture of the sentence in relation to the problem of expressing climax." The chief difficulty in teaching a child to speak is "to persuade it to abandon the wordless sentence."

It is this belief in the music of the sentence and its primacy over the word which gives Rebecca West's writing at its greatest its incomparable rhythmic fluidity and, at its worst, its imprecise rhetoric. As she wrote, "a great many quite good plays could be performed with rhythmic howls in the place of dialogue and lose nothing by the change." When she was unsure of her ground, Rebecca herself took refuge in rhythmic howls—the equivalent of "vamping till ready" on the piano. (This was what Wells had disliked about some of her writing.)

Readers who knew nothing of her theory of sentences have nevertheless felt their magic. Kay Boyle read and reread *The Judge*: "I read it as a textbook, studying the shape of the sentences." There are in *The Judge*, as in all Rebecca's books, long Proustian sentences which probe uneasy states of mind like a tongue on a sore tooth, exploring not only the states of mind but their physical expression. Here a young girl anxiously watches an unhappy middle-aged woman: "So she was shaken and distressed by the fine face, which looked discontented with thinking as another face might look flushed with drinking, and by the powerful yet inert body which lay in the great armchair limply but uneasily, as if she desired to ask a question but was restrained by a belief that nobody could answer, but for lack of that answer was unable to commit herself to any action."

The architecture of her complex sentences is more graceful when, as often, there is a central caesura, as in this one from her report on the Nuremberg trials, designed to illustrate the fact that the value of an experience—in this case the Allied occupation of Berlin—does not depend on the number of people who are affected by it: "If a man stranded on a desert island should become a saint under the coco-nut palms but is never rescued, it should not be pretended that what happened to him is of no importance; for if that be conceded, then nothing is important, since humanity is stranded on this desert world and will certainly never be rescued." The drama critic Kenneth Tynan wrote that in her serious journalism Rebecca West's "mastery of the long, analytical sentence is unrivalled in the history of ephemeral literature."

The long, bitter, indiscreet sentences that Rebecca unwound in letters in the latter half of her life, and which eased her unbearable tension, represent a disorder of her commitment and creativity; they are a lifetime's artistry running amok. As her diary notes indicate, she was aware of it. She told Emily Hahn on one occasion: "For goodness sake burn this letter. I have an awful feeling that my epistolary sins will find me out."

Her writing for publication was unaffected, though her self-confidence was undermined. She wrote to Lord Beaverbrook asking him to instruct his journalists to treat her gently when she was due to be profiled in the *Daily Express* on the publication of *A Train of Powder* in 1955.

In August of the same year, Anthony brought his wife, Lily, to England to see his children and to meet Rebecca and Henry. Anthony had another novel coming out in the United States; when his mother asked him about it, he said it was "a light book."

8

This "light book," *Heritage,* was a fictionalized account of Anthony's childhood and youth. It is the story of an illegitimate child confused and damaged by his upbringing. His mother is a famous actress, Naomi Savage—a character modelled on Rebecca. Naomi's theatrical mannerisms, her unpredictability, her physicality, her charm, her style, her frightening changes of mood, her unconscious untruthfulness . . . all this, for Anthony, was Rebecca. The boy idolizes her, but cannot rely on her. When Naomi marries the Colonel, she takes on the role of a country lady in a great house and plays it beautifully. Just when the boy has come to trust the Colonel and the promises of security and inherited wealth, his mother tires of her role, abandons the marriage, and returns to the stage.

While the implication that Naomi/Rebecca grows tired of her dull but devoted husband was potentially explosive for Henry's self-esteem, Rebecca never, in all her diatribes against *Heritage,* touched on this aspect. What shattered her was the portrait of a woman who was wantonly irresponsible and even unkind to her son, and the fact that Anthony had made what amounted to a public announcement of his unhappiness as a child. The portrait of Naomi is not, in other ways, unflattering or demeaning; Wells (depicted as Max Town) has all his irresponsibility and egotism laid bare, Odette Keun (Lolotte) cuts a ludicrous figure, and there are sneers at most of the rest of the Wells family, portrayed as dreary and limited. For everyone involved, *Heritage* had the impact of a brick thrown through a window—which was precisely what its author intended. There is an epigraph at the beginning of the novel:

> These are long vendettas,
> a peculiar people, neither forgivers
> nor forgetters. . . .

The long letters flowed once more from Rebecca's typewriter. To Anthony himself:

> I really do not see what else I could have done but leave you at that school. . . . It was evident to me from *Heritage* that you remembered our lives together as extremely cheerless, and blamed me for this. . . . You appear to blame me for the breach with H.G. . . . I am sure I loved you and have always loved you. But I cannot interpret these things as anything but evidence that you hate me and have always hated me. . . . You are a gift to me—but in your book you did everything you could to withdraw that gift.

Kitty West, witnessing Rebecca's misery, reproached her former husband for his maliciousness. He replied: "I found that I wanted to write that book not to pay off old scores or anything of that kind but simply to describe areas of feeling that I know about." He was sad if the result was painful to others.

Most of Rebecca's friends, in receipt of her epistles filled with pain and anger, tried to belittle the harm done or intended. "I'm sorry, John," she replied to Gunther, "but nothing will make me believe that Anthony loves me or did not write in malice." Dorothy Thompson warned her that "a mother cannot hate her own son without doing *herself* the most serious injury," and urged Rebecca to pull herself together. These attempts to cool the situation elicited scorching responses from Rebecca: "Dear Dorothy, you are being rude, and very silly."

Dorothy had reminded her that *Heritage* was a *novel*, something that Rebecca would just not allow for; she actually complained because many incidents in the book were "invented"—as indeed they were, if only because Naomi's career as an actress required a fully worked-out theatre setting and appropriate episodes. The Colonel, except in his "overwhelming goodness and his obtuseness," was not the real Henry, since he was a member of the landed gentry from birth, and the heir to ancestral acres.

Harold Guinzberg of Viking assured her that no one in New York was gossipping. "The book is having a moderate, but not a wild, success. No one has any different view about Rebecca West, person or great writer, than he had a couple of months ago." Nevertheless, he advised her by telegram against making a planned visit to the United States, "assuming you don't want reporters questioning or otherwise stimulate personal publicity which thus far is negligible."

Charles Curran was another who stressed that *Heritage* was a novel, and gave sensible advice: "Don't talk or write about it to anyone, don't let it be supposed that you care a curse about it. . . . No matter how devoted you were, and I'm sure you were, you took on a job that was utterly impossible from the moment that he was born." Rebecca was incapable of not talking about it, not writing about it. Curran touched the heart of the matter in a letter to their mutual friend Emily Hahn: "If I were in her [Rebecca's] place, I wouldn't care a damn. But . . . she has several skins fewer than any other human being, it's a kind of psychological haemophilia, which is one reason why she writes so well, and why she is so vulnerable."

Rebecca thought she knew, quite definitely, that Anthony meant to hurt and punish her, however he presented his case to Kitty and others.

The introduction he wrote to the new edition of *Heritage,* after her death, confirms Rebecca's view:

> The truth of how things were between my mother and myself
> was that from the time that I reached the age of puberty, and
> she came to the point of a final rupture with my father, she
> was minded to do me what hurt she could, and that she re-
> mained set in that determination as long as there was breath
> in her body to sustain her malice.

The outside observer may feel that the boot was on the other foot. Gip and Frank Wells and their wives were, like Rebecca, anxious to prevent the publication of *Heritage* in England, and between them they suc-ceeded. Rebecca was outraged when Beaverbrook summoned her to his presence and asked her to reconsider, since he wanted to serialize the book in the *Express.* Frank Wells wrote her a friendly letter saying that, while he had always liked his half-brother, Anthony, and would always be pleased to see him, "I have never had any illusions about the odder side of his character," and the book was "very wicked."

"I have no love for Anthony and no hate," Rebecca wrote in the aftermath. "I have a passionate concern with him in a no man's land where love and hate do not exist, only vertigo." The vertigo went on and on: "my heart bumps and thumps, and I get up from the desk and walk about rubbing my hands. This is as poor a way of spending my middle sixties as my worst enemy could have devised." As the years passed, An-thony published many well-written autobiographical articles, in both Britain and the United States, always hostile to his mother, which never failed to upset and madden her all over again. "Motherhood is the strang-est thing, it can be like being one's own Trojan horse."

9

Rebecca may have indemnified herself, Anthony, and all artists when she wrote in *Black Lamb and Grey Falcon:* "We must admit that sometimes human beings quite simply lie, and indeed it is necessary that they should, for only so can poets who do not know what poetry is compose their works." Art, she wrote in *The Strange Necessity,* was "one way of collecting information about the universe," and she described in that book, in a discussion of Proust, how lived experience is transformed into fictional truth. Proust's "governing fantasy," she wrote, very nearly coincided with reality. The same was true of her own. Yet it is "very nearly" that which maddens the near and dear of those novelists who use their own families as raw material. They do not see the alchemy of art, they see travesty and betrayal. If Anthony hurt Rebecca with *Heritage* in 1955, she hurt Lettie with *The Fountain Overflows* in 1956.

The original agreement with her publishers for this novel, a fictionalized version of her childhood, had been made ten years earlier, but, as she said in 1952, "I have a feeling that the powers of darkness do not want me to finish it." She intended it as the first of three or four volumes of an ambitious "Saga of the Century," taking the story up to the Second World War and the Holocaust. Her plan was not just to trace the development of her heroine but to give a picture of a changing society and of Europe in flux politically and morally. Possible models were Proust's *A la recherche du temps perdu* and, closer to home, the sequence of novels written by her friend G. B. Stern about several generations of a Jewish family, based on her own.

She was making her fair copy of the second volume the year after *The Fountain Overflows* came out; some months later, there was only "half the linking chapter left to do"; her publishers expected the manuscript at any moment. But she never delivered. Although enough of the contribution of the saga was found among her papers to make two posthumously published novels, *This Real Night* and *Cousin Rosamund,* she never in her lifetime chose to let the manuscripts out of her hands, or to complete the project, though she went on adding to it almost to the end.

The Fountain Overflows has proved the most popular of Rebecca West's novels; it has the universal appeal of all well-realized family stories. Although it is of the greatest autobiographical interest, the weight of Rebecca's intention is carried by two characters who, though they had originals in real life, are wholly designed for her purposes. Cousin Rosamund—lovely, serene, instinctual, not clever—represents pure goodness, which is even more important than the music to which the heroine of the "saga" and her sister devote their lives. Richard Quin, the sisters' younger brother, is the adorable little brother Rebecca never had, the adorable boy that Anthony was or might have been, a golden boy unique in her fiction in that in him "pure goodness" is embodied in an attractive male.

Both Rosamund and Richard Quin are without sin, and doomed to be destroyed by the evil in the world—while the others fight out the battle between good and evil within the microcosm of their flawed selves. "The point is," Rebecca wrote in her synopsis, "that Mary and Rose [versions of Winnie and Rebecca herself] represent all that can be got out of art, all that art can do: which is not everything. There is something else, the work of the spirit, which was done by Rosamund and Richard Quin."

Rebecca covered a lot of paper explaining that the Aubrey family in *The Fountain Overflows,* apart from Mrs. Aubrey, who was her own mother, was not the Fairfield family. It would not be the compelling novel that it is if imagination had not taken over from memory and documentation; in any case, Rebecca was incapable of describing even an encounter in the village shop without invention, and when she later embarked on writing her memoirs, meaning to set down facts, she composed a family romance which soared rapidly into the realms of fiction.

But her novel was at least as strongly based on a mythologized perception of a personal past as *Heritage* was. Unlike Anthony's minor novel, it is a generous book. For literary quality, humour, evocation of place and period, of the intimate agony of family life, and of the break-up of a marriage as seen through a daughter's eyes, the book with which it can best be compared is another family story written in mid-century, *The Man Who Loved Children** by Christina Stead, an author whom Rebecca West admired without qualification. A flamboyant, fallible father is at the centre of Christina Stead's novel, as of Rebecca's; and, like Rebecca's, it discharges resentments.

Disingenuously, or optimistically, Rebecca dedicated *The Fountain Overflows* to "My sister Letitia Fairfield." The detested eldest sister in the book, Cordelia—pretty, smug, disapproving, inartistic—looks and behaves exactly as Rebecca described Lettie in her conversation and in her letters, memoirs, and notebooks; "the picture of my mother and Lettie

---

* Published in 1940 in the United States, 1966 in Britain.

were certainly drawn from life, and your mother contributed to Mary," she told Alison Macleod after Lettie's death.

Having perceived, or invented, her sister Lettie, Rebecca could not leave her alone. Among her unpublished papers examined after her death was a story, "The Short Life of a Saint," in which it is left to the reader to decide whether it is the self-righteous, self-sacrificing elder sister who is the saint, or the misunderstood, pregnant, unmarried one. Many friends presumed that the complacent woman in her story "The Salt of the Earth"* (who is so tactlessly interfering and hurtful towards her less fortunate relations that she is murdered by the husband who loves her) was also a version of Lettie. Rebecca denied this. She may in an odd way have been telling the truth. Every novelist, taking into account characters based on real people as well as wholly imagined ones, must always at some level be writing out of a knowledge—sometimes hidden—of herself or himself.

But poor Lettie recognized Rebecca's version of her in the hateful Cordelia of *The Fountain Overflows*. In reply to a letter which has not survived, Rebecca wrote: "I was so sorry that I upset you and caused you to feel such horrid doubts. Of course I love you dearly and am, as well, very grateful to you for your constant kindness and affection. But I will admit that you do sometimes exasperate me. . . . As for Cordelia. I am quite overcome. I cannot think of anything less like you."

She cited as evidence incidents in the book that had no parallels in Lettie's real life—precisely the sort of evidence that she had disallowed, and taken as further evidence of treachery, in Anthony's *Heritage*. "The only thing you had in common with Cordelia was an affection for the children's awful aunt. . . . I hoped you would like the book and can't help hoping you still will." She brazened it out, and Lettie, who was less Balkan than her little sister, did not nurse resentment.

It might have been cold comfort to tell Lettie that it was Rebecca's ruling fantasies that helped to make her a major writer, though that was true. Within the structure of a traditional family novel, she made poetic sense of the central drama of her childhood—not principally the question of Lettie, but the painful enigma of her father and of her parents' failed marriage. *The Fountain Overflows* bears witness to one of her own stated

* In *The Harsh Voice*.

purposes as an author: "My work expresses an infatuation with human beings. I don't believe that to understand is necessarily to pardon, but I feel that to understand makes one forget that one cannot pardon."

The Fountain Overflows was a commercial success. Macmillan, in England, sold thirty-three thousand copies in the first two months, and it was a Book Society Choice. Viking, in the United States, gave it a first printing of forty thousand copies, and reprinted almost at once. Rebecca West's face was on the cover of the *Saturday Review,* and the book was a Literary Guild selection. It beat the blockbuster *Peyton Place* to first place in the bestseller list of the New York *Herald Tribune* for two weeks in early 1957. It was serialized in the *Ladies' Home Journal* for a fee of $35,000. "I bought Henry a beautiful Daimler coupé, the first new car we have ever had, a tender antelope of a car."

10

One of the ways Rebecca tried to stanch what Curran called her "psychological haemophilia" was through the Roman Catholic Church. She wanted to find "a technique which will enable me to come into contact with God." Drawn though she was to the Orthodox Church by her Serbian sympathies, she felt their rites and traditions were "too remote from me to be a useful technique." A chance conversation with a Polish Franciscan monk in Cahors, while on holiday in France, had been a revelatory experience; she began taking instruction, initially with Fr. Gervase Mathew of Blackfriars in Oxford, in 1950.

Eighteen months later she had thrown in her hand. The reasons she gave were comedic. She could not become a Catholic, she told the Hutchinsons, because of the "constant and degrading contact with priests who are homosexuals sublimating their troubles in intellectual pretensions." Nor did she like literary Catholics. Evelyn Waugh "made drunkenness cute and chic, and then took to religion, simply to have the most expensive carpet of all to be sick on." As for Graham Greene, he "repre-

sents God as behaving in a manner quite incredible unless it is supposed
He has a hangover. So you get perversity and cruelty enthroned. I DON'T
LIKE IT."

She had always accepted the simplest part of the Christian doctrine—"that goodness is adorable and that there is an evil part in man
which hates it, that there was once a poor man born of a poor woman
who was perfectly good and was therefore murdered by evil men, and in
his defeat was victorious." But the crucifixion, a most potent image for
her, was also what held her back. She loathed the doctrine of the Atone-
ment—that our sins are forgiven by God in return for the voluntary sacrifice of Jesus on the cross.

The core of *Black Lamb and Grey Falcon* is about this problem. In
Yugoslavia she saw a black lamb being slaughtered on a bloodstained rock
in a Muslim fertility rite, and was horrified by the senseless killing, the
"beastly retrogression." Yet it was familiar to her: "All our Western
thought is founded on this repulsive pretence that pain is the proper price
of any good thing." St. Paul "tinkered incessantly with the gospel till he
made it appear as if cruelty was the way of salvation," and St. Augustine,
"in his desire to establish cruelty in a part of holiness," had tried to find
a logical basis for "the abominable doctrine of St Paul." In her book on
St. Augustine she had protested against the "eerie talk of buying favours
from the gods by suffering," and written of Christianity as "a threat to
reason." It was the savage irrationality of the crucifixion which defeated
her. "We are continually told to range ourselves with both the crucified
and the crucifiers, with innocence and guilt, with cruel love and kind
hate." She was nauseated by Christians "bleating" about the blood of the
Lamb.

Her own cosmology was a matter of eternal duels—between light
and darkness, good and evil, life and death, female and male. She did not
refer much to right and wrong, a formulation which assumes a more
limited scale of values and an acceptance of human criticism; the opposing forces that raged in her universe and within herself were seen as
grandly impersonal. Yet she had written in 1933 that she had "what
Christians call the will to belief," and saw in "the gaunt figure on the
cross" a metaphor for human aspiration—"the same tension . . . the
same heroic attempt to cover all, to know all, to feel all." Unable to accept

redemption through a bloody bargain between God and man, she remained a heretic: a Manichaean in spirit, seduced by the dualism that has permeated most Western philosophy.

Manichaeism, widespread in the Graeco-Roman Empire from the third century A.D., is based on a belief in two separate cosmic kingdoms: light is goodness, darkness is evil. Each kingdom has its ruler, and they are at war. According to the myth, Satan invaded the kingdom of light and particles of light mingled with the darkness. Matter is the prison of light, and the material world exists so that man may fight to separate the darkness from the light in himself and so be united with God.

"It is a beautiful myth, and how nearly it corresponds to a basic fantasy of the human mind is shown by its tendency to reappear spontaneously in age after age." It had the practical advantage "of presenting the ordinary human being with a hypothesis which explains the extraordinary and unpleasant things which are constantly happening to him," wrote Rebecca in her book on St. Augustine. He was a Manichaean in his youth, and the "recognition of dualism as a source of distress" was imported into Christianity by him. Students of Rebecca West's writing cannot help being struck by how consistently these concepts pervade her own imagery, and her thinking and feeling about morality, politics, art, gender, neurosis, and herself. She seemed to find insufficient comfort in the thought that the world might only exist at all because opposing forces are held in equilibrium and that nothing can exist without a notional opposite. Only the existence of art persuaded her of the possibility of any equilibrium at all, which was why art mattered so much.

Ideas of duality are expressed in her very early writing; in an article written during her time with Wells, she used a formulation that was to be repeated over the years: "We are each of us an amalgam of the will to live and the will to die." It may have been her mother's death, which had been a struggle, that reinforced this thinking; it may have been a ready response to Freud's *Beyond the Pleasure Principle*, published in 1920, in which he set out his theory of the death instinct. Her own dualism was diagnosed by Wells, as was the fact that she seemed too often in thrall to the kingdom of darkness: "It is your nature to darken your world. . . ." In Wells's *Mr Britling Sees It Through* (1916), mild Mr. Britling specifically mentions Manichaeism when thinking of the horrors of war: "Is man stretched quivering upon the table of the eternal vivisector for no end—and without pity?"—an image which foreshadows Rebecca's idea of all humanity stretched in tension on the cross.

It was in that repository of the essential Rebecca West, *Black Lamb and Grey Falcon*, that Rebecca discussed Manichaeism most fully, as "actually an extremely useful conception of life." The trouble was that man neurotically connived with the darkness, embracing gloom and death instead of pleasure and life. The whole of modern history, she wrote, could be deduced from the "popularity" of Manichaeism with its "preference for hate over love and for war over peace." There is a chicken-and-egg problem with her arguments. She blamed Manichaeism as a human construct for causing man's self-destructiveness, while seeming, often, to accept its validity as an *a priori* interpretation of the universe.

Having failed to come to terms with the Roman Catholic Church, Rebecca continued in her formal adherence to the Anglican Church, in which she had been reared, persisting in her hope that the transcendent pleasure given by music and art meant that God was really good and all-powerful and that the universe had "a beneficent explanation" against all the odds. "I feel there is a God," she wrote when she was over eighty, "and that He is defeated and that one should go with Him down into defeat." A month before she died, unhappy and frightened, she told her niece, Alison, what her basic quarrel with God was: He had made her so that she could not possibly refrain from committing sins, and now she was being hideously punished for them.

God for Rebecca West was the ultimate intimate enemy. She pitted herself against Him as if she were a critic and He a recalcitrant artist whose performance did not live up to its reputation. She had "been" God, playing with conkers in the Streatham garden. "Of course what one really wants is to play God," she had written, longing to juggle with the historical record in *Black Lamb and Grey Falcon*. Her acute awareness of the metaphysical world suggests that she had a genuinely religious temperament and that she was, as she wanted to be, "in contact with God," even though she found Him no more satisfactory than any of the other males with whom she had an intimate relationship. But she believed that it was not just agreeable but correct to love the light—which meant pleasure, celebration, peace, laughter, love, "fresh lobster"—and this conviction irradiates her best writing as it irradiated her, and the people who loved her, in the good times.

11

In an article entitled "I Believe . . ." Rebecca demonstrated how closely religion and politics were linked in her mind: "I believe in the Christian conception of man and the French Revolution's interpretation of his political necessities." Her obsession with the threat of communism in the 1950s puzzled and distressed some of her old friends, but it becomes comprehensible in the context of her metaphysical universe. It was not for her a question of party, policies, or personalities, and she could identify with extremists of any colour; in her novel *The Birds Fall Down* she showed in action the emotional closeness between political fanatics, however opposed their beliefs. Evil must be identified, and then it must be combatted. She was at one here with her father's hero, Edmund Burke, who wrote, "All that is necessary for the triumph of evil is that good men do nothing."

Rebecca, who saw many unremarkable events as shocking dislocations, as "evil," had no trouble in reconciling her politics with the mysticism of William Blake, her favourite poet, or in reconciling life-and-death matters with her music-hall humour and home-economics metaphors. Communism had become for her the locus of the darkness that might extinguish the light; as Jung wrote, "Our fearsome gods have only changed their names: they now rhyme with *ism*." Evelyn Hutchinson understood how her crusade also channelled something "welling up from elsewhere"; it was "a displacement of old feelings." She wrote to him: "My own theory is that the international organizations of Nazism and Communism fulfilled the needs of a lot of people who wanted to rebel against the father and the mother and their own country."

Being Rebecca, she translated feeling into action. She read and reviewed everything she could lay her hands on about the accusations of
spying for the Russians made by Whittaker Chambers against Alger Hiss,
succeeding in getting one book, *The Strange Case of Alger Hiss,* by a former British Lord Chancellor, Lord Jowett, withdrawn by its American
publisher, Doubleday, because of "inadvertent serious factual error." This
was the period of the James Bond novels, and Rebecca's activities reflected the prevailing atmosphere of global conspiracy. A letter arrived for
her from Room 005 of the War Office: "I have reason to believe that you
are aware of certain facts relating to the case of Alger Hiss, which I
would very much like to have the opportunity of discussing with you."

She took part in radio and TV discussions about the threat of communist infiltration, and compiled cuttings-books of material about the
growing anti-communist drive in America, and the resulting anti-
American feeling in Europe. She had sent to her the U.S. Senate reports
on subversion in government departments and all the proceedings of the
Committee on Un-American Activities in the House of Representatives.
She claimed to have read 105 volumes of the official records for the series
of articles she wrote under the heading "The Facts Behind the Witch
Hunts" for the *Sunday Times* in the spring of 1954; these articles were
reprinted in *U.S. News & World Report,* and caused a furore.

They were widely taken as an endorsement of Senator Joseph
McCarthy and the methods of his investigative committee. In fact she
had written to Dorothy Thompson, "I see no sense in what McCarthy
does," and deplored his bullying tactics; and, as she said to J. B. Priestley,
"I had from the beginning regarded him [McCarthy] as a stupid and violent demagogue." Her point was that, although the investigations might
be unpleasant, communism was worse. "The articles provoked hostility
as I knew they would. It took as much courage to write them as any action
I have ever performed in my life."

Evelyn Hutchinson wanted her to write to *The New York Times,*
disassociating herself from McCarthy and refuting the accusations that
she defended his activities; but she was more ready to condemn those
who used McCarthyism as a "smear word," as she put it, in an effort to
sabotage every investigation of communist infiltration in the United
States. She received a lot of hate-mail. Francis Biddle wrote "an article
on the spy scandals which included an attack on me" which particularly

upset her "because it was he who first at Nuremberg told me the whole story of infiltration."

Rebecca interpreted the hostility as an expression of fear. "People are terrified of the next war. They want to give in, as the French gave in to the Germans. They want nobody to say a word against Russia." Neutrality to her was impossibly craven, as was the belief that "totalitarianism is not really bad, not black but grey—and the United States a darker shade of grey. It is a horrible state of dishonesty and fear." She compiled a private list of closet communists mainly in British public life which tended to include anyone who had crossed swords with her and which, were it not for her own high seriousness, would be hilarious. It included large numbers of members of Parliament, government officials, and journalists, "one half (about) of producers and executives of Rank and Korda," and the "vast majority" of the BBC. (About some of them, of course, she was dead right.)

Even in the year of the witch-hunt articles, she said in reply to a reader attacking her for her article on Ethel and Julius Rosenberg in *Picture Post:* "I am a Socialist, and have been so for 44 years"—though "I must admit I am prejudiced by the way that the Russians have invariably killed off all the Socialist leaders of every country they have taken over." She ended her life unable to hold any "formal political faith" at all: "I just try to serve the cause of liberty as I can, in the style of Eliza in *Uncle Tom's Cabin,* who leaped from ice-pack to ice-pack as the bloodhounds bayed behind her." What appeared as a fundamental change of direction seemed to her no great change at all; and just as her religious position could be deduced from the Black Lamb, so her political creed was already formulated in her elaboration of the image of the Grey Falcon.

The Grey Falcon is a reference to a Serbian poem about the conquest of the Serbs by the Turks at Kossovo in 1389. Before the battle, Prince Lazar is given by Elijah, disguised as a falcon, the choice between an earthly and a heavenly kingdom; he chooses the latter, and builds a church instead of deploying his armies. The Turks attack and the Serbs are massacred. Rebecca wrote in *Black Lamb and Grey Falcon* that the story showed that "what the pacifist really wants is to be defeated," and related it to the weakness of liberal left-wing philosophy. "They want to be right, not to do right. . . . They want to receive the Eucharist, be beaten by the Turks, and then go to Heaven."

It was possible that "those who are born into the world with a preference for the agreeable over the disagreeable are born also with an impulse towards defeat"; she mourned for those who would not impose their
rightness and so become "Christ and Judas at once." Liberal thinking set
up the principle that "doom was honourable for innocent things"; she and
her left-wing friends had regarded themselves as "far holier than our Tory
opponents because we had exchanged the role of priest for the role of
lamb," and failed in the "chief moral obligation of humanity, which is to
protect the works of love." These arguments made her religious position
even more unorthodox; she clearly thought Prince Lazar was wrong to
choose a heavenly kingdom and lose an earthly one—which was precisely
what the gospel of Christ demanded.

She trusted no one, not even herself, to "cast off this infatuation
with sacrifice." She was writing, in *Black Lamb and Grey Falcon,* about
the moral obligation to combat Nazism. Ten years later it was communism, and Rebecca was even firmer in her certainty that she, and the
West, must not play the seductively irresponsible role of the sacrificial
lamb. During the 1960s she received the papers of the Philadelphia-based
Council Against Communist Aggression; its executive secretary, Arthur
G. McDowell, said she was "the only person I know" who had read the
entire Warren Commission Report (on the assassination of John. F. Kennedy). Admiral H. G. Rickover sent her details of each new U.S. nuclear
submarine as it became deployed.

At one level she suspected that her strenuousness was excessive. In
the farther recesses of her mind there was nothing about herself that she
did not know. In 1959 she wrote a powerful short story, "Parthenope,"*
in which the heroine, the only sane member of an insane family, takes
extreme action to save her sisters from being committed to a lunatic asylum. Her male admirer assures her that there is "nothing wrong" with
her. "Is there not?" Parthenope asks. "There is an extravagance in the
means my sanity took to rescue their madness that makes the one look
uncommonly like the other."

---

* *The New Yorker,* 7 Nov 1959; reprinted in *Rebecca West: A Celebration* (1977).

12

One of the people Rebecca pronounced a communist was the film director Roberto Rossellini. In late 1952 she was hired by David O. Selznick to go to Rome to work with Rossellini on a projected film of Colette's *Duo,* to star his then wife, Ingrid Bergman, and George Sanders. Henry went with her, and they were put up at the Grand Hotel. But from Rebecca's first meeting with Rossellini and Bergman the collaboration was doomed. Rossellini did not seem to want the treatment she had prepared; he did not intend following Colette's story-line, and Rebecca disliked both him and his proposed story, though she worked on it.

She found Rossellini "the most unappetising male on this earth"; he had "thin arms and legs and a paunch, a fish mouth and fish eyes, and black bootlaces of hair streaked over a lard-white scalp." Ingrid Bergman was beautiful but "stupid and oddly gauche and mannerless (half-German by the way, Hamburg on her mother's side, which explains a lot)." Rebecca later wrote a personal letter to Bergman telling her that she would get nowhere in her career so long as she worked with Rossellini. She herself was paid off handsomely, but ended her visit in the Salvador Mundi Hospital with bronchitis and colitis.

In Paris, on the way home, her French agent, Odette Arnaud, gave a party for her, at which she regaled the company with horror stories about Rossellini and Bergman. Janet Flanner, meeting her for the first time, found Rebecca "rather strange, at least to one knowing her only now, and not formerly, when perhaps she was less determined to have only her own view of individuals predominate." Rebecca's reaction to "the New Yorker woman Janet Flanner" was even more of a put-down: she "disconcerted me by being 6 months older than me and looking like a little old lady. I would have put her down as 70–75. Her hair was dyed sky-blue but it didn't help."

Janet Flanner shed an unwittingly ironic light on the manner in

which Mr. and Mrs. Henry Andrews presented their marriage to outsiders. She commented with unwarranted surprise that Rebecca in Paris
shared a bed with "her elderly husband"; she added: "She said he always
demanded a double bed. He leered slightly at me as she said it, pleased
to be considered so sensual, doubtless."

This glimpse of Henry is complemented by an account of him written only three weeks earlier by Bernard Berenson, with whom the An-
drewses had spent Christmas in the midst of the Rossellini debacle.
Berenson wrote in his diary that they seemed to have been everywhere
and known everyone. "He [Henry] particularly speaks faultless German,
excellent French, and gets on in Italian. He seems particularly to have
known every Englishman intimately that I have known but superficially.
He knows his Classics in art as well as literature, French cathedrals for
example, and all that is in them. All that and a businessman, an *homme
d'affaires,* and not the least a professional *érudit* or *homme de lettres.*" He
seemed to Berenson "a Faustian individual."

Rebecca and Henry travelled together a good deal in the 1950s—to
Liechtenstein to visit Paul Gallico, to Venice, to Spain, to Mexico, where
they visited Frieda Lawrence, "full of fire and vitality." They went to Yale,
where Rebecca gave three lectures*—on the interaction of political and
religious ideas in imaginative literature, ending with Proust and Kafka—
and visited the Hutchinsons ("You are the green pastures of my life").
They made frequent brief trips to France, and were particularly happy in
the northern cities of Amiens and Rouen; they took the car, and were
sometimes accompanied by Anne Charles, Lettie, and Winnie's scientist
son, Norman (Bobby) Macleod. Rebecca was fond and proud of her
nephew and was, in the end, to make him the principal beneficiary of her
will.

In 1953 Anne Charles was married from Ibstone, like a daughter of
the house, and was succeeded by Miss Griffie-Williams, "a curious des-
iccated nymph, a beautiful girl that had been dried in the cool oven with
the herbs." She stayed three years; afterwards there were good secretaries
at Ibstone and less good ones, but the idylls of earlier arrangements were
seldom recaptured. Ibstone House was continually improved; they built a
terrace outside the drawing-room, and bought two eighteenth-century

---

* Expanded into *The Court and the Castle* (1958).

lead sphinxes, with the faces of Madame de Pompadour and Madame Dubarry, to stand upon it. The house was often written up and photographed for magazines; it was a grand and gracious place now, well kept, decorated in shades of apricot, peach, and celadon green, filled with good furniture and with pictures stacked several deep on the walls—"a house for the happy marriage of two people who love a home and have discovered the immortal roots of country living," as *Housewife* had it.

They gave big parties, and for the annual regatta at nearby Henley they would hire a launch and give elaborate picnics. Henry was a wine connoisseur: everything was of the best. There were three thousand bottles wedged solid in the cellars at Ibstone. They were entertained in turn—sometimes by the Dashwoods of West Wycombe, and by the Astors at Cliveden, who were their grandest neighbours. (Rebecca still felt that she was not fully accepted by traditional English society.) At Fleur Cowles's London flat, Rebecca sat on a sofa with Helena Rubinstein, "a woman of 86 whose beautiful face is going back to the monkey." Cary Grant came and talked to them, but the guest of honour was Karen Blixen (Isak Dinesen), "very beautiful, like a deer or a bird, but wasted by age and some sort of distress. Not the sort of distress I would have divined from her books."

At Ibstone with Henry, often in the sort of distress one might divine from her books, Rebecca found peace in long walks through the fields and woods with Albert, her dog: "My labrador was my best friend, and no cliché." She felt herself a part of the countryside around Ibstone. The world was a beautiful stage-set, only the play was wrong. "The most beautiful hours of all my life, no love transcended them, was when the snow fell thick on our valley and then froze hard. Day after day my labrador and I walked over the white fields. . . ." Her old friend from the drama academy, Greta Mortimer, had a cottage nearby. One mild February, in the high woods near Watlington, they looked down across the Vale of Oxford, white now not with snow but with thousands of hawthorn trees in flower, and they agreed that the beauty of the moment made up for "all we've been through."

13

Henry, that "Faustian individual," never ceased to seem problematic to Rebecca. He was the kindest and most hospitable of men. To some people he seemed a bore—he was nicknamed "Chinese Torture" by what remained of the Bloomsbury group—but most guests were grateful for his friendliness and attention. He was generous—women friends received lace handkerchiefs by the dozen, chocolates by the kilo, scent by the half-litre.

His liking for young women made him a nuisance. "Daddy" could become "coy in the way WE DO NOT LIKE," as Rebecca put it, in the presence of pretty girls. He "stood too close," said Ruth Lowinsky's daughter Clare. In the village young women learned to move quickly to evade his over-friendliness, and new secretaries had to put their foot down at once if they were not to be embroiled in sentimental dalliance. His accounts reveal that he bought a lot of jewellery in the last fifteen years of his life, and though Rebecca had some beautiful rings and necklaces, not all that he bought was destined for her. Yet his old-fashioned manners, his conventionality, and his obvious regard for Rebecca made it impossible for most friends and relations to guess at this side of his life.

What he did was to transfer some of his superfluous devotion; and Rebecca kept up a brave face in public. She genuinely liked Henry's last attachment, Gerd Larsen, who was ballet mistress at Covent Garden. Henry bought two identical expensive handbags, one for Gerd and one for Rebecca. When the women met, each with her new bag, Rebecca carried off the situation by exclaiming in rich tones of delight: "Oh how *lovely!* We've *both* got one!" But she minded; she told Pamela Frankau once that "the total lack of jealousy signified a mental disorder." Her perpetual cataloguing of Henry's inadequacies was at once a cause of his wandering and, on her part, a hitting back.

It was not his philandering but his eccentricity and vagueness, worsening as the years passed, that made Rebecca tell intimates such as Charles Curran that she sometimes felt like walking out on him. She— busy, successful, famous, capable, impatient—was not an easy wife for someone like Henry, who had no regular occupation and no practical skills. He needed a great deal of affection and reassurance, and could only go at his own pace. Rebecca suggested that he write a book about banking, to occupy his time, but this became yet another unfinished project. "I have of course constantly to correct him. But I don't know how not to do that; I have to correct him because he is deaf, primarily, and also because he is very slow-witted. Not unintelligent, but slow."

But they wrote to one another virtually every day when apart— "Darling Ric," "My dearest Rac." In public they called each other "My dear." They made a good team as kind "parents" to younger people in trouble. In 1957 Ruth Lowinsky, Rebecca's close friend of thirty years, a "fountain of charity and wisdom," died suddenly. Rebecca and Henry took over much of the responsibility for helping Justin, Ruth's young son, find his place in the world. Rebecca's reciprocated affection for Justin—and her distress over Anthony—made her think that "parents and children are the victims of a theory of causality that is bogus. It is nice if you have a good time with your parents or your children"—but that's all that could be said. She and Henry did better with young people who happened not to be their own children, and in these undertakings they were as one. To many of their friends and their friends' children they were fairy godparents. They helped, for example, to pay for the education of Merlin and Christopher Holland, the grandsons of Oscar Wilde. When the marriage of a friend in the village broke down and she came to Henry and Rebecca at Ibstone, they sat each holding one of her hands and told her, "This is your home." There are many similar stories of their generosity.

Ibstone House itself was a source of shared pride—and of dissension. "I cannot get a full swathe of work done, however I try. But Henry loves the chores of the day, which however fall very heavily on me. But still I love Henry, which is something and something again." In 1955 they celebrated their silver wedding with a dinner party for forty; after dinner the soprano Marion Studholme sang Rebecca's favourite aria—Susanna's "small white star of a song," "*Deh' vieni non tardar,*" from *The Marriage of Figaro*. The celebration was a vote of confidence in her marriage—which was not so very different from many marriages.

In 1959 Rebecca West went to Buckingham Palace to receive the crowning honour of her professional life. Mrs. Henry Andrews emerged as Dame Cicely Andrews, better known to the world as Dame Rebecca West. In reply to one of the many letters of congratulation, she said that she was surprised to be, for once, in the position of "teacher's pet"; she had accepted the honour because "it seems to be a pleasant, picturesque thing in itself" and because it should do something for the prestige of women journalists, "who are a downtrodden class."

When, shortly after she became a Dame, she chose her favourite records for Roy Plomley's radio programme "Desert Island Discs," she chose as her one luxury to take with her to the imaginary island a stone head from the Far East that had been given to her by her husband, because it was "wise and calm—like my husband." She was being neither ironic nor hypocritical. The ideal Rebecca clung to the ideal Henry, however much the selves that they were in everyday life fell short of those ideals. They could achieve serenity together even in the everyday, as Rebecca's diary attests: "Had supper by TV with Henry—very happy, as we are sometimes."

PART SIX

Dame Rebecca

1

In the spring of 1960 Dame Rebecca went to South Africa on her own for three months to write a series of articles for the *Sunday Times*. She was pleased to go, since life at Ibstone had been particularly chaotic; the current secretary, for whom Henry had a soft spot, turned out to be in need of psychiatric treatment. "This is a marvellous, marvellous rest," Rebecca wrote to Charles Curran from Johannesburg—which was "pure Chislehurst" in its suburban comforts.

No one else could have considered her tour a "rest." After a month in Johannesburg she went on to Cape Town, Durban, Bloemfontein and Basutoland, visiting mines, factories, housing-projects, kraals, schools, and talking to whites and Africans of every shade of opinion. She regarded Apartheid "with contempt as pure idiocy and provocative of endless suffering," as she wrote to Henry, but met many whites who seemed to be doing what they could to improve the Africans' conditions of life. These new friends were nearly all from the Jewish community: "You cannot believe how superior the Jewish population is to all others out there."

It was the spring of the Sharpeville massacre, and Rebecca by chance was at the Johannesburg Agricultural Show on 9 April when an attempt was made on the life of Prime Minister Hendrik Verwoerd, the architect of Apartheid. Rebecca's report of the incident was on the front page of the *Sunday Times*, above the second of her "major series" of articles, "In the Cauldron of Africa," which now seemed to be a personal triumph for her.

Her third article, "A Return to Barbarism," was a report on the trial for treason of a number of people most of whom were members of the African National Congress (ANC). She accused one of the judges, Mr. Justice Kennedy, of putting questions to an African witness "in a form which in England is more often heard from the floor of the court than from the bench"; she paraphrased two of his alleged questions which, in her view, led the defendant towards an acknowledgement that to argue for adult franchise at all was in itself treasonable and an incitement to violence.

Mr. Justice Kennedy wrote to protest that he had asked no such questions; he would take legal action unless the *Sunday Times* printed a correction and an apology. The transcript of the trial was sent for; it did not bear Rebecca out. The case was settled out of court for £3,500 and an apology, to Rebecca's disgust, because she thought the *Sunday Times* should have stood by her. She let it be known that she doubted the "intactness" of the official record. But in a private notebook she wrote that she had been outside the courtroom at the crucial moment, and that the questions were reported to her by other people.

Lettie had advised her to concede gracefully, and was therefore ostracized by Rebecca for a year; Rebecca played the part of the bored younger sister at the family party for Lettie's eightieth birthday in 1965. But she did send some photographs of the distinguished Dr. Letitia Fairfield to the National Portrait Gallery—and sent her a cheque to buy a wig, "which I assure you you will find most useful—but mind you have it cleaned regularly."

Life magazine cancelled a syndication arrangement for her African articles after the Kennedy row; but Rebecca made a success on Edward R. Murrow's "Small World" television programme, one fan writing to applaud her "smashing indictment of Apartheid" and wishing that "public questions could always be discussed with such clarity, understanding and distinction." Her African mission had exhilarated her. "How fortunate we are," she wrote to Emanie Sachs (now Emanie Arling Philips) "to have so many shots in our locker, and to be able to fire them off!" Travelling through South Africa, often in extreme discomfort, she had "all the joy I would have felt at such an experience in my early youth." She was nearly seventy.

She wrote no more for the *Sunday Times*—and was signed up at once to review books for the *Sunday Telegraph*. It was home life that exhausted her. "If I were a male author," she wrote to Emily Hahn, "and one of my reputation (except that like you I'd have a far higher reputation if I were male) everybody would be damned sorry for me if I had a wife who acted as Henry does; and I have the most passionate desire just TO GO AWAY." Yet Ibstone was still a precious place—with her borders of white petunias by moonlight, and the view of "stubble-fields shining silver-gold under the sunlight with a frame of dark-green trees round every field."

2

She did go away as she longed to, but generally with Henry. In January 1962 they were at Sandy Lane Hotel in Barbados. T. S. Eliot and his young second wife, Valerie, were there too, and Rebecca and Henry, from their own room, watched the Eliots playing patience on their verandah. "He looks incredibly old for 73, she inappropriately looks like Nell Gwynne (really very beautiful)." On a cool wet night they invited the Eliots to dine at the Colony Club, which was open on three sides: "Eliot sat at the table in his raincoat, suggesting a poem of another style than his, beginning 'I am the raincoat and the rain.'" He was already ill.

They returned home via New York, where Rebecca lectured at Columbia, and met Diana Trilling for the first time; they also saw Anthony and Lily. Late in 1962, after attending the first Writers' Conference ("a shambles") at the Edinburgh Festival, Rebecca went to the Bircher Benner Clinic in Zurich, whose claims rested on muesli and holistic medicine, to see if her gall-bladder pain could be eased. Staying with Noel Coward at Les Avants afterwards, she was in pain again. Coward had arranged to take treatments from the eighty-year-old Dr. Paul Niehaus—the famous rejuvenating "monkey-gland" treatment, in fact injections of cells from a sheep embryo. Rebecca went into the clinic too, and stayed five days. "Keep this under your hat," she begged Emanie.

The clinic, she said, was like a set for *The Magic Flute*, and Dr. Niehaus was "the son of the illegitimate daughter of the Crown Prince Frederick," Queen Victoria's son-in-law. The patients lay face downwards on their beds while Dr. Niehaus flitted from room to room "giving the injections himself with incredible rapidity. I hope I will not bring blushes to your cheeks," she told the Hutchinsons, "if I say I was reminded of the loves of the birds." Back at Ibstone, "I feel fresh. I am able to write more easily and better than for years (I think) in spite of all my interruptions, I am not depressed by my depression, if you know what I mean."

But a year later her gall bladder had to be removed, and after the operation she had a recurrence of her hallucinatory disturbances. She thought she was lying in the Church of the Madonna dell'Orto in Venice, where Tintoretto is buried. "The walls were covered with frescoes by Tintoretto, representing a confusion of armies streaming over a huge cornfield dotted with sheaves." (She thought she was dying: Tintoretto's nightmarish *The Last Judgement* is among the paintings by him in Madonna dell'Orto.) Behind the doctors round her bed she saw that the church was full of sixteenth-century Venetians, all looking at—*whom?* "I paused because my three names clashed in my head, Cicely Fairfield, Cicely Andrews, Rebecca West, I could not choose between them."

She also thought that Henry was poisoning her with the soup that he had sent in daily from the Empress Restaurant in Berkeley Street in his anxiety to make her comfortable. But her convalescence was sweetened by a week at the Ritz ("incredible bedlinen") and by the presence at Ibstone of "Timmy" Richardson, a kind and cheerful secretary whom Rebecca loved but who was not appreciated by Henry. Rebecca's Christmas letter to Alison Macleod summed up the situation at the end of 1964 in comic-opera terms:

> Henry hates my secretary.
> My secretary hates Henry, his secretary, and the farmer's wife, who is a daily.
> Henry's secretary hates me, my secretary, the farmer's wife, and Miss Gibbs, the alternate daily, but loves the gardeners and the farmer.
> Miss Gibbs hates Henry's secretary, the farmer's wife, the farmer, and the gardeners, but loves my secretary.
> The farmer's wife hates us all, but flatters us in a rich Irish brogue so bogus it ought to be called an Irish bogue.
> The gardeners hate us all but don't flatter us in any accent. . . . Henry's doctor says I ought to sack my secretary but my Swiss couple will leave if she does and the dog adores her.
> Oh Merry Merry MERRY Christmas.

Yet that Christmas she was able to go with Leo Lerman of American *Vogue* to the first night of Marlene Dietrich's show in London, and adored it: "She is Helen of Troy." Henry's doctor diagnosed that he had suffered a slight stroke, and that his increasing forgetfulness and erratic behaviour were due to arteriosclerosis. He had not learned to drive a car until he was in his forties, and had driven their old Rolls at twenty miles an hour. As he grew older, deafer, and blinder, he drove faster and faster. In the goodness of his heart he was always keen to drive Rebecca to her engagements. Often he got lost, and she was late. There were collisions, the odd prosecution.

Rebecca longed for the magistrates to forbid him to drive, but no one seemed prepared to deprive this courteous elderly gentleman of his license. Henry remained not only likeable but impressive: also, he was the husband of Dame Rebecca West. He was a member of the international Mont Pélerin group of economists, historians, philosophers, and journalists, presided over by Friedrich von Hayek; Rebecca marvelled that "he appears before bankers and industrialists as if he had some great firm behind him, whereas he has nothing but his own name—and he left the City before the Second World War."

3

Throughout the early 1960s Rebecca was working on the last novel that was to be published in her lifetime. Back in 1943 she had begun a novel about treachery, "which seems to me more and more the root of all our human misery." At the end of the war she told G. B. Stern that "everything is falling into the pattern of my new novel, it is really frightening"—and real-life treason took over from fiction for her, for many years. (Even in the 1960s she was still on the trail, reporting the Vassall Tribunal and the Stephen Ward affair.) She had her treason novel all planned out in the 1940s, plus a sequel. But the sequel took on a life of its own—or, rather, of her own—and turned finally into *The Fountain*

Overflows. When she had difficulties with the planned sequels of *The Fountain Overflows* she turned back, twenty years on, to her abandoned novel about treachery: an example of how much of a writer's work can grow from the same tangled roots.

What had sparked off her treachery novel, *The Birds Fall Down*, was a book of memoirs by a tsarist Russian, tutor and adviser to Nicholas II, which she had picked up casually to read in bed. Her version of him became an old tsarist count in exile in Paris at the turn of the century; the pre-revolutionary web of international intrigue, betrayal, and terrorism is seen through the eyes of his half-English granddaughter. In the course of conversations and confrontations, the novel reveals black treachery not only in political life but in the mean secrets of private life. It is a novel of ideas and a mystery story, in which the greatest villain is the "intimate enemy," and no one, not even the innocent heroine, can retain integrity and survive.

The Birds Fall Down can be read as a fictional companion-piece to *The Meaning of Treason*, but it is not a work of propaganda; its whole force is towards demonstrating the inevitability of the Russian Revolution of 1917. Rebecca had never been in Russia, though she had met Russians in exile in France during the 1920s. When drafting the novel, she consulted Moura Budberg, Wells's Russian mistress and most probably a double agent herself, about names for her characters: "Gorin" and "Kamensky" were both suggested by Moura. The double agent in the novel was based on the real-life Ezno Azeff, whom Rebecca had first heard about from Ford Madox Ford.

The novel most comparable with *The Birds Fall Down* in terms of international scope and grasp of period is Sybille Bedford's *A Legacy* (1956), and Mrs. Bedford wrote praisingly to Rebecca that her novel "has everything: characters, living people, the sense of history and movement of history, time, action, Fate." Paul Scott, author of the Raj Quartet, wrote to Rebecca acknowledging "unconscious mimicry," and saying that *The Birds Fall Down* gave him courage to continue with his own ambitious project, which was "all about history and politics, as well as people"; he had her example in mind when facing the problem of dealing with prolonged conversations in trains.

The train-conversations in Rebecca's novel are very long indeed; this is a story that unfolds at its own inexorable pace. But it is also dramatically visual, and in 1978 was adapted as a BBC television serial with Felicity Deane playing the young girl. Rebecca took the keenest interest in the production, and accompanied cast and crew to Paris, enjoying giving advice to the director on ambiguous points of detail: "There was I, at 85, sitting on a cane-bottomed chair in the Avenue Kléber, at half-past twelve at night, being asked to produce a working model of an obscene gesture."

She had worked on the novel at the desk in her bedroom late into the night, with Henry sleeping in the adjoining room. Gwenda David, Viking's representative in London, was of service to her in applying the brakes to her runaway manuscript; when Rebecca wrote in old age that she had been fortunate in her women friends, she was thinking particularly of Gwenda David. When *The Birds Fall Down* was finished, in March 1966, she feared it was "the most lugubrious novel ever written, bar none." But it was the *Yorkshire Post* Book of the Year, and a Book-of-the-Month selection in America. She was awarded the Benson Medal of the Royal Society of Literature, and made an Hon. D. Litt. of New York University. She told Charles Curran at the end of the year in which it was published, "Up till now I have made £53,000 out of *The Birds*."

She relaxed by practising her arithmetic. "I bought a little book at Smith's in Marlow and I'm working through the exercises. I am inspired to confidence by the fact I get nearly all the answers right. There's life in the old dog yet." Max Lerner, in the New York *Post,* wrote, "I find her, in her seventies, racier in her talk, more peppery in her polemics and less stodgy in her thinking than most of the bright young men I know."

Throughout the 1960s some of Rebecca's excess energy was poured into her feud with Anthony. Periods of reconciliation and regret alternated with periods of recrimination, on both sides. Rebecca was committed to Kitty's children; she ended her manuscript "Synopsis of Later Memoirs" with the simple sentence "I love my grandson Em [Edmund] very much." She refused to recognize Lily's children and, with misguided loyalty, poured out her rejection of them in letters to Kitty. She wrote terrible things about Lily. For most of this time Anthony's behaviour, so far as his letters to his mother are concerned, could not be faulted. Not until after Rebecca's death did he and Lily see her letters to Kitty—and to Lily West, Dame Rebecca was, in retrospect, a malevolent monster.

How could she behave so unwisely, or so badly? How could she rec-

oncile her belief in the sacredness of the "works of love" and, in Mozar-
tian terms, her love for the role of Susanna, with her strenuous
impersonation of the Queen of the Night? "I do things which are wrong
because I think they are right—and of course I fool myself into thinking
they are right—but if I couldn't fool myself I don't think I would do
them." In the mid-1960s she decided to make a new will. Doubled-edged
discussions with Anthony by mail about how she should dispose of her
assets became mixed up with strongly worded advice about how Caroline
and Edmund should pursue their careers. Rebecca felt that every decision, and every detail of Anthony's financial position, should be discussed
and decided with her. Her attitude provoked the first tough letter from
fifty-four-year-old Anthony for some time:

> It's hard for any of us to understand why you cannot believe
> that we are doing anything in a reasonable and orderly fashion
> for ourselves. . . . You are much loved by all of us, but you do
> not make loving you an easy task when you try to force the
> facts of our lives into the pattern of your ideas of what our lives
> should be. . . . I cannot live someone else's dreams or submit
> to being rewritten.

But when Rebecca read what Anthony wrote about her, both in
factual and fictional form, and even when he was writing about other
women (such as Madame de Staël or George Sand), she felt that it was
she who was being rewritten, she who was being made the subject of
someone else's dreams, and of his nightmares. She was "copy" for Anthony as he was not for her. There was no way she could have redeemed
herself in his eyes, as there was no way he could have redeemed himself
in hers. They had mythologized each other, as Rebecca had mythologized
Aunt Sophie Blew-Jones. Even their intermittent rapprochements, ago-
nizing in their tenderness and remorse, seemed to serve chiefly as spring-
boards for even deeper plunges into outrage and recrimination. It is hard
not to conclude that, in spite of the real unhappiness involved, the ven-
detta was in a perverse and obscure way transformed into a source of
psychological justification, even a source of energy, by both of them.

4

At Ibstone, Henry and Rebecca engaged a new farm manager. Bob Langford, finding the accounts in a mess, discovered the extent to which Henry had been cheated by employees and stock-dealers over the years. Within six months he had turned the operation round to break even. The house was shabbier now, but still beautiful. Henry and Rebecca went on buying, not only paintings but silver, ceramics, and jade. The yard still filled with Rollses and Bentleys when they gave parties. Rebecca continued to improve the garden; Henry, hearing that she wanted more daffodil bulbs, ordered her a ton and a half. Albert the Labrador died, and was replaced by Annie, a West Highland terrier, a gift from Justin Lowinsky.

For Christmas 1967 they went up to Rebecca's nephew, Bobby Macleod, and his wife, Marion, in Edinburgh. While they were away, the house was burgled; the loss that hurt most was Henry's collection of jade. Nothing was recovered. The robbery was the beginning of the end of Ibstone. In the autumn of 1968 Henry was taken into Wycombe General Hospital, where he died on 3 November. The death certificate gave the cause of death as "1) Carcinoma of colon 2) Uraemia and renal calculus." He was seventy-four. They had been married thirty-eight years.

Rebecca gave him a great send-off. The twelfth-century church at the nearby village of Fingest (Ibstone has no church of its own) was full. "We had a quite gorgeous funeral for Henry—somehow the Vicar let me rewrite the Burial Service and I patched together the Anglican and the Orthodox Serb Church and had priests of both churches and it was quite beautiful." Her grandson Edmund and his wife came over from America. Rebecca wore a black veil, and there were trumpeters; Douglas Woodruff, who had been their best man, wrote an obituary for the *Times* headed "Banker and Patron."

Bob Langford helped Rebecca sort out Henry's clothes. There were thirty almost identical dark suits from Savile Row, each with money in the waistcoat pocket, ready for tipping. £187 was extracted from the waistcoats. As an old man in the village said, "He was a comical old bugger, but he was a gentleman." That would have pleased Rebecca, who had been afraid he was not. She was shaky in the days after the funeral, huddled over an electric fire with a shawl round her shoulders, Annie the terrier at her feet.

Before Henry's illness, they had been planning to sell Ibstone; now she got rid of it at once, except for two cottages on the estate, which she gave to Alison Macleod. She also sold the larger and more important furniture, and over a thousand books. She offered Anthony some first editions, an eighteenth-century embroidery that had hung over the drawing-room mantelpiece, a carpet that she believed to be Aubusson, and some Piranesi prints that Wells had given her.

Henry left Anthony no money. Wells had left him little, on the understanding that he would be Henry's principal legatee—but the quarrels of the intervening years had put a stop to that. Yet Anthony wrote an understanding letter to his mother about Henry: "Although the demons in my unconscious always made me very ambivalent towards him, I do know how very nice his nice side was, and I wouldn't have been so powerfully jealous of him if I hadn't known how much there was in him to love and like. My jealousy made me think of him as all dog and an intruding enemy who took you away, but I know a whole lot of him was a pussinger and a nice one." Rebecca replied to "My dear pussinger" with an equal affectionate acceptance. The truce did not hold. Anthony was soon exploring his childhood in print again, this time describing his rejecting grandmother. "She loved him so," Rebecca mourned in her diary. "He liked a pineapple upside-down pudding she made. THIS IS AWFUL." It was this betrayal that made her instruct her solicitor to remake her will yet again, "omitting any benefit to Anthony."

5

Rebecca wrote Emanie Arling Philips a long letter describing not only her grief and emptiness after Henry's death but also her regret that she had so often been impatient with a man who was frail both physically and psychologically. Henry had been difficult, "yet I do feel that all the time I was living with a man who was superior to almost anybody else I have known, far, far superior to H.G. (who, I think, loved me more, but I don't know.)" Going through Henry's private papers made her sad for him. "He so wanted to be someone, he had such gifts. It all went to nothing."

She was unhappy on her own account too, as she discovered evidence of the extent and nature of his philandering. She had to rethink her whole marriage. She felt it had been partly her own fault, for not giving him more time and attention; but self-reproach was soon extinguished by bitterness. "I find to my astonishment that an unhappy marriage goes on being unhappy when it is over." From most friends, and from her family, she concealed her misery. "I pretend to have been happily married to Henry, whereas I was wretched with him, and have never known anything as near happiness as the relief I felt when he died." The single item among his papers that hurt her most was a photograph of Irene Ravensdale, Lord Curzon's daughter, taken in the mid-1930s outside Amiens Cathedral. Amiens had been "a special place" for Henry and Rebecca: "When we first became lovers I lay in his arms in a hotel room and we listened to the nightingales. . . . I cannot bear this." There had been many other women as well, some of them family friends, some of them from humbler walks of life. Charles Curran made a valiant attempt to comfort her. Rebecca replied with a statement of bleak feminist realism:

> What you don't understand is that I *understand* the male attitude but don't *like* it. I don't think it's pleasant for a husband

whose wife is successful to feel an irresistible compulsion to go off with a tart. Wouldn't it be repulsive if Lady Churchill's reaction to her husband's glory had been to go home to sleep with a waiter? Isn't the male attitude mean, silly and dirty? What I feel is the catch about this vale of tears is that there is something so desperately unloveable, even unlikeable, about the male sex.

Charles was one of the few creditable specimens she had met, she told him; most men she had known had been silly "as women rarely are."

> But there is the most powerful pressure on woman to get tied up with them. The lot of a lone woman in society is uncomfortable. Henry had in his good days a sweetness which was very unusual, and I loved him. . . .
>
> But why did I have to marry at all? I would have been better off if I had not married him or anybody else. Men are not good companions or allies on a long haul. They always bring trouble. There is no real reason why any woman who can keep herself should marry.

The "real reason" why Rebecca had married was not a reason at all, but a need and a hope. She loved love, and she had longed for the emotional security she felt she had lacked in her childhood and in her years with Wells. Though she had believed men to be "poor stuff" from her girlhood, a house without a man in it was to her incomplete, and her sense of herself depended on her attractiveness: even as an ill old woman, she responded to a male presence in her drawing-room with an upsurge of animation. A few months before she died she was thinking about the difficult years after she left Wells, and decided that no man then had treated her as a normal human being. "And the only way any male could have been a useful friend to me would have been to marry me, which nobody did for seven years, which was ridiculous. I would have been a good wife to almost any man, to live decently in a house with children."

It was not until Henry had been gone for six years that Rebecca resolved her feelings about her marriage, writing in her diary: "It is a curious thing that in the last week or so I have so deeply realized that I love Henry. I know all about him, but what about that—I love him, and it is a great comfort." It was to Emanie that she had poured out most of her anger, and when her letters were returned after Emanie's death, she placed a signed statement with them in her files, recording her gratitude for Henry's "kindness and sweetness and sympathy" in the early years of their marriage and stressing that she loved him dearly even though "he was a very inconvenient husband for a woman writer."

Her self-questioning about the usefulness of marriage for women emerged, humourously, in her journalism. She began a review of Eva Figes's *Patriarchal Attitudes* by saying, "There is, of course, no reason for the existence of the male sex except that one sometimes needs help with moving the piano." Half a century earlier she herself had planned to write a book about the balance of power between men and women; she never wrote it, but her thoughts on the subject are loud in everything she did write. An anthology could be compiled from *Black Lamb and Grey Falcon* alone of her meditations about relations between the sexes.

She wrote in that book that man was not sure about the existence of his own soul, and must therefore "be reassured, hour by hour, day by day," by the assumed inferiority of women. If they draw strength from this belief, it is better to let them have it; for if women use "full capacities of mind and body," his confidence is eroded. "There is no known remedy for this disharmony," and there may never be a society where men are men and women are women without women's having to conceal their true selves. If they do not do so, some men become womanish and turn away towards their own sex.

Although Rebecca was devoted to many homosexuals as individuals and as couples, homosexuality in men distressed her because it represented the failure of the sexes to come to any understanding. Yet she always knew how imperfectly she herself fitted into any traditional stereotype of femininity, and how unreal gender distinctions could be. She knew in old age that her behaviour was still sometimes inappropriate by conventional standards. "Why do I spoil things by noisiness and impulsiveness?" she wrote in her diary after a banquet where she sat between the influential lawyer Lord Goodman and Lord Hill of the BBC and was "naughty"—i.e., combative and assertive. "I wish I was aware of the impression I made and could control it."

She had extravagantly admired Virginia Woolf's *Orlando,* a fantasy about one person playing a multiplicity of gender roles; and in a 1974 review of Jan Morris's *Conundrum,* the autobiography of a successful transsexual, she wrote cheerfully: "I would have liked to become a man at the age of just under fifty, and would have felt myself simply doing something amusing out of the pages of Ovid's *Metamorphoses.*" In a private notebook she added that most women do "become" men as they get older, only the clever ones conceal it. She expressed this in print in more general terms a year before she died: human beings carry "too much cargo," and "we cannot handle our contradictions, our distressing multiplicity of characteristics"—and so we conceal them. Rebecca West would have liked to be loved as a woman by a man who knew her "distressing multiplicity" and remained unshaken. She never resolved the general problem of men and women, and in the first page of her memoirs (unpublished in her lifetime) wrote a sad sentence: "I was never able to lead the life of a writer because of these two over-riding factors, my sexual life, or rather death, and my politics."

6

When Henry died Rebecca was nearly seventy-six, and felt that she would soon follow him: "I am sitting on my suitcase at a railway station." She did not sit on it for long. She went to Monte Carlo with Ruth Lowinsky's daughter Clare; she went to Mexico, which she had first visited with Henry. Mexico fascinated her, and she wrote thousands of words about it, but never published them. She went to Dayton, Ohio, to see a favourite cousin of Henry's; she went to see her successful cousin David Ogilvy (of the advertising firm Ogilvy and Mather) in France; she went to Beirut, to see Merlin Holland, who was working there.

With Lettie, she went for the first and last time to Ireland, her father's homeland, where she was guest of honour at the PEN International Congress in 1971. She was disappointed by Dublin but not by Kerry, her father's county, "just the country I have always longed for."

At home in her comfortable London flat, 48 Kingston House North, she appreciated the tranquillity. "I sit and eat yoghurt in the evening and look down on the marvellous gardens next door and feel rested and happy." She took modern London in her stride, enjoying the plays of Pinter and Alan Ayckbourne, and finding the nude musical *Hair* "a very poor version of the kind of thing one saw in Berlin nightclubs just before the Weimar Republic collapsed." As for the ubiquity of four-letter words, all she questioned was whether their allegedly liberating influence could affect world peace: "Millions of people were saying *fuck* when America went into Vietnam; and that the number may have slightly increased since then seems no reason for hoping that America will get out of Vietnam."

She gave herself great birthday treats in the early 1970s—sometimes two, a luncheon party at the Empress followed by a dinner party at home. She gave parties on the Private View day of the Royal Academy's summer exhibition, and her eightieth birthday was celebrated in multiple ways, culminating in a dinner given for her at the Garrick Club. The Booker Prize was inaugurated in 1969, and Dame Rebecca was one of the judges for the first two years.

The reviews she wrote for the *Sunday Telegraph* in her early eighties were among the liveliest of her whole life. She did not write like an old person; she never, as her last literary editor, Nicholas Bagnall, observed, lost her "unmistakeable pounce"; her style was so much her own from first to last that "if you were shown something of hers which you hadn't read before, you wouldn't be able to date it." She reviewed a lot of modern literary biography, and since she had known practically everyone she was able to settle a few old scores and pay tribute where it was due; she was prodigal with anecdotes and reminiscence, never pompous, never tentative.

She was able, in these late review articles, to consolidate her opinions of the literary worth of her dead contemporaries. She praised, for example, the originality and historical importance of the early novels (*Main Street* and *Babbitt*) of her old admirer Sinclair Lewis, while stressing the mess he made of his later life and writing career. She was adamant that Arnold Bennett's *The Old Wives' Tale* was one of the best English novels ever written, while revealing her dislike of Bennett as a man. Michael Arlen's writing was "a mixture of the genuine article and advertising copy"—just as it was only by chance, she had written long before, that Jean Giraudoux "became a writer instead of a designer of smart luggage."

The inventiveness of her imagery was undimmed. The poet W. B. Yeats, whom she had met at the Lynds' in her youth, was "an old fraud"; his unattainable mistress, Maud Gonne, was a great lit-up bus "crashing through the lights to give aid to Cathleen ni Houlihan [Ireland]" while Yeats himself was just "someone waiting at a bus stop in a drizzle as the pitiless vehicle went by, golden and glowing, through the dampness of the night."

She thought that it was the "brutalization" of modern fiction that had led to the popularity of biography, but already in the 1960s was appalled by both the amount and the quality of most biographical writing. "Can it be that even now, when the number of people reading and writing biographies at any given moment must exceed the number of people suffering from the common cold, it is not yet realized that a biography is not simply the life of any human being? One can write *The Diary of a Nobody* and achieve a classic, but 'The Life of a Nobody' is nothing." She condemned the "impudence" of the "psychoanalytic takeover bid" for biography. "As in the case of divine revelation, and as also in the case of tea-leaf reading, there is no concern here with sheer brute evidence."

Rebecca West had enormously strong literary likes and dislikes. From first to last she had loathed Tolstoy, both the man and his books. "I will declare with my last breath," she wrote in 1923, "that *War and Peace* is a stodgy pudding of events mixed by a loveless zestless boring egotist who wanted to write a big big book." Six years before that, she had told Sylvia Lynd that she had read *War and Peace* twice "and found nothing but stuffed Tolstoys, and such lots and lots of them." About *Resurrection* "I cannot speak but only yawn," while *Anna Karenina* seemed written "simply to convince Tolstoy that there was nothing in this expensive and troublesome business of adultery." For Dostoevsky, in contrast, she had nothing but praise: "The serenity of *The Brothers Karamazov*, the mental power of *The Possessed*, the art of *The Raw Truth!*"

She was still dismissing Tolstoy in the 1980s as "a monster of hypocrisy." A non-literary basis for her antagonism may be deduced from what she told Bertrand Russell about H. G. Wells: "I am aware from my knowledge of him that he has a violent anti-sex bias like Tolstoy's—you punish the female who provokes your lust." Her antagonism was also part of her general disinclination to accept "great men" at the world's valuation. Reverential postures did not come naturally to Rebecca West. If W. B. Yeats was an old fraud, T. S. Eliot was a *poseur;* and she refused to join in any "Byron-worship," complaining of Byron's "dreary caddishness, his meanness about money, his pert incivilities and his disloyalties." In these cases her antipathy to the writer as a person disqualified him in her eyes as an artist.

Even where she praised excellence, she preferred to cut it down to manageable dimensions. The novelist Ivy Compton-Burnett, for example, was like a family retainer: "all her stories are nanny stories about how awful the family is, she was very, very clever." She wrote of Iris Murdoch that "one can think of no other contemporary novelist who could have touched her achievement"—but only after filling several column-inches with a witty send-up of the gothic excesses of Murdoch's *A Severed Head.*

In *A Room of One's Own,* a feminist polemic, Virginia Woolf had speculated about the obscure life that would have been led by Shakespeare's brilliant sister, had he had one. Similarly, Rebecca railed against the injustice done to the genius of the real-life sister of the composer Mendelssohn; she was always alive to unrecognized genius and to opportunities denied. In social life, when someone was being praised on all sides, she would say, almost perversely, "But did you know his brother?" (Or his sister, or cousin—in any case, a person of whom no one present had heard.) "He was the only *really* interesting member of that family." In her literary judgements, she likewise reserved her unqualified commendation for writers whom she found admirable but who were not in the public eye.

In the 1920s she had championed the cause of H. M. Tomlinson, a relatively neglected novelist then as now, whose *Gallion's Reach* (1927) she praised as "another turn in the spiral of perfection." In the last years of her life, when asked whom among modern novelists she most enjoyed reading, she would cite A. L. Barker—author of *The Middling, A Source of Embarrassment, The Heavy Feather*—whom she admired wholeheartedly, "but I'm the only person who does, so far as I can make out." (In fact, A. L. Barker has a considerable body of loyal readers, even if not as yet a vast commercial success.)

An enemy might surmise that her praise of the unrecognized or unrewarded, in life or in literature, was a device to diminish the stature of those successful figures with whom she felt in competition. But Rebecca's more maverick likes and dislikes grew out of her lifelong fellow-feeling with losers and underdogs and her lifelong inclination to look for excellence beyond the narrow confines of the accepted canon. Of the acknowledged "great men" among the moderns, only Proust was beyond criticism. "The greatness of Proust! One cannot exaggerate it," she wrote in the 1920s, and never changed her mind.

But Nicholas Bagnall rarely knew, when he sent Dame Rebecca a book for review, what her reaction was going to be. Her opinions were sometimes so personal that they seemed to have no outward consistency or logic. Week after week, her tendentious, high-spirited articles enlivened the sober *Sunday Telegraph*. It was not until her eyes began to give trouble that reading and writing became anything of a strain. She had an operation for cataracts at the London Clinic, where most of the patients were rich Arabs: "One had the impression that there were camels padding up and down the corridors."

7

The Wells family had sold H.G.'s letters and papers to the University of Illinois. Dr. Gordon N. Ray, responsible for establishing the Wells archive at Illinois and a Wells collector himself, was designated as the official biographer. He had first approached Rebecca in 1958, and it was borne in on her how little control she had over how her affair with Wells would be presented to posterity, particularly by Anthony. Ray kept in touch, and visited Ibstone in 1962; in 1970, at a meeting with him in New York, she agreed to lift her restriction and give him access to her letters from Wells in the Beinecke Library at Yale, "on condition that I can pass whatever he may write about them." Ray then suggested that he should write a different book altogether, just about the relationship: this became *H. G. Wells and Rebecca West* (1974). Rebecca's additional condition was that he should not consult Anthony at all.

Evelyn Hutchinson questioned the wisdom of Rebecca's releasing the intimate details of her early life to the public. The fact was, she explained, "that the stories broadcast by Anthony have to be refuted, and also the wholly false picture of the situation by the Mackenzies.* . . . And I want to do everything I can to get the situation as I want it before I die."

She did her damnedest. In his preface Ray told how she "corrected errors of fact, filled in the inevitable omissions of a narrative based on fragmentary materials, and set down with her accustomed force and wit how she herself regarded this part of her life." He wrote of their "collaboration" with gratitude, but his task was not easy. Dame Rebecca wrote him immensely long letters commenting on his drafts, sometimes in a third-person narrative form, sections of which were incorporated into his text. He retained his integrity ("She does not agree in every instance with my interpretations of fact or my analysis of her writings") and the result was a readable book which did very well indeed. Rebecca made no money out of it; she charged a "reader's fee," a 2 percent royalty, which went to the London Library.

The book received a lot of notice, not all of it sympathetic. Lillian Hellman, who had "always had reservations about Miss West," criticized Rebecca for betraying the secrets of the bedroom, and quoted with approval the attack on Rebecca made by Ruth Hale when Rebecca first went to New York in 1923: "We thought of you as an independent woman but here you are looking down in the mouth because you relied on a man to give you all you wanted and now that you have to turn out and fend for yourself you are bellyaching about it." Anthony reviewed the book antagonistically, and used legal sanctions to regain possession of two drawings done for him by Wells in 1921, which had remained among Rebecca's papers and were reproduced in the book. In the same stiff letter to her publishers, he referred to "the exceptionally offensive nature of the book itself," which "holds me up to derision and contempt by suggesting I was

*Norman and Jean Mackenzie, *The Time Traveller: The Life of H.G. Wells* (1973). In fact she reviewed it generously—and sent the reviewing fee to the London Library, in keeping with her determination to make no profit from her association with Wells.

conceived in malice" ("in an angry moment," Rebecca had suggested
to Ray).

Rebecca had begun writing her own memoirs in 1971. The working
title became "Parental Memoirs," because memory and reminiscence so
fueled her novelist's imagination that she elaborated scenes and conversations from her parents' youths with a fluency that produced the manuscript of a long book before she had got further than her own early
childhood. There were numerous drafts, variant versions, and genealog-
ical digressions, not only about her parents' families but about Henry's.
Like the Cousin Rosamund saga, the memoirs were never completed and
never abandoned.

She continued to fill notebooks with stories and unfinished novels,
drafts of letters, tables of verbs in foreign languages, exercises in algebra
and arithmetic, recipes and reviews, all jumbled up together, with the
occasional startling one-liner: "What is Harold Wilson but a laddered
stocking?" She wrote poems, which meant a great deal to her; those she
wished to preserve she copied out repeatedly. Working on one she called
"The Universal of the Rose" in 1974, she wrote in her diary: "I wish I
could understand why people don't like my poetry, it seems to me it's very
good." She said that she once sent a poem, pseudonymously, to *The Times
Literary Supplement* and had it rejected.

The only scraps of her poetry known to be published provided titles
for two of her own books. There were the three lines quoted at the beginning of *The Harsh Voice,* attributed to Richard Wynne Errington; and,
unable to find a title for her last published novel, she wrote six lines
which included her eventual title *The Birds Fall Down.* These lines were
attributed to Conway Power (the name she generally appended to her
poetry, even in her private notebooks), from a non-existent poem called
"Guide to a Disturbed Planet." When the novel was published she had
fun deflecting the inquiries of readers who wanted to know how to find
the works of Conway Power. One was told a long story: Conway Power
was a landowner in a remote area who had written thousands of poems
and destroyed most of them. He had left some of them with her, given
his property to a nephew, and gone abroad. "If I can trace the book (if
there is a book) I'll let you know."

Although Conway Power's output contained some magical phrases,
and some lacerating flashes of self-knowledge, there was an old-fashioned

heaviness about it which explains why it never found a public. Rebecca would have liked to be known as a poet. She would have liked to master every art. In her widowhood she sketched trees and flowers, but she had not inherited her father's artistic skills. Even the countless photographs she took on her trips abroad were unremarkable. But she drew, or doodled, as obsessionally as she wrote. There is among her papers a box of repetitive drawings, all on one of three themes: "The Umbrella Lady," a dancing woman with two umbrellas, becoming airborne; "The Trolls," sets of grouped figures shaped like commas; and a sequence depicting robots in a garden—inhabitants of Conway Power's "disturbed planet," perhaps.

Her correspondence was still huge. Some of her letters were never posted, because they were too rude. To Malcolm Muggeridge, for example: "It is indeed improbable that we shall see one another again in this world, if I can help it. You are at any time a revolting personality. . . ." Conversely, she wrote a sensitively respectful letter to a stranger, the former television personality Isobel Barnett, who had been arrested for shoplifting. The pathetic case had attracted maximum publicity. There but for the grace of God, thought Dame Rebecca. This letter was never posted because no sooner was it written than the announcement came that Lady Barnett had committed suicide.

Throughout the 1970s Dame Rebecca commented on current events, writing articles on Watergate, on the rise of Mrs. Thatcher. She gave frequent interviews. Honours continued to accrue; she was a Fellow of Saybrook College, Yale; a member of the American Academy of Arts and Sciences; an honorary doctor of Edinburgh University. In May 1980 she was "swept into the orbit of one of the most glorious episodes in British history," as she put it in the *Sunday Telegraph*. For the last time she was, during the siege of the Iranian Embassy, at the centre of events in her familiar role of eye-witness reporter, at the age of eighty-seven.

The Iranian Embassy was only a hundred yards from Kingston House. From her kitchen window, Dame Rebecca watched policemen with guns in the back garden trying to negotiate with terrorists who were threatening to blow up their hostages and the building. A cordon was put round the area; Dame Rebecca and her neighbours were evacuated before the SAS stormed the embassy, but she was back in her flat in time to see "swaddled corpses" lowered from the burnt-out building.

8

In 1978 she had had her first contact with Virago, the feminist publishing house, which was to reissue many of her books in an extended publishing programme that continued after her death. In 1982 Virago, in association with Viking, also published, under the title *The Young Rebecca,* a collection of her earliest articles and reviews from the *Freewoman* and *Clarion* years which, half a century and more later, had lost neither their pertinence nor their impertinence. "I hate reading my old stuff," Dame Rebecca wrote in her diary, "but I realized as I turned over the pages how cracking good they are." In 1981 she was "electrified" to find herself being promoted as one of the twenty writers on the Book Marketing Council's "Best of British" list, since she had felt that for years there had been "a sort of conspiracy of silence about my work." Rebecca West lived to know that her books had meaning for her grandchildren's generation.

Lettie died in 1978, aged nearly ninety-three. The beloved middle sister, Winnie, had died in 1960. Alex Woollcott, one of her first American friends, had died in 1943, and Ross of *The New Yorker* in 1951; Rebecca was never quite at ease with his successor, William Shawn. Harold Guinzberg of Viking died in 1961, and "what he's meant to me in the last few years is beyond telling. With Alex Woollcott and Ross and Ruth Lowinsky all the best of my life has gone." Dorothy Thompson died in 1961. "When I think how calm and happy she was when I first met her I could weep—but we all start as grazing land and end up as ploughed fields."

Doris Stevens died in 1963, Pamela Frankau in 1967, Fannie Hurst in 1968, John Gunther in 1970, A. D. Peters (Rebecca's London agent for forty-three years) in 1972, G. B. Stern in 1973, Emanie Arling Philips in 1981. Lord Beaverbrook died in June 1964. The previous December, he had asked if he might send her "a case of the best claret going. I have two cases left. One for you and one for me." It was a happy ending—except that eleven years later Rebecca was thrown into disarray by an idle question put to her by a woman at a party: "Would you like to have had an affair with Beaverbrook?" This gave Rebecca a sleepless night. She had a great many agitated, sleepless nights, going over and over the past in her mind.

Visitors poured through her flat: academics, social lions, interviewers, admirers, researchers, London friends, friends from Ibstone days, the relations. Few of her near and dear were immune from being condemned, in her diary, as stupid, mad, evil, or communist on the evidence of some ill-judged remark—only to be gloriously reinstated after a subsequent and happier visit. One young relative who fell from grace permanently was Edmund, the adored grandson. In the mid-1970s he divorced and remarried. Rebecca rejected his second wife as violently as she had rejected Anthony's Lily, her irrational hostility stemming from her terror of broken marriages in the family and of men's "abandoning" women.

She picked up the threads with other younger relations, such as Christina, sister of David Ogilvy; they were the grandchildren of Uncle Arthur Fairfield and the detested Aunt Sophie. Christina's second marriage was to the art historian James Byam Shaw, and Rebecca rejoiced in the fact that they were so elegant and "respectable," in a way that many of her relations and Henry's were not. Another late friend was Stanley Olson, a young American expatriate who first came to see her in 1974 in connection with his biography of Elinor Wylie. She came to rely on his attentive friendship, and was to designate him as one of her biographers.

The people with whom she was happiest were not grand or famous or literary, but those for whom she need put on no performance, such as John Milloy, her regular driver. Dearest of all were "my darling Margaret Hodges," her wartime secretary, and Margaret's husband, John. Their house in Kent, which she had helped them buy, was her best refuge. "I was sorry to go. Longed to stay much longer with them. . . . And they have a bent towards happiness. It is heaven to see them moving about their house and garden, loving it."

"I hate going out into the grand world, I feel sick and inadequate. If only I could lose weight and look elegant." Her appearance mattered to her in her eighties nearly as much as it had at eighteen. After a dinner at Lady Kelly's: "People liked my dress (which is a dressing-gown I got at Harvey Nichols, cut up with nail-scissors and pieced together with Scotch tape!)" For the party Macmillan gave for her on the publication of the anthology volume *Rebecca West: A Celebration* in 1977, she had a dress specially designed by the Japanese couturier Yuki. At the age of eighty-five, taking Madge Garland along as her adviser, she invested in a new mink coat.

Her visitors, in the last years, waiting in the drawing-room at Kingston House, might be disturbed by loud groans of "Oh *God*, oh *God*" from the bedroom, as Dame Rebecca divested herself of the old dressing-gown in which she worked and strove to dress herself, crippled by arthritis, in pain from diverticulitis; "Oh *God*, oh *God*" again as, with her housekeeper's help, she rummaged for her hearing-aid and the right pair of spectacles. But then Dame Rebecca made her entrance, in a gold-braided kaftan, supported on a malacca cane, two or three pairs of spectacles swinging on cords round her neck, and proceeded to give the visitor the time of his life. It was hard to leave, and she would limp to the door to see her guest out—the impossible questions, the imperious opinions, and the laughter still pouring from her. Only when the door closed did the power cut out, and Dame Rebecca collapsed into grey exhaustion.

Dame Rebecca never mellowed. As one temporary housekeeper noted, "Her life, even now, is black and white and crimson and purple and wild." Her last secretary, Diana Stainforth, never thought of her before her final illness as an old lady: "she was just a lady who happened to be old." Doris Lessing, the last new friend to be important to Rebecca, saw both the glory and the frustration of her old age: "All that wit and brilliance and fire in prison."

A year before she died, Dame Rebecca wrote to the charity Age Concern asking if they could recommend "anywhere in the nature of a home for old people with substantial incomes which would take me in and give me care and some measure of comfort." (She did have a substantial income: her estate, when her will came to be proved, was in the region of £770,000.) That she was able to remain in her own setting was due to the care and devotion of a small number of people: Justin Lowinsky, Diana Stainforth, and, most important of all, her housekeeper Mrs. Monro, recently widowed and a Scot: Tessa Monro shared Dame Rebecca's liking for detective stories, had a salty tongue and infinite patience.

9

Dame Rebecca had chosen her grave in 1974, driving down to Brookwood Cemetery, near Woking in Surrey, with Gwenda David. She liked Brookwood for its look of a Victorian country estate, "beautiful rhododendrons and beautiful trees, some yews, but most other kinds, pines, oaks, and some superb and unusual azaleas, the graves far apart, bracken (they tell me the bluebells are wonderful)." She bought for £200 a plot near a pink hawthorn, "subject to enquiries about the health of the hawthorn tree."

She finished her last book, *1900*, in early 1981, with difficulty. Each major effort after this left her with less strength to recover. In May 1982 she was devastated by an unsympathetic interview by Leslie Garis in *The New York Times* into which had been incorporated an interview with Anthony, of a predictable kind, and some disparaging remarks about Henry from Malcolm Muggeridge. From this she never fully recovered. Yet that summer she wrote a whole short story, "Edith"—a post-nuclear story, which is to say a pre-death story, but infused with hope. She never lost her humour; when the faint words of the Einstein-like "wise man" of science, in whom lies the survivors' only chance, are finally heard, they are: "Can anyone tell me what is happening?"

With many rejected drafts and much groaning, she completed in September 1982 an article for *Vogue* on what it felt like to be ninety—her ninetieth birthday fell that Christmas. In spite of the trouble writing now caused her, the end result was punchy and ironic, and included a funny story, crisply told, about a long-ago lunch given by Charles Curran for herself, Henry, and Mae West. Her last book review, immediately afterwards, was written in desperate confusion, the jumbled drafts pieced together by Diana Stainforth. "I'm too tired, I can't go on," she said to Diana, and wept.

She had written in her youth that "it is necessary that we should all

have a little of the will to die, because otherwise we would find the performance of our biological duty of death too difficult." She found the
performance of this biological duty horribly difficult. The great engine
was breaking up, but there were still months to get through. She could
not bear to be left alone. "I must have someone in the house—to cling
to, I suppose, but also to be fond of. My dependence on Tessa is a grave
problem to me."

In the last stages, Tessa Monro took no time off at all. For her last
three months, bedridden after a hip operation, Dame Rebecca was unhappy and confused, her hyperactive mind tormenting her with dislo-
cated memories, terrors, and illusions. Her ninetieth birthday passed
without the possibility of a celebration.

In January 1983, when Alison Macleod was by her bed, Dame Rebecca said she wanted to see Anthony. Alison tried to ascertain whether
she meant it; she retracted the next moment. "Oh, what's the use, if he
hates me so much? . . . He's a bad boy, but he's the love of my life." Then
she fell asleep. In a less lucid phase, she scribbled on a pad: "Dear H.G.,
I know you have Anthony there, but I don't care so long as he is happy. I
love him so much." Another day she asked for her mother, in clear formal
tones: "Is Mrs Charles Fairfield here?" Sometimes she was aware of her
condition, and distressed that she was dying so slowly.

Her death, like her life, was a battle. She described in *Black Lamb
and Grey Falcon* how during the air raids of World War II she would put
on a gramophone record, "and from it there radiates the small white star
of light" which is Susanna's aria at the end of *The Marriage of Figaro* as
she waits in the garden. Bombs and destruction cannot consume the music; the attention "does not relinquish the small white star of the song,
which is correct, permanent, important. 'Yes', we say in our beings, heart
and mind and muscles fused in listening, 'this is what matters.'"

The best of Rebecca West and of her writing—not always correct,
but permanent, important—underwrites the promise of peace and pleasure made by music. "This is what matters." A woman—"I paused because my three names clashed in my head, Cicely Fairfield, Cicely
Andrews, Rebecca West, I could not choose between them"—died on the
morning of 15 March 1983, released, one must believe, into the kingdom
of light.

Her dead body was buried in the place that she had chosen. Her live spirit was celebrated at a service of thanksgiving in St. Martin-in-the-Fields on Trafalgar Square. The church was packed. Her books remain, and are read. This is what matters.

NOTES

There are two main archives of Dame Rebecca West's letters and papers. One is in the McFarlin Library at the University of Tulsa; this contains all the material that was in her possession in her London flat at the time of her death; when I was doing the research for this book it was still in London. The other archive, composed of letters and papers presented by Dame Rebecca in her lifetime, is in the Beinecke Library at Yale. When Dame Rebecca named her two biographers, she did not specifically state that the restriction she had placed on some of her papers in the Beinecke Library should be lifted, and the authorities at Yale have not felt able to break their agreement with her. Her stipulation was that certain papers should be seen by no one until after the deaths of her husband (who died in 1968) and of her son, Anthony West.

The most important among these papers are some diaries, her letters from H. G. Wells, and her correspondence with her husband. When Gordon N. Ray wrote his *H. G. Wells and Rebecca West*, she lifted the restriction for him; the quotations from Wells's letters to her in my book are taken from Ray's, apart from a few other collections. Some diaries, and some letters to and from her husband also survive apart from those in the Beinecke. Dame Rebecca was such a prodigious writer of letters and autobiographical notes, and the mass of material available to me was so overwhelming, that the limitation noted above came to seem less than disastrous.

The letters from Charles Fairfield, and the correspondence between Rebecca West and her mother, sisters, and other relations are in the possession of her niece, Alison Macleod, unless otherwise indicated in the Notes. The letters from Rebecca West to Professor and Mrs. Evelyn Hutchinson (and theirs to her) are in the Beinecke Library at Yale. Unless otherwise indicated, book publishers cited in the notes are British.

I should like to thank the following institutions, and their librarians and archivists, for access to their collections, for permission to use material, and for their helpfulness and efficiency: The Beinecke Rare Book and Manuscript Library, Yale University (in particular Marjorie Wynne); the Humanities Research Center, University of Texas at Austin; the Berg Collection, New York Public Library; the Lilly Library, Indiana University; the George Arents Research Library, Syracuse University; Georgetown University Library; the Robert H. Taylor Collection, Princeton University Library; the Margaret Clapp Library, Wellesley College, Massachusetts; Smith College, Massachusetts; The Library, University College, London; Stadtsarchiv, Hanover; the International Institute of Social History, Amsterdam; the University of Sussex Library; the Central Library, Southend-on-Sea; the London Library.

The correspondence between Rebecca West and her son, Anthony West, is quoted by kind permission of her son, Anthony West. For permission to quote from the letters and published works of H. G. Wells I am grateful to A. P. Watt Ltd. on behalf of his literary executors. For permission to quote from the published letters and diaries of Virginia Woolf I am grateful to the author's estate and The Hogarth Press. The letters from Rebecca West to Professor Evelyn Hutchinson and the late Margaret Hutchinson are quoted by kind permission of Professor Hutchinson.

The Dyson Papers are quoted by permission of Elaine Bate; Sylvia Lynd's unpublished memoirs, and Rebecca West's letters to Sylvia Lynd, by permission of Maire (Lynd) Gaster; Rebecca West's letters to Sara Melville by permission of Mary Melville; her letters to John Gunther, and John Gunther's letters and diaries, by permission of Jane Gunther; and her letters to Marie Belloc-Lowndes by permission of Susan Lowndes Marques and Elizabeth Lady Iddlesleigh. Her letters to June Head are quoted by permission of June (Head) Fenby, and to Anne Charles by permission of Anne (Charles) McBurney. All these letters and documents were, at the time of writing, in the private collections of the aforementioned. Other sources of quoted material are gratefully acknowledged in the Notes.

ABBREVIATIONS

Tulsa   The Rebecca West Papers, Special Collections Department, McFarlin Library, University of Tulsa.

Yale   The Beinecke Rare Book and Manuscript Library, Yale University Library.

Texas   The Humanities Research Center, University of Texas at Austin.

Berg   The Berg Collection, New York Public Library.

Syracuse   The George Arents Research Library, Syracuse University.

Indiana   The Lilly Library, Indiana University.

Georgetown   The Douglas Woodruff Papers, Special Collections Division, Georgetown University Library.

Amsterdam   International Instituut voor Sociale Geschiedenis (International Institute of Social History), Amsterdam.

INTRODUCTION

Page xv, "a woman as a woman," "argument that is not there," and "necessary to achieve it":

xvi   C. G. Jung, "Women in Europe," *Aspects of the Feminine* (tr. R. S. C. Hull), Routledge and Kegan Paul 1982.

xvi   "some benign, some abhorrent": *Black Lamb and Grey Falcon*, vol. II, p. 519.
      "anything like her before": G. P. Wells (ed.), *H. G. Wells in Love*, Faber 1984.

xvii "whom I like I love": *The Strange Necessity*.
      "in their pockets": *Black Lamb and Grey Falcon*, vol. II, pp. 417–18.

PART ONE: CISSIE

I owe much general information about the family to Norman and Alison Macleod and to RW's memoirs, unpublished at the time of writing.

 9 "what romance was": *Black Lamb and Grey Falcon*, vol. II, p. 478.
10 "surrounded by London": to Dorothy Thompson, 15 Aug 1948. Syracuse.
11 "surrounded by rhododendrons": Diary, 10 Sep 1971. Tulsa.
12 "we knew nobody": Diary, 17 Feb 1974. Tulsa.
    "liberalism and conservatism": "My Father," *Sunday Telegraph*, 1962.
13 "loneliness to loneliness": Notebook 19. Tulsa.
16 "to know in Havana": Charles Fairfield's press-cuttings. Tulsa.
18 . . . glamorous parent: descriptions of RW's parents from Memoirs. Tulsa.
19 "drunken comets": "My Father."
    "I ever knew": Tom Pillans to RW, 15 Nov 1916. Tulsa.
20 "any fun for me" and "into his warmth": "My Father."
    "the Holy Ghost": to Hugh Walpole, 19 Sep 1928. Texas.

Page 20   "relationship with me": Notebook J. Tulsa.

21   "wife and children": Memoirs. Tulsa.

22   "I don't know" and description of the Heinemanns and their house: to Valenza
         (Heinemann) Lancaster, 11 Jan 1954. Courtesy of Tara Heinemann.

23, 24   "no father at all" and "bare of possessions": Memoirs, typescript D. Tulsa.

25   "a vital issue" and "about his subject": *Black Lamb and Grey Falcon*, vol. II, p. 544.
     "that we survive": "Greenhouse with Cyclamens III," *A Train of Powder.*
     "understatements and misstatements": *St Augustine.*
     "on his senses": *Sunday Telegraph*, 17 June 1962.

26   "more which do not": "Greenhouse with Cyclamens III," *A Train of Powder.*
     "alternative hypotheses": "Mr Setty and Mr Hume," *A Train of Powder.*

27   . . . of that street: for an understanding of the social geography of Edinburgh I am
         indebted to David Daiches, *Edinburgh*, Hamish Hamilton 1978.

28   "been an agony": Notebook 138. Tulsa.
     "whisky-sodden uncle": Memoirs, typescript E. Tulsa.
     "destroyed all traces": to E. and M. Hutchinson, Feb 1955.

29   "late at night": Memoirs, typescript E. Tulsa.
     "blast of burning air": to E. and M. Hutchinson, 4 Dec 1953.

30   "Ile de Pâques": *Figaro Littéraire*, 19 March 1955.
     "slow and pale!": Tulsa.

34   "my sturdy pack-horse build": *Black Lamb and Grey Falcon*, vol. II, p. 276.
     "always known it": *Vogue*, 17 April 1944.
     "an actress!": to Lettie, 18 April 1910.

35   "ruined my early life": to G. B. Stern. Tulsa.

36   "who became several": Notebook J. Tulsa.

37   "pinched Edinburgh accent": to Clare Stanley-Clarke, summer 1962. Courtesy of
         Clare Stanley-Clarke.
     "thought nothing of it": to Jean Overton Fuller, 27 March 1962. Tulsa.
     "more suitable to do than writing": EBC interview with Bill Moyers, 8 July 1981.
     "I have ever seen": to Jean Overton Fuller, 27 March 1962. Tulsa.

38   "not got any": *Black Lamb and Grey Falcon*, vol. II, p. 478.

39   "the human will" and "relations with Christ": "The New God," typescript article
         ?1915. Tulsa.
     "like a bolster": *Cosmopolite*, 14 April 1938.
     "reactionary ideas": to editor of *The Author*, 9 May 1946. Tulsa.
     "inflamed by flirtation": to Charles Curran, 6 Feb 1955. Tulsa.

40   "hole in the world": Violet Hunt, *The Flurried Years*, Hurst and Blackett 1922.
     "in our language" and "albino-ish": *Sunday Telegraph*, 7 May 1972.
     "any of us deserve": *Daily News*, 2 April 1915.
     "hair-raising and wicked": Brigit Patmore, *My Friends When Young*, Heinemann
         1968.

41   "5 pink ostrich feathers": Jane Lisserdale and Mary Nicholson, *Dear Miss Weaver*,
         Faber 1970.
     "get any poetry?": to Dora Marsden, n.d. 1912. Dyson Papers.

Page 41 "an innocent child": *Sunday Telegraph,* 26 May 1968.

42 "their best to revolt" and "not strictly accurate": to Dora Marsden, n.d. 1913.
    Dyson Papers.

"miserably poor stuff": "The Sex War," *Clarion,* 4 April 1913.

"what satire was": EBC interview with Bill Moyers, 8 July 1981.

"and the aristocracy": *Clarion,* 4 Feb 1913.

43 "looting the till!": to *New Freewoman* office, n.d. 1913. Dyson Papers.

PART TWO: PANTHER

47 "wholesome weekly irritant": H. G. Wells to Dora Marsden, 1913. Dyson Papers.

"a little effaced": to Harold Rubinstein, 2 Oct 1912. Courtesy of Hilary Rubinstein.

"Fame!": to Harold Rubinstein, 13 Nov 1912. Courtesy of Hilary Rubinstein.

"Wasn't it glorious?": to Harold Rubinstein, 11 Jan 1913. Courtesy of Hilary Rubinstein.

48 "Old Maid's mania": *Freewoman,* 19 Sep 1912.

"kissed each other": G. P. Wells (ed.), *H. G. Wells in Love,* Faber 1984.

49 "your great adventure": HGW to RW, Feb 1913.

"my own fault": to Dora Marsden, June 1913. Dyson Papers.

"dig up the corpse": to Dora Marsden, August 1913. Dyson Papers.

"beautiful boof toreros": postcard to Lettie, 29 May 1913. Tulsa.

"don't want to come home": postcard to Lettie, 4 June 1913. Tulsa.

50 "wish you liked me": to HGW, June 1913.

"an inferior bull": to Dora Marsden, Sep 1913. Dyson Papers.

"all these things": notes for Gordon N. Ray, Notebook 16. Tulsa.

"disappointed with things": "Trees of Gold," *New Freewoman,* 15 June 1913.

"on my cinders": HGW to RW, June 1913.

51 "more ambitious play": *New Freewoman,* 1 Oct 1913.

"much better in future": to Dora Marsden, late 1913. Dyson Papers.

"back of his soul": *Black Lamb and Grey Falcon,* vol. I, p. 170.

52 "or useful connections": to Victoria Glendinning, 8 Sep 1975.

"and sallow guest": to Violet Hunt, 1914. Berg.

"was wholly mine": *H. G. Wells in Love.*

53 "wonderful of lovers": HGW to RW, Dec 1913.

"to have a child": HGW to RW, 14 Jan 1914.

"adjustment of any sort": *H. G. Wells in Love.*

54 "and insulting them": to Dora Marsden, late 1913. Dyson Papers.

"never meeting H.G.": Diary, 21 April 1971.

"loathe and hate journalism": to T. Adcock of *Bookman,* 1913. Yale.

55 "Bless you": Anthony West to RW, 12 March 1974. Tulsa.

"innumerable difficulties": dictated by Lettie to Alison Macleod, 21 Oct 1976.

56 "must be right": Memoirs. Tulsa.

57 "did not practise towards us": to Winnie, 1946.

"she hated her": *H. G. Wells in Love.*

Page 57 "none the worse for that": Diary, 18 Feb 1971.

58 "in Fleet Street": to Violet Hunt from Hunstanton, 1914. Berg.

"of anyone else": Gordon N. Ray, *H. G. Wells and Rebecca West*, Macmillan 1974.

"fever to subside": *H. G. Wells in Love.*

"devoted to me": ibid.

60 "in his pram": Sylvia Lynd, unpublished memoirs.

61 what I really need": to Sylvia Lynd from Alderton, Hatch End.

"intellectually and artistically": G. B. Shaw to Mrs. Patrick Campbell, 4 Sep 1916.

62 "loyalty to literature": HGW to Hugh Walpole, 1917. Quoted in Norman and Jeanne Mackenzie, *The Time Traveller: The Life of H. G. Wells*, Weidenfeld and Nicolson 1973.

"tea-cosy I have ever met": quoted by RW, *Sunday Telegraph,* 5 Sep 1971.

"in the language": Susan Lowndes (ed.), *Diaries and Letters of Marie Belloc-Lowndes*, Chatto and Windus 1971.

"the old ladies": to Sara Melville, 1917.

"hardly my fault!": Rupert Hart-Davis, *Hugh Walpole*, Macmillan 1952.

63 "no one to back me": Diary, 27 Aug 1971.

"using our wills": "Greenhouse with Cyclamens II," *A Train of Powder.*

"my love for you": HGW to RW, 12 June 1914.

"an ultimatum": HGW to RW, July 1914.

64 "Do it again!": Sylvia Lynd, unpublished memoirs.

"little boy can have": Lettie's statement to Alison Macleod, 21 Oct 1976.

"no such consolations": Diary, 29 April 1917.

65 "Hey nonny nonny": Sylvia Lynd to Mrs. A. R. Dryhurst.

66 "but it is": to J. B. Pinker, 1917. Texas.

"for the Century": to S. K. Ratcliffe, 1917. Yale.

67 "*Lovely* guns!": RW to Sylvia Lynd, 1917.

"seems very happy": to S. K. Ratcliffe, 9 Aug 1918. Yale.

68 "of different species": HGW to RW, 13 Sep 1917.

"will to power": *Daily News,* 1918.

"sore over it": to Sylvia Lynd, 10 Oct 1917.

"on with my work": to Kitty West (Katharine Church), 20 May 1944. Courtesy of Katharine Church.

"hate waiting about": HGW to RW, 1918.

69 "kindness and condescension": to Sylvia Lynd, 1917.

"best I could do": notes for Gordon N. Ray. Tulsa.

"proletarian resentments": *The Meaning of Treason.*

70 "inconveniently isn't here": to Sylvia Lynd, 1918.

"into serfdom?" to S. K. Ratcliffe, 12 March 1918. Yale.

"erroneously imagined her": Max Beerbohm to G. B. Shaw, 28 June 1918. Copy. Tulsa.

71 "so it's all right" and "this pleasure also": to Sara Melville, 1918.

"bright intellectuality to me": Thomas Hardy to HGW, 27 Jan 1919. Yale.

72 "halfdays and evenings": *H. G. Wells in Love.*

Page 72, 73 "those that remained" and "from my case": "An Experience," ms. Tulsa.

73 "at my door": to E. and M. Hutchinson, 3 Aug 1962.

73, 74 "against Rebecca" and "to my embraces": *H. G. Wells in Love.*

"to do that now": HGW to RW, late 1920.

"as I do": to Sara Melville, late 1920.

"a *backward* boy": HGW to Winnie Macleod, 16 Dec 1920. Courtesy of Alison Macleod.

"dear good Anthony": postcard to Anthony West, Nov 1920. Collection of Alison Macleod.

76 "sick distraught female": HGW to RW, late Nov 1920.

"hymenic indiscretions": Harris Wilson (ed.), *Arnold Bennett and H. G. Wells,* Hart-Davis 1960.

"undiluted happiness": notes for Gordon N. Ray. Tulsa.

"anything else in the world": HGW to RW, 30 April 1921.

"and he lost": Diary, 1921. Tulsa.

77 "as a child might do": "Elegy." Reprinted in *Rebecca West: A Celebration.*

"in any generation": *New Republic,* 27 Feb 1915.

"a plum-silly book": *New Statesman,* 8 July 1922.

"very pink friends": "Oranges to Oranges," *Ending in Earnest.*

"and perhaps might": D. H. Lawrence to RW, 7 Oct 1929. Tulsa.

78 "dowdy *Lady Chatterley's Lover*": to E. and M. Hutchinson, 25 Oct 1960.

79–80 "live after death": to Marie Belloc-Lowndes, 30 Aug 1921.

80 "you can imagine": to Reginald Turner, 1921. Yale.

"terrible nose-bleeding": to Marie Belloc-Lowndes, 19 Jan 1922.

81 "turn around in the streets": HGW to RW, Dec 1921.

"absolutely insane extent": to Lettie, 22 Jan 1922.

"enormous earnings": Norman and Jeanne Mackenzie (eds.), *Diary of Beatrice Webb,* vol. III, Virago 1984.

"to keep away": HGW to RW, 20 March 1922.

82 "ever since Porlock": G. B. Stern to Lettie, 1923. Collection of Alison Macleod.

"household chores together": Gordon N. Ray, *H. G. Wells and Rebecca West.*

"a decent inn": to Marie Belloc-Lowndes, summer 1922.

83 "the damn bitch": to Sylvia Lynd from Alderton, Hatch End.

"materialized that gig": *H. G. Wells in Love.*

84 "it didn't happen": Anthony West in conversation with Victoria Glendinning, 1983.

"deliberate in the world": *H. G. Wells in Love.*

"or each other": H. G. Wells, *Secret Places of the Heart,* Cassell 1922.

85 "for two years": *H. G. Wells in Love.*

"of many a talent": to unknown recipient from Porlock, 1922. Tulsa.

"he is reading": W. Somerset Maugham to RW, 1922. Tulsa.

86 "very shaggy": Virginia Woolf to Lady Ottoline Morrell, 18 Aug 1922. Nigel Nicolson (ed.), *The Letters of Virginia Woolf,* vol. 2, Hogarth Press 1976.

"eaten me for breakfast": to Victoria Glendinning in conversation.

"love of ten years": Gordon N. Ray, *H. G. Wells and Rebecca West.*

Page 87   "weeks of childish dependence": to S. K. Ratcliffe, 21 March 1923. Yale.

be read as overstatements: quotations from Anthony West, *H. G. Wells: Aspects of a Life,* Hutchinson 1984.

"a major catastrophe": notes for Gordon N. Ray. Tulsa.

88   "hearing Tito Gobbi sing": "The Real H. G. Wells," *Sunday Telegraph,* 17 June 1973.

"the male mind" and "the modern woman": *Hearst's International-Cosmopolitan,* Nov 1925.

"get what they can" *Black Lamb and Grey Falcon,* vol. I, p. 415.

"out of our relationship": *H. G. Wells in Love.*

90   "it was H.G.": Notebook 15. Tulsa.

"and spoilt it": HGW to RW, Dec 1923.

"came from her": *H. G. Wells in Love.*

91   "coming back to him": HGW to RW, late 1923.

PART THREE: SUNFLOWER

For Anthony West's memories of his boyhood, here and in later sections, I am grateful to him for conversations in New Haven, London, and New York in 1983 and 1984. For details of the early career of Lord Beaverbrook I am indebted to A. J. P. Taylor, *Beaverbrook,* Hamish Hamilton 1972. I am indebted to Yvonne Kapp for memories of the Hôtel Josse in the summer of 1926, and to June (Head) Fenby and Anthony West for memories of life at the Villa Mysto.

95   "all so interesting": to the Sinclair Lewises, 9 Dec 1923.

"slim like lilies": to Winnie, 2 Nov 1923.

"to interrupt it": to Arnold Bennett, 21 Nov 1923. Wilson Harris (ed.), *Arnold Bennett and H. G. Wells,* Hart-Davis 1960.

96   "both places, of course": A. J. P. Taylor, *Beaverbrook.*

97   "to be husband and wife": Memoirs, notebook F. 1970s. Tulsa.

98   "or more roses": Harriet Cohen, *A Bundle of Time,* Faber 1969.

"opulent Oriental type": to Lettie, 8 Feb 1924.

"on the East Side": to Fannie Hurst, mid-1920s. Texas.

"years of distraction": to Fannie Hurst, 30 Oct 1933. Texas.

99   "poor old donkey": to Fannie Hurst, late 1923. Texas.

"playing Juliet very successfully" and "idea he loved me": to Fannie Hurst, 12 June 1924. Texas.

100   "you intellectual women!": Lawrence Langner to RW, 10 April 1924. Tulsa.

"with a blonde": RW to Reginald Turner, 6 Oct 1921. Yale.

"with Marion Davies": to Lettie, 3 April 1927.

"made him impotent": ibid.

102   "I deserved it": *Spectator,* 1 Nov 1946.

"happened to me in America": to Mina Curtiss, 2 June 1924. Smith College.

"want peace really": Emanie Sachs to RW, 1924. Tulsa.

Page 102 "curly blond hair": Marcia Davenport, *Too Strong for Fantasy*, Charles Scribner's Sons (New York) 1967.

"seen since Spain": to the Sinclair Lewises, 9 Dec 1926. Syracuse.

103 "handling at the moment": Major Bryant to Lettie, 17 March 1924. Collection of Alison Macleod.

104 "a very good time": HGW to Winnie, 13 April 1924. Collection of Alison Macleod.

"The strain of them, I mean": Enid Bagnold to Roderick Jones, 28 March 1924. Courtesy of Anne Sebba.

"love for you" and "Phantom Panther": HGW to RW, 4 June 1924 and 3 Aug 1924.

"to tell him that?": HGW to RW, 30 Oct 1924.

"for ten years": telegram returned to RW by A. J. P. Taylor. Tulsa.

"of my manner": to Winnie, 17 Nov 1924.

105 "a lot of Christians do": Maxine in *Sunflower*.

"the refined palate": to Winnie, 17 Nov 1924.

"that isn't there": to Sylvia Lynd, 22 July 1925.

"keep in the wave": to Lettie, 27 Feb 1925.

106 "silly bitch!": Frank Harris to Emma Goldman, 15 Sep 1924. Amsterdam.

"for their friends": Emma Goldman to Stella Ballantine, 19 Dec 1924. Amsterdam.

"a generous spirit": Emma Goldman to Stella Ballantine, 26 Dec 1924. Amsterdam.

107 "dinner a good show": to Winnie, 17 Nov 1924.

"no outlet for her gifts": to Sherry Kahan, 13 Aug 1973. Copy. Tulsa.

"when I am with her": Emma Goldman to Stella Ballantine, 2 June 1925. Amsterdam.

108 "for seventy-four years": to editor of *Who's Who*, 14 July 1982. Copy. Tulsa.

109 "afraid of her": John Gunther to Helen Hahn, 21 Dec 1924.

"brilliant yellow flowers": John Gunther to Helen Hahn, 24 March 1925.

110 "in Monte Carlo": to S. K. Ratcliffe, Nov 1925. Yale.

"Mrs John Barrymore" and "New York indeed": to Sara Melville, summer 1926.

111 "in the swimming tank": to Reginald Turner, Sep 1927. Yale.

112 "bored with one another": William Gerhardie to Lord Beaverbrook, 14 Sep 1926. Courtesy of Michael Holroyd.

114 "wrong with the school": to John Gunther, summer 1926.

"think like the *Daily Mail*": to Sylvia Lynd, 1920s.

115 "under a spotlight": to Lettie, 2 Nov 1926.

"more than a year!": to John Gunther, Nov 1926.

"understand my jokes": *The Strange Necessity.*

116 "I've loved anybody": to Carl Van Vechten, 29 Dec 1926. Berg.

"with van Druten": to Fannie Hurst, Dec 1926. Texas.

"with yellow flowers": to John Gunther, Dec 1926.

"How *good* he was": Diary, 25 April 1975.

"give him pain": "Greenhouse with Cyclamens II," *A Train of Powder.*

117 "don't know what it is": to Fannie Hurst, 21 Dec 1926. Texas.

"happen to him like that!": "Toller," *Ending in Earnest.*

"the Book of Tobit": to Winnie, 25 Nov 1924.

Page 118   "commits me to humanity": to Fannie Hurst, 21 Dec 1926. Texas.

"one has no foothold": to Lettie, 1928.

"greatly interfered with": to Lettie, 25 March 1927.

119   "gifts and power": *Sunflower* ms. book. Tulsa.

120   "I have ever met": *London Calling,* 9 June 1928.

"see it at Agay": to Hamish Hamilton, 1927. Tulsa.

"centenarian gardener": to Fannie Hurst, summer 1927. Texas.

"for many years": *The Strange Necessity.*

"servant called Kate?": to Lettie, summer 1927.

121   "some attaché's little joke": to Marie Belloc-Lowndes, 19 July 1946.

122   "for vast sums": to Winnie, Nov 1927.

destroyed it at once: A. J. P. Taylor to Victoria Glendinning, 25 Oct 1983.

"Mrs Wells should have died": to Fannie Hurst, Dec 1927. Texas.

123   "suppress it for years": to Fannie Hurst, early 1928. Texas.

"*work* you've been doing lately": G. B. Stern to RW, 1928. Tulsa.

"ordinary English": New York *Herald Tribune,* 12 Jan 1930.

124   "in all his manifestations": to E. and M. Hutchinson, 8 Nov 1960.

"most avuncular postcard": postcard from G. B. Shaw to RW, 13 July 1928. Tulsa.

125   "as you are read": HGW to RW, 17 July 1928.

"a silly name": HGW to RW, mid-June 1928.

"cockney imagination": Anthony West, *H. G. Wells: Aspects of a Life,* Hutchinson
1984.

"sit down on it and think": HGW to RW, 3 Aug 1928.

"women won't like you": Wilson Harris (ed.), *Arnold Bennett and H. G. Wells.*

126   "Beethoven and Mozart": *Black Lamb and Grey Falcon,* vol. I, p. 646.

"a harmony with it": ibid., p. 522.

"how to live": Arnold Bennett, *Evening Standard,* 9 Aug 1928.

"lowest form of insult": to Fannie Hurst, 27 Aug 1928. Texas.

127   "nobody sees it": to Sylvia Lynd, 1928.

128   "will be wonderful": to John Gunther, 1928.

"awfully nice" and "looks good": Anthony West to RW, 1928. Tulsa.

129   "not going to die": Anthony West in conversation with Victoria Glendinning.

"to get over": to S. K. Ratcliffe from Cromer, summer 1928. Yale.

"father of my dreams": Anthony West, *H. G. Wells: Aspects of a Life.*

130   "ever had in my life": draft letter to Gordon N. Ray. Notebook 16. Tulsa.

131   "would probably have happened": Bertrand Russell to RW, 10 Sep 1929. Tulsa.

"overshadowing personality": Pamela Frankau, *I Find Four People,* Ivor Nicholson
and Watson 1935.

"nicely warmed Mediterranean": to Sylvia Lynd, 31 Aug 1929.

132   "and mitigate it": "Mr Smithers." *Ending in Earnest.*

"plunged into the pot": Beverley Nichols to RW, 2 July 1976. Tulsa.

"ached about the middle": Pamela Frankau, *I Find Four People.*

"blue eyes and large whiskers": ibid.

"to be a lesbian": Diary, 10 Jan 1975. Tulsa.

Page 132 "baking in the sun": Anthony West to Victoria Glendinning, 1984.

133 "by being a male": Anthony West to Victoria Glendinning, 1984.

"as well as mother them": "What I Think of Marriage," *Daily Mail,* 10 Oct 1929.

"I or my mother possessed": Anthony West to Victoria Glendinning, 1984.

134 "a fantasy, not a novel": to Winnie, 1929.

"crazy entertainment": to Sylvia Lynd, 31 Aug 1929.

"intellectual trance": HGW to RW, 13 Sep 1929.

"named *Harriet Hume*": RW, Introduction to Harriet Cohen, *A Bundle of Time.*

135 "very 'automatic' writing": to Sylvia Lynd from Villa Mysto, summer 1929.

"as highly unsympathetic": to Hugh Walpole, 19 Sep 1928. Courtesy of Sir Rupert
Hart-Davis.

"certain to crush one don't": to Fannie Hurst, 27 Sep 1929. Texas.

"meant Max to me": to Fannie Hurst, 1929. Texas.

136 "with Max in any way": to A. J. P. Taylor, 15 June 1968. Copy. Tulsa.

"love Rebecca": telegram to Fannie Hurst. Texas.

PART FOUR: MRS. HENRY ANDREWS

Documents confirming the basic facts of RW's account of Henry Andrews's background
are among her papers at Tulsa. Background to her political and personal involvement in
Yugoslav affairs is also taken principally from her files in Tulsa. For the account of life at
Ibstone House during World War II, I am particularly indebted to Margaret Hodges.

139 "the most alarming": Vera Brittain, *The Testament of Friendship,* Macmillan 1940.

"sweet, kind and loving": "Synopsis of Later Memoirs," unnumbered notebook
1973. Tulsa.

140 from the Far East: A. C. Poynton, *Wallace Brothers,* Oxford University Press 1974.

"lacks all discernment": Henry Andrews to Mary Andrews, 10 June 1916. Tulsa.

141 "he cares most": Earnest Breakwell to Mary Andrews, 26 March 1917. Tulsa.

"bear reprinting": *Oxford Magazine,* 21 Feb 1919.

"only derision": Draft Memoirs, notebook 2D. Tulsa.

142 "of France and Spain": Memoirs, notebook B. Tulsa.

"the right person": to Monica Stirling, 1946. Tulsa.

"of a playwright": Memoirs, notebook B. Tulsa.

143 "it's perfect": to June Head, Feb 1930.

"from each other": "Sensible Folks," sent to Pinker 17 Oct 1930. Ms. Tulsa.

"to build me up": to S. K. Ratcliffe, Oct 1930. Yale.

144 "bought everyone else's": C. A. (Sappho) Dawson Scott, unpublished diary, 1 Nov
1930. Courtesy of Marjorie Watts.

"the word 'banker'": to Jilly Cooper, 26 July 1976. Copy. Tulsa.

"altogether it's lovely": to Lettie from Genoa, Nov 1930.

"and I did it": to Victoria Glendinning, 1 Nov 1975.

145 "my mother-in-law's" and "from Selfridges": to Winnie, early 1931.

"with their blessings": Henry Andrews to RW, 2 July 1931. Tulsa.

Page 146   "a trial for a time": to Fannie Hurst, 30 Oct 1933. Texas.

"forget things all the time": to Winnie, July 1932.

"a positive advantage": Vera Brittain, *Time and Tide,* 18 Oct 1930.

"a trumpeting ass": to Prof. Hansi Pollack, 2 May 1960. Tulsa.

"approves the match": to Reginald Turner, 30 Oct 1930. Yale.

147   "bang-on way" and "writhed with impatience": Anthony West in conversation with
Victoria Glendinning.

"sublimated entrance hall": Louise Morgan, *Everyman,* 5 Nov 1931.

"I don't care": to Winnie, 29 March 1930.

148   "a great man": to HGW from Orchard Court. Copy. Tulsa.

"psychoanalyst in Europe": to Roy Harrod, 25 Aug 1932. Courtesy of Lady Harrod.

"to please him": to Roy Harrod, 25 Aug 1932.

"So be it": HGW to Anthony West, 14 April 1932. Copy. Tulsa.

"run after him": HGW to RW, 20 April 1932. Copy. Tulsa.

"I was arty": Anthony West in conversation with Victoria Glendinning.

149   "can't have *two*": to Victoria Glendinning, 3 Dec 1976.

"through a glass darkly": Anthony West to RW, marked by her: "Anthony in America first visit." Tulsa.

"eleven and a half pounds": Beatrice Kaufman and Joseph Hennessy (eds.), *The
Letters of Alexander Woollcott,* Cassell 1946.

149–50   "nice and amiable": to Reginald Turner, early 1935. Yale.

150   "critic that she also is": *Ending in Earnest.*

151   "unpardonable in an adult": *Daily Telegraph,* 6 May 1932.

"light up post-war England": *The Strange Necessity.*

"a weeping willow": ibid.

"Max Beerbohm was of his": *Ending in Earnest.*

"at a parking place": ibid.

"indefensible as infanticide": *The Strange Necessity.*

152   "eternal views about life": *Ending in Earnest.*

"mountain-pony sturdiness": ibid.

"at your service": George T. Bye to RW, 4 June 1935. Tulsa.

"of scattered books": Rupert Hart-Davis (for Jonathan Cape) to A. D. Peters,
20 Feb 1935. Texas.

153   "great classical artist": *St Augustine.*

"curious callousness": to Norman Macleod, 14 Feb 1933.

"all his clubs": to Mr. Pinsent, 3 July 1938. Tulsa.

154   "recorded in literature": *Black Lamb and Grey Falcon,* vol. II, p. 206.

155   "and great intelligence": Virginia Woolf to Vanessa Bell, 25 May 1928. Nigel
Nicolson (ed.), *The Letters of Virginia Woolf,* vol. 3, Hogarth Press 1977.

"a child by Wells": Virginia Woolf to Rosamund Lehmann, 2 July 1928. *The Letters
of Virginia Woolf,* vol. 6, 1980.

grateful, happy letter: Virginia Woolf to RW, 10 Nov 1928. Uncollected. Tulsa.

"of rare gifts": Ms. contribution to Joan Browne for *Recollections of Virginia Woolf.*
Tulsa.

Page 155   "hoofmarks of Wells": Virginia Woolf to Lady Ottoline Morrell, 31 Dec 1933. *The Letters of Virginia Woolf,* vol. 5, 1979.

"to feed a dog off": to Victoria Glendinning in conversation, 2 April 1976.

"the direction of doubt": New York *Herald Tribune,* 7 Feb 1932.

155–6   "fuller of bitterness": to Sylvia Lynd, 1932.

156   "mutual one of ours": Fannie Hurst to Carl Van Vechten, enclosing RW's letter, 3 Feb 1937. Berg.

"wit and rhythm": John Gunther, Diary, 1 Jan 1936.

"appearances": Anne Oliver Bell (ed.), *The Diary of Virginia Woolf,* vol. IV, Hogarth Press 1982.

157   "floodlit by electricity": ibid.

"English ruling class": courtesy of Alison Macleod.

158   "makes much headway": Virginia Woolf to Vita Sackville-West, 19 Aug 1939. *The Letters of Virginia Woolf,* vol. 6, 1980.

"ourselves are happy": to Fannie Hurst, 30 Oct 1933. Texas.

"shoot all the Jews": to Winnie, 1931.

"the whole world today": *New York Times,* 12 May 1935. See also *Time and Tide,* 24 Aug 1935, for a more critical view.

159   "talked to each other": to Fannie Hurst, 23 July 1929. Texas.

"forms of slavery": Ms. synopsis of *The Thinking Reed.* Tulsa.

"as possible": *Booklover,* Feb/March 1936.

160   "at their throats": A. J. P. Taylor, *A Personal History,* Hamish Hamilton 1983.

161   "to have cancer?": *Nash's* magazine, 25 June 1936.

162   "never the massacrer": *Black Lamb and Grey Falcon,* vol. I, p. 22.

163   "and my time": report to Colonel Bridge of the British Council, 1936. Copy. Tulsa.

"open on my lap": to Marcia Davenport, 21 Nov 1941. Courtesy of Marcia Davenport.

"a complete folly": ibid.

164   "its blackened foundations": *Black Lamb and Grey Falcon,* vol. II, p. 496.

"about Rebecca West": John Gunther to RW, 6 Oct 1944. Tulsa.

165   "might be a Serb": *Black Lamb and Grey Falcon,* vol. I, p. 15.

obstinate, unattainable: paraphrased from letter in French to RW from Stanislav Vinaver, 1938. Tulsa.

"hedges of wild roses": to Henry Andrews, 1 June 1938. Tulsa.

166   "put to of late": to Henry Andrews, 10 June 1938. Tulsa.

"as well at home": postcard to Henry Andrews, 1 June 1938. Tulsa.

"prolongation of delight": *Black Lamb and Grey Falcon,*.vol. I, p. 236.

"very little homosexuality": ibid., p. 207.

"women still women": ibid., p. 215.

"'behave like a Serb'": ibid., vol. II, p. 522.

167   "up to 12 or 14": Ruth Lowinsky, Nov 1939. Tulsa.

"we and the farm still exist": to Ruth Lowinsky, 7 Dec 1939. Tulsa.

"to bombed London": *The New Yorker,* 14 Dec 1940.

168   "violation of the law": *Black Lamb and Grey Falcon,* vol. I, p. 287.

Page 169   "flover for you": Lela Gavrilović to RW. Tulsa.

"lame cobras": *Ladies' Home Journal,* 12 Jan 1940.

170   "during my lifetime": Henry Andrews's will, 7 Oct 1966. Tulsa.

171   "British sympathies": *Black Lamb and Grey Falcon,* vol. II, p. 532.

"astonishingly misinformed": Neil Balfour, letter, *South Slav Journal,* March 1980.

"the Ministry of Information?": to Richard Sykes, 10 Nov 1980. Copy. Tulsa.

"the British authorities": letter, *The Times Literary Supplement,* Jan 1981.

172   "glowingly of him": Prince Androj to RW, 16 March 1982. Tulsa.

174   "Eastern Europe to Russia": to Winnie, autumn 1943.

So had Tito: see Nora Beloff, *Tito's Flawed Legacy,* Gollancz 1985.

175   "the right moment": to Lettie, 1948.

"to me personally": Diary, 30 Jan 1945. Tulsa.

"that particular debt": to Paul Palmer, 21 Sep 1949. Tulsa.

"send me a farthing": draft letter to Churchill, 29 Aug 1949. Tulsa.

176   "the smell of skunk": *Black Lamb and Grey Falcon,* vol. I, p. 128.

"its every page": Clifton Fadiman, *The New Yorker,* 25 Oct 1941.

"monumental chronicle": *New York Times Book Review,* 26 Oct 1941.

"our modern world": San Francisco *Chronicle,* 9 Nov 1941.

178   "on the ground": Mary Ellmann, *Thinking About Women,* Macmillan 1969.

a "private dream": *Black Lamb and Grey Falcon,* vol. I, p. 25.

"if I were you!": ibid., p. 209.

"the war thus far": Lewis Mumford to RW, 28 Sep 1944. Tulsa.

179   wrote Lady Mosley: *The European,* July 1956.

"organ after organ": to Joseph Hergesheimer, 17 April 1941. Texas.

"that kind of ill-health": *1900.*

180   "enjoyment of life": *Time and Tide,* 8 June 1941.

"without indiscretion": to John Gunther, 1941.

"no longer fear death": Diary, 14 April 1942. Tulsa.

"bayonet in his ribs": to Stanislav Vinaver, 14 Dec 1936. Tulsa.

"not enough subscribers": *Sunday Telegraph,* 18 Dec 1979.

181   "too innocent to be loved" and "symbols of a natural life": Diary, 14 April 1944.
          Tulsa.

her published article: *The New York Times,* 16 April 1944.

183   "they are superb": to Winnie, 1940s.

"in case of invasion": to G. B. Stern, 1941. Tulsa.

"made everything fun" and "and go under": Margaret Hodges to Victoria Glendin-
          ning in conversation.

184   "pulling at me": Anthony West to RW, July 1940. Tulsa.

"in his spare time": to Margaret Rhondda, 28 July 1940. Texas.

185   "problem to solve": to Kitty West (Katharine Church), 20 May 1944. Courtesy of
          Katharine Church.

"the damned precursors": Memoir notes adapted 5 April 1970 from Diary for 1944.

twenty-page letter to Lettie: 20 Sep 1944.

Page 185 to degrade her: see Anthony West, Introduction to *Heritage*, new ed., Secker and
   Warburg 1984.

186 "to make him happy": to Kitty West (Katharine Church), July 1944. Courtesy of
   Katharine Church.
   "at her tired feet": Marilyn French, *Beyond Power: Women, Men and Morals*, Cape
   1985.
   "taken him from me": Diary, 30 March 1945.
   "he should be careful": to Lettie, 20 Sep 1944.
   "got hold of": Anthony West, *H. G. Wells: Aspects of a Life*, Hutchinson 1984.
   "tragic part in our lives": to Anthony West, 1972. Copy. Tulsa.

187 "pretty well without me": to Marjorie Wells, 21 Aug 1946. Gordon N. Ray, *H. G.
   Wells and Rebecca West*, Macmillan 1974.
   "he then knew": loose typescript. Tulsa.
   "exploit that association": to Society of Authors, 25 May 1966. Copy. Tulsa.

PART FIVE: REBECCA WEST

191 "citadel of boredom": "Greenhouse with Cyclamens I," *A Train of Powder.*
   "it may inflict": *Virginia Law Review,* Dec 1957.
   "huge parties": "Greenhouse with Cyclamens I," *A Train of Powder.*

192 "that gorgeous bridge": to Winnie, 29 Aug 1950.
   "my terrific discontent": to Dorothy Thompson, 31 Aug 1946. Syracuse.
   "repudiating me" and "after the first years": "Synopsis of Later Memoirs," unnumbered notebook. Tulsa.

193 "happiness in sex": ibid.
   "right hand is doing": A. L. Rowse, *Glimpses of the Great,* Methuen 1985.

194 "known as nations": obituary notice of Francis Biddle, *Times,* 5 Oct 1968.
   "rasping but rich": *The Meaning of Treason.*
   "minute shred of ceremony": ibid.

195 "curl with terror": to Winnie, 12 Dec 1949.
   "than I do": Tulsa.
   "be anything worse": to Cyril Connolly, 1 Nov 1964. Copy. Tulsa.

196 "give him protection": *The Meaning of Treason.*
   "and a roof": "Opera in Greenville," *A Train of Powder.*
   "on social change": *The Meaning of Treason.*
   "permanent opposition": ibid.
   "to the infantilist": ibid.
   "interested in them": BBC radio, "Frankly Speaking," Feb 1953.

197 "millinery or glovemaking": to Mr. Watt, 19 May 1959. Copy. Tulsa.
   "exceptional value": *The Meaning of Treason.*
   "view of eternity": ibid.
   "tremor of the extremist": V. S. Pritchett, *New Statesman,* 24 Sep 1949.

Page 198   "on many levels": Joseph Barnes, *The New York Times Book Review*, 30 Nov 1947.
              "best for everybody": to Anthony West, early 1947. Copy. Tulsa.
       199   "advanced drunkenness": to Anne Charles, 12 April 1947.
              "an old man": John Gunther, Diary, 13 April 1947.
       200   "a great deal": Cole Leslie, *The Life of Noël Coward*, Cape 1976.
              "a fair measure": to E. and M. Hutchinson, 5 July 1947.
       201   "on the proofs" and "might fall into": *Evening Standard*, 7 Dec 1951.
              "a great paper": ibid., 20 May 1977.
              "lost a shoe": to Dorothy Thompson, 20 Sep 1958. Syracuse.
              "any matches": *Evening Standard*, 10 Nov 1947.
       202   "cracked old women": to John Gunther, 4 Nov 1947.
              "silly doctrinaires": ibid.
              "against their clatter": *Evening Standard*, 20 Oct 1947.
       203   "between Fascism and Communism": ibid., 29 Sep 1947.
              "know what to think": to Dorothy Thompson, 1947. Syracuse.
              "greasy oxtail soup": to Charles Curran, 1959. Tulsa.
              "over many years": to Winnie, 1949.
       204   "part of the darkness": to Charles Curran, 26 Jan 1949. Tulsa.
              "think of them!": to Charles Curran, 1949. Tulsa.
              "feel very bereft": to Marie-Noële Kelly, 7 June 1982. Courtesy of Lady Kelly.
       205   "pleasures of defamation": to Charles Curran, 1950s. Tulsa.
              "then nothing matters": to E. and M. Hutchinson, 5 July 1947.
       206   "what I have not had": Diary, 9 March 1963. Tulsa.
       207   "that disagreeable people": to Winnie, 3 Jan 1950.
              "all there together": to Dorothy Thompson, spring 1949. Syracuse.
              "an unpleasant situation": to Charles Curran, 6 July 1949. Tulsa.
              "knowledge of the Germans": to Anne Charles, June 1949.
       208   "it was lovely": to John Gunther, 1 Aug 1949.
       209   "this has come about": to Rache Lovat Dickson, 1957. Tulsa.
              "a bad slip": to G. B. Stern, 6 March 1950. Tulsa.
              "marvellous ham": Diary, 1 March 1950.
              "I'm frayed": to G. B. Stern, 6 March 1950. Tulsa.
              "given any more": to Charles Curran, 14 April 1959. Tulsa.
              "not arrogant but pitiable": *This Real Night*.
       210   "origins are shameful": Anthony West to Henry Andrews, 3 Sep 1949. Copy. Tulsa.
              "waste of my youth": to Lettie, 5 Nov 1949.
              "exhilarating relationship" and "literary enemies": to John and Myfanwy Piper,
                 1 Sep 1949. Copy. Tulsa.
       211   "and really rich": to Winnie, 22 Nov 1949.
              "trouble with their children": Dorothy Thompson to Harold Ross, 17 Feb 1950.
                 Syracuse.
              "fretting for him": to John Gunther, 9 July 1951.
              "not believe his senses": to Winnie, 8 May 1952.

Page 212   "gratitude for me": Diary, 5 Feb 1950. Tulsa.

"down to the ground": to E. and M. Hutchinson, 15 April 1963.

"the wordless sentence" and "nothing by the change": *The Strange Necessity.*

"shape of the sentences": Robert McAlmon and Kay Boyle, *Being Geniuses Together,* new ed., Hogarth 1984.

213–24   "never be rescued": "Greenhouse with Cyclamens II," *A Train of Powder.*

214   "ephemeral literature": Kenneth Tynan and Cecil Beaton, *Persona Grata,* Wingate 1953.

"find me out": to Emily Hahn, 3 Jan 1959. Indiana.

"a light book": to E. and M. Hutchinson, Oct 1955.

215   "withdraw that gift": draft letter to Anthony West, 1955. Tulsa.

216   "that I know about": Anthony West to Kitty West, 1955. Copy. Tulsa.

"write in malice": to John Gunther, 8 Sep 1955.

"the most serious injury": Dorothy Thompson to RW, 27 Jan 1955. Tulsa.

"and very silly": to Dorothy Thompson, 1 Feb 1955. Tulsa.

216   "couple of months ago": Harold Guinzberg to RW, 10 Nov 1955. Tulsa.

"thus far is negligible": telegram, Harold Guinzberg to RW, 15 Oct 1955. Tulsa.

"he was born": Charles Curran to RW, 8 Nov 1955. Tulsa.

"so vulnerable": Charles Curran to Emily Hahn, 1955. Copy. Tulsa.

217   "sustain her malice": Anthony West, Introduction to *Heritage,* new ed., Secker and Warburg 1984.

"very wicked": Frank Wells to RW, 12 April 1956. Tulsa.

"only vertigo": to E. and M. Hutchinson, 26 Sep 1956.

"could have devised": to Emily Hahn, 4 April 1958. Indiana.

"one's own Trojan horse": to E. and M. Hutchinson, 20 Aug 1959.

218   "compose their works": *Black Lamb and Grey Falcon,* vol. I, p. 117.

"to finish it": to E. and M. Hutchinson, 22 June 1952.

219   "done by Rosamund and Richard Quin": synopsis of "Cousin Rosamund: A Saga of the Century." Tulsa.

220   "contributed to Mary": to Alison Macleod, Feb 1980.

"anything less like you" and "you still will": to Lettie, 2 Jan 1957.

221   "that one cannot pardon": "A Visit to My Godmother," BBC Radio, 1963, revised version, "A Visit to a Godmother," *Rebecca West: A Celebration.*

"tender antelope of a car": to E. and M. Hutchinson, 26 Sep 1956.

"a useful technique": to E. and M. Hutchinson, summer 1950.

"intellectual pretensions": to E. and M. Hutchinson, 22 June 1952.

222   "I DON'T LIKE IT": to Doreen Wallace, 12 Aug 1952. Courtesy of Prof. G. E. Hutchinson.

"defeat was victorious": *Black Lamb and Grey Falcon,* vol. II, p. 85.

"beastly retrogression": ibid. p. 204.

"any good thing": ibid., p. 205.

"cruel love and kind hate": ibid. For the full argument see pp. 186–210.

"to feel all": *Letter to a Grandfather.*

Page 223 "the will to die": "Hypocrisies," very early ms. article for *The Red Book*. Notebook
14. Tulsa.

224 "useful conception of life": for RW on Manichaeism see *Black Lamb and Grey Falcon*, vol. I, pp. 175–9.

"down into defeat": Diary, 12 April 1974. Tulsa.

225 "his political necessities": *Sunday Chronicle,* 17 Dec 1944.

"rhyme with *ism*": C. G. Jung, "Women in Europe," 1927.

"of old feelings": Prof. G. E. Hutchinson to Victoria Glendinning in conversation,
1983.

"their own country": to E. and M. Hutchinson, 1 Sep 1953.

226 "discussing with you": from War Office official, 10 Jan 1951. Tulsa.

"what McCarthy does": to Dorothy Thompson, 16 June 1953. Syracuse.

"violent demagogue": to J. B. Priestley, 22 June 1955. Texas.

"in my life": to E. and M. Hutchinson, 12 June 1953.

227 "story of infiltration": to E. and M. Hutchinson, 4 Dec 1953.

"dishonesty and fear": to E. and M. Hutchinson, 3 Oct 1954.

"have taken over": *Picture Post,* 17 Jan 1953. Copy. Tulsa.

"bayed behind her": Washington *Post,* 26 April 1979.

227, 228 "go to Heaven" and "the works of love": for the whole argument see *Black Lamb and
Grey Falcon,* vol. II, pp. 186–210.

228 "infatuation with sacrifice": ibid.

229 "explains a lot": to E. and M. Hutchinson, 29 Jan 1953.

"individuals predominate": 18 Jan 1953. Janet Flanner, *Darlinghissima: Letters to a
Friend,* ed. Natalia Danesi Murray, Random House (New York) 1985.

"it didn't help": to Anne Charles, 8 Feb 1953.

230 "so sensual, doubtless": Janet Flanner, *Darlinghissima.*

"Faustian individual": *Sunset and Twilight: From the Diaries of Bernard Berenson
1947–1958,* Hamish Hamilton 1964, entry for 25 Dec 1952.

"with the herbs": to E. and M. Hutchinson, 26 Sep 1956.

231 "roots of country living": Barbara Vise, *Housewife,* July 1951.

"divined from her books": to E. and M. Hutchinson, 5 Dec 1957.

"the white fields": Memoirs, notebook 20. Tulsa.

"all we've been through": Greta (Wood) Mortimer to Victoria Glendinning in conversation, 1983.

232 "WE DO NOT LIKE": to Anne Charles, 25 June 1953.

"a mental disorder": Pamela Frankau, *I Find Four People,* Ivor Nicholson and Watson 1935.

233 "not unintelligent, but slow": to Charles Curran, 10 Nov 1953. Tulsa.

"or your children": to Emily Hahn, 23 Jan 1958. Indiana.

"something again": to Dorothy Thompson, 30 April 1953. Syracuse.

234 "a downtrodden class": to Douglas and Mia Woodruff, 5 Jan 1959. Georgetown.

"as we are sometimes": Diary, 25 May 1963. Tulsa.

PART SIX: DAME REBECCA

Page 237 "pure Chislehurst": to Charles Curran, March 1960. Tulsa.

"endless suffering": to Henry Andrews, March 1960. Tulsa.

"others out there": to Ralph Carlisle, 15 Aug 1960. Tulsa.

"from the bench": *Sunday Times,* 24 April 1960.

238 "cleaned regularly": to Lettie, 2 Aug 1966.

"understanding and distinction": James M. Cain to RW, 27 April 1960. Tulsa.

"my early youth": to Emanie Arling Philips, 1960. Tulsa.

"TO GO AWAY": to Emily Hahn, 15 June 1960. Indiana.

239 "round every field": to Bruce and Beatrice Gould, 28 Aug 1961. Copy. Tulsa.

"'and the rain'": to E. and M. Hutchinson, 29 Jan 1962.

240 "loves of the birds": to E. and M. Hutchinson, 6 Dec 1962.

"know what I mean": to E. and M. Hutchinson, 12 March 1963.

"choose between them": Draft Memoirs, unnumbered notebook. Tulsa.

"incredible bedlinen": to Anthony West, 12 May 1964. Copy. Tulsa.

"MERRY Christmas": to Alison Macleod, 21 Dec 1964.

241 "Helen of Troy": to E. and M. Hutchinson, 5 Dec 1964.

"Second World War": to Clare Stanley-Clarke, 6 Sep 1962. Courtesy of Clare Stanley-Clarke.

"our human misery": to Leonard Woolf, 1940s. University of Sussex.

"really frightening": to G. B. Stern, 26 Sep 1945. Tulsa.

242 "time, action, Fate": Sybille Bedford to RW, 20 Feb 1967. Tulsa.

"as well as people": Paul Scott to RW, 15 Aug 1975. Tulsa.

243 "an obscene gesture": *Sunday Telegraph,* 8 Oct 1978.

"bar none": to E. and M. Hutchinson, 31 March 1966.

"out of *The Birds*": to Charles Curran, 20 Dec 1966. Tulsa.

"old dog yet": to Dachine Rainier, 9 Aug 1966. Copy. Tulsa.

"young men I know": Max Lerner, New York *Post* 17 Oct 1966.

244 "would do them": to Lulu Friedman, late 1961. Copy. Tulsa.

"to being rewritten": Anthony West to RW, 23 Dec 1964. Tulsa.

245 The death certificate: dated 3 Nov 1968. Tulsa.

"quite beautiful": to Emanie Arling Philips, 27 Nov 1968. Tulsa.

"Banker and Patron": *Times,* 12 Nov 1968.

246 "and a nice one": Anthony West to RW, late 1968. Tulsa.

"THIS IS AWFUL": Diary, 16 Jan 1971. Tulsa.

"any benefit to Anthony": Diary, 15 Jan 1971. Tulsa.

247 "but I don't know": to Emanie Arling Philips, 6 Nov 1968. Tulsa.

"went to nothing": to Anne McBurney, late 1968.

"when it is over": to Emanie Arling Philips, 15 Dec 1968. Tulsa.

"when he died": Memoirs, notebook 20. Tulsa.

"cannot bear this": Memoirs, typescript A. Tulsa.

248 "herself should marry": to Charles Curran, 18 Nov 1968. Tulsa.

"a house with children": Diary, 24 July 1982. Tulsa.

Page 249   "a great comfort": Diary, 2 Nov 1974. Tulsa.

"a woman writer": memo marked "Sent to Yale 6.1.78," in file of RW's letters
  to Emanie Arling Philips, returned to RW after EAP's death. Tulsa.

"moving the piano": *Sunday Telegraph,* 28 June 1970.

"disharmony": *Black Lamb and Grey Falcon,* vol. II, p. 48.

"noisiness and impulsiveness?": Diary, 24 June 1971. Tulsa.

"could control it": Diary, 25 June 1971. Tulsa.

250   "Ovid's *Metamorphoses*": *The New York Times,* 14 April 1974.

"multiplicity of characteristics": *Sunday Telegraph,* March 1982.

"and my politics": Memoirs. Tulsa.

"a railway station": to Marie-Noële Kelly, 24 Nov 1968. Courtesy of Lady Kelly.

"always longed for": to Sir Rupert Hart-Davis, 18 Sep 1971. Courtesy of Sir Rupert
  Hart-Davis.

251   "rested and happy": to Emanie Arling Philips, 18 June 1969. Tulsa.

"Weimar Republic collapsed": to Emanie Arling Philips, March 1970. Tulsa.

"out of Vietnam": *Censorship: For and Against* (pamphlet), Hart (New York), 1971.

"to date it": Nicholas Bagnall to Victoria Glendinning, 11 May 1986.

252   "dampness of the night": *Sunday Telegraph,* 28 Aug 1977.

"sheer brute evidence": *Sunday Telegraph,* 14 May 1967.

"a big big book": to Francis Hackett, Jan 1923. Texas.

"art of *The Raw Truth!*": to Sylvia Lynd, 1917.

253   "provokes your lust": to Bertrand Russell, Sep 1929. Copy. Tulsa.

"and his disloyalties": "Curious Idolatry," *Ending in Earnest.*

"very, very clever": Interview with Marina Warner, 1981, *Writers at Work: The
  Paris Review Interviews,* sixth series, Secker & Warburg 1985.

"touched her achievement": *Sunday Telegraph,* 10 June 1962.

"spiral of perfection": *The Strange Necessity.*

"so far as I can make out": Interview with Marina Warner, 1981.

254   "down the corridors": to Emily Hahn, 11 Feb 1975. Copy. Tulsa.

"write about them": to E. and M. Hutchinson, Jan 1970.

255   "before I die": to E. Hutchinson, 10 Oct 1973.

"of her life" and "of her writings": Gordon N. Ray, Preface, *H. G. Wells and Rebecca West,* Macmillan 1974.

quotation from Ruth Hale: Lillian Hellman, *The New York Times Book Review,*
  3 Oct 1974.

256   "conceived in malice": Anthony West to David Garnett of Macmillan, 8 June
  1975. Copy. Tulsa.

"it's very good": Diary, 2 March 1974. Tulsa.

257   "a revolting personality": to Malcolm Muggeridge (not sent), 23 June 1981. Tulsa.

"in British history": *Sunday Telegraph,* May 1978.

258   "cracking good they are": Diary, 22 Jan 1982.

"silence about my work": to Lennie Goodings, 17 Nov 1981. Copy. Tulsa.

"my life has gone": to Hamish Hamilton, 19 Oct 1961. Tulsa.

"ploughed fields": to John Gunther, 12 July 1961.

Page 259 "one for me": Lord Beaverbrook to RW, 31 Dec 1963. Tulsa.

"affair with Beaverbrook?" Diary, 25 April 1975. Tulsa.

"loving it": Diary, 10 Aug 1975. Tulsa.

"and look elegant": Diary, 5 March 1974. Tulsa.

260 "with Scotch tape!": Diary, 5 March 1974. Tulsa.

"purple and wild": Teodora Weber, unpublished memoir of RW, spring 1979.

"happened to be old": Diana Stainforth, unpublished memoir of RW's last six months.

"measure of comfort": to secretary of Age Concern, 2 Feb 1982. Draft. Tulsa.

261 "hawthorn tree": Diary, 13 June 1974. Tulsa.

unsympathetic interview: *The New York Times: New York Times Magazine*, 4 April 1982; reprinted in *Woman's Journal*, Aug 1982.

"what is happening?": "Edith: Or the Bomb-story," unpublished ms. Tulsa.

article for *Vogue:* American *Vogue*, Feb 1983.

"can't go on": Diana Stainforth, unpublished memoir of RW's last six months.

262 "too difficult": "Hypocrisies," very early ms. article for *The Red Book*. Notebook 14. Tulsa.

"problem to me": Diary, 14 Jan 1982.

dying so slowly: account of RW's state of mind and quotations from the diary of Alison Macleod, 22 Dec 1982–15 March 1983.

"'this is what matters'": *Black Lamb and Grey Falcon*, vol. II, pp. 523–4.

"choose between them": see p. 240. Draft Memoirs, unnumbered notebook. Tulsa.

MAJOR WORKS BY REBECCA WEST

FICTION

The Return of the Soldier. London: Nisbet & Co 1918. New York: The Century Co 1918.
The Judge. London: Hutchinson 1922. New York: George H. Doran 1922.
Harriet Hume. London: Hutchinson 1929. New York: Doubleday, Doran 1929.
War Nurse (anonymously). New York: Cosmopolitan Book Corporation 1930.
The Harsh Voice. London: Jonathan Cape 1935. New York: Doubleday, Doran 1935.
The Thinking Reed. London: Hutchinson 1936. New York: Viking Press 1936.
The Fountain Overflows. London: Macmillan 1957. New York: Viking Press 1956.
The Birds Fall Down. London: Macmillan 1966. New York: Viking Press 1966.
This Real Night (posthumously). London: Macmillan 1984. New York: Viking Press 1985.
Cousin Rosamund (posthumously). London: Macmillan 1985. New York: Viking Press 1986.
Sunflower (posthumously). London: Virago Press 1986. New York: Viking Press 1987.

NON-FICTION

Henry James. London: Nisbet & Co 1916. New York: Henry Holt 1916.
The Strange Necessity. London: Jonathan Cape 1928. New York: Doubleday, Doran 1928.
Ending in Earnest: A Literary Log. New York: Doubleday, Doran 1931.
St Augustine. London: Peter Davies 1933. New York: Appleton 1933.
Black Lamb and Grey Falcon. London: Macmillan 1942. New York: Viking Press 1941.
The Meaning of Treason. New York: Viking Press 1947. London: Macmillan 1949.
The New Meaning of Treason. New York: Viking Press 1964. London: Macmillan 1965
  (with title *The Meaning of Treason*, revised edition).
A Train of Powder. New York: Viking Press 1955. London: Macmillan 1955.
The Court and the Castle. New Haven: Yale University Press 1957. London: Macmillan
  1958.
1900. London: Weidenfeld & Nicolson 1982. New York: Viking Press 1983.

IN PRINT IN 1987

Macmillan: *Black Lamb and Grey Falcon*, *This Real Night*, and *Cousin Rosamund*; also
  Rebecca West: A Celebration (anthology, 1977).
Virago: All Rebecca West's other fiction except *War Nurse*; also *The Meaning of Treason*,
  revised edition, *A Train of Powder*, and *The Young Rebecca: Writings of Rebecca West
  1911–1917*, ed. Jane Marcus (1982).

INDEX

A NOTE ABOUT THE AUTHOR

Victoria Glendinning is the author of three other biographies: *Elizabeth Bowen, Edith Sitwell: A Unicorn Among Lions,* which won the Duff Cooper Memorial Prize and the James Tait Black Memorial Prize, and *Vita: The Life of Vita Sackville-West,* which won the Whitbread Prize. She contributes reviews and articles to newspapers and journals in both Britain and the United States, particularly the London *Times* Literary Supplement, and *The New York Times* and Washington *Post* book reviews. She has four sons and lives in London and Hertfordshire with her husband, the Irish writer Terence de Vere White.

A NOTE ON THE TYPE

This book was set in a digitized version of Fairfield, a type face designed by the distinguished American artist and engraver Rudolph Ruzicka (1883–1978). This type displays the sober and sane qualities of a master craftsman whose talent has long been dedicated to clarity. Rudolph Ruzicka was born in Bohemia and came to America in 1894. He designed and illustrated many books and was the creator of a considerable list of individual prints in a variety of techniques. Composed by Graphic Composition, Inc., Athens, Georgia. Printed and bounded by Murray Printing Co., Westford, Massachusetts. Typography and binding design by Iris Weinstein.